THE GUNNE

THE GUNNERS

DAY-TO-DAY LIFE AT HIGHBURY

RICHARD LERMAN AND DAVID BROWN

MAINSTREAM
PUBLISHING

EDINBURGH AND LONDON

First published in Great Britain in 1998 by
MAINSTREAM PUBLISHING COMPANY (EDINBURGH) LTD
7 Albany Street
Edinburgh EH1 3UG

ISBN 84018 039 0

A catalogue record for this book is available from the British Library

Typeset in Times
Printed and bound in Great Britain by Butler & Tanner Ltd

Writing this book, one of four that are being published simultaneously by the same authors, has been no hardship for us. When we had not been writing about Arsenal, we would have spent the time discussing the fortunes of the Gunners. Much of the time, we did anyway.

Quite simply, long before it became trendy to attach oneself to the fortunes of a football club, we were hauling up and down motorways supporting Arsenal in the days before the club's first double. The views and comments about events and players are, therefore, personal and have not been culled from any reference book. It has not been our intention to be controversial, rather our aim is to be factual, but we feel we have to express an opinion where necessary and if that causes upset to any reader then we sympathise but stand by our views.

Several eminent authorities have recorded the history of Arsenal Football Club as it progressed from humble beginnings in the munitions factory in Woolwich, through the all-conquering teams of the thirties, the double winners of the early seventies and on to Arsène Wenger's cosmopolitan champions.

All of the publications, vintage and current, have been organised on one of two themes.

The usual football club history book is laid out chronologically from past to present, developing chapter by chapter the story of the journey to prominence (or in some cases oblivion) and the characters that shaped the destiny of the club and the team.

Alternatively, a player-by-player analysis or a who's who will attempt to list, in alphabetical order, all or sometimes just the key participants who have taken part in the building of the organisation or the events on the field.

We believe that *The Gunners* introduces a third, and new, concept to the study of football clubs.

Simply, by using a diary format, we have attempted to catalogue the important events, the landmarks along the way for both the club and its players and the highs and lows as they occurred on a day-to-day basis from formation to the present.

Obviously in a topic as large as the one we have attempted to cover there will be a debate about what material should be included and what should be left out. It would not have been practical to include details on every player that has ever worn the red and white shirt of Arsenal. We have had to establish criteria that only those who have played a minimum number of games, or have been recognised for some other aspect of their career, be included. If, as we suspect, this has led to the omission of many fine players who for one reason or another did not make it into these pages, we apologise to them, their families and their supporters.

As previously stated, it has not been our policy to be contentious, we have desired to present a factual account of the history of this great club and, in so doing, some subjective decisions have had to be made. However, if any reader should consider we have made a glaring omission or a factual inaccuracy, we should be glad to address these matters with correspondence via our publisher, so that we might include any changes in a future edition of this book.

Finally, although we are sure that our view of certain players will not be shared by all, we would hope that the greater sentiment, that the club and the team are bigger and of more importance than any single individual, will emerge and be embraced.

We believe that Peter Hill-Wood was absolutely right when he recently maintained that Arsenal were and always have been the pre-eminent club in Great Britain. With Monsieur Wenger's guidance we now look forward to conquering Europe.

This is the first time that the authors, Richard Lerman and David Brown, have worked together. This book, and three other titles from the same partnership, form part of a series on football that Mainstream Publishing are issuing where the material is organised in diary format.

Richard Lerman was previously involved (as co-author) in the production of the Arsenal Official Programme Guide and publishes a monthly magazine called *Boot* which serves as a forum for collectors of football-related memorabilia, programmes etc. He is married with three sons (all keen football enthusiasts) and lives in North London.

David Brown is also married but with two young daughters (neither of whom have any interest in football) and lives in Kent.

Together, both men travel the length and breadth of Great Britain and Europe driven by their obsession with Arsenal Football Club and the pursuit of further glory.

ACKNOWLEDGEMENTS

Richard Lerman and David Brown would like to thank the following who have helped us in the research and for providing us with the material to make this book possible: first and foremost to Andy Kelly, for the use of his extensive database of matches that the club have played in. Andrew Miller with his input especially on the first Double year in 1971. Marc Norden for helping with the painstaking task of proof-reading and highlighting our mistakes, Les Easterbrook, John Roberts and Stuart Lerman. We would also like to thank the many readers of *Boot* magazine, which specialises in football memorabilia (6 Denmark Road, London, N8 0DZ), who have provided us with material for this publication.

Last but not least, we would very much like to thank Graham Betts for his efforts in organising this project together with all the staff at Mainstream Publishing.

1894	Liverpool	A	Division 2	0–2
1895	Darwen	A	Division 2	1–3
1896	Hastings	A	Friendly	12–0
1897	Darwen	A	Division 2	1–4
1898	Blackpool	A	Division 2	3–3
1900	Barnsley	A	Division 2	1–1
1901	Newcastle United	A	Friendly	1–5
1903	Stockport County	A	Division 2	1–0
1904	Stockport County	A	Division 2	0–0
1906	Bolton Wanderers	A	Division 1	1–6
1907	Sheffield Wednesday	A	Division 1	1–1
1908	Sunderland	A	Division 1	2–5
1910	Liverpool	A	Division 1	1–5
1912	Manchester United	A	Division 1	0–2
1913	Sunderland	A	Division 1	1–4
1914	Notts County	A	Division 2	0–1
1915	Barnsley	A	Division 2	0–1
1916	Millwall Athletic	A	London Combination	0–3
1919	Millwall Athletic	A	London Victory Cup	1–0
1921	Bradford City	H	Division 1	1–2
1923	Blackburn Rovers	A	Division 1	5–0
1927	Cardiff City	H	Division 1	3–2
1929	Sunderland	A	Division 1	1–5
1937	Bolton Wanderers	A	Division 1	5–0
1938	Everton	H	Division 1	2–1
1940	Charlton Athletic	A	League South 'A' Division	6–2
1944	Portsmouth	A	Football League – South	1–2
1948	Bolton Wanderers	A	Division 1	1–0
1949	Manchester United	A	Division 1	0–2
1955	West Bromwich Albion	H	Division 1	2–2
1966	Fulham	A	Division 1	0–1
1972	Everton	H	Division 1	1–1
1974	Newcastle United	H	Division 1	0–1
1980	Southampton	A	Division 1	1–0
1983	Swansea City	H	Division 1	2–1
1985	Tottenham Hotspur	H	Division 1	1–2

Steve Williams made his debut for the Gunners (as substitute) having signed from Southampton the previous day.

1986	Tottenham Hotspur	H	Division 1	0–0
1987	Wimbledon	H	Division 1	3–1
1988	Portsmouth	A	Division 1	1–1
1990	Crystal Palace	H	Division 1	4–1
1991	Manchester City	A	Division 1	1–0
1992	Wimbledon	H	Division 1	1–1
1994	Wimbledon	A	Premier League	3–0
1997	Middlesbrough	H	Premier League	2–0

JANUARY 2ND

1892	Cowlairs	H	Friendly	1–2
1893	Glasgow Thistle	H	Friendly	1–2
1897	Chatham	H	FA Cup qualifying round 5	4–0
1904	Blackpool	A	Division 2	2–2
1909	Notts County	H	Division 1	1–0

1912 Alexander Graham joined Arsenal as a professional after playing for Larkhall United in Scottish junior football.

1915	Wolverhampton Wanderers	H	Division 2	5–1
1926	Tottenham Hotspur	A	Division 1	1–1

1927 Peter Goring was born in Bishops Cleve, Gloucestershire.

1928	Tottenham Hotspur	H	Division 1	1–1
1932	West Bromwich Albion	A	Division 1	0–1
1933	Sheffield Wednesday	A	Division 1	2–3
1937	Huddersfield Town	H	Division 1	1–1
1943	Portsmouth	H	Football League – South	5–0
1954	Aston Villa	H	Division 1	3–0
1960	Wolverhampton Wanderers	H	Division 1	4–4
1965	Wolverhampton Wanderers	H	Division 1	4–1

1971 Arsenal were drawn away at Huish Park to play non-league Yeovil Town in the 3rd round of the FA Cup but adverse weather conditions caused the match to be postponed.

1978	Ipswich Town	H	Division 1	1–0

Peter Simpson made his final senior appearance as substitute. He had played 370 (10 goals) League, 53 (1 goal) FA Cup, 33 (3 goals) FL Cup and 21 (1 goal) European matches. 'Stan', along with Geordie Armstrong, never got the international recognition their consistently high standards of performance merited and both were overlooked in favour of less worthy candidates.

A pillar in the defence of the Fairs Cup and Double winning teams.

1982	Tottenham Hotspur	A	FA Cup 3rd round	0–1
1984	Norwich City	A	Division 1	1–1
1988	Queen's Park Rangers	H	Division 1	0–0
1989	Tottenham Hotspur	H	Division 1	2–0
1993	Yeovil Town	A	FA Cup 3rd round	3–1
1995	Tottenham Hotspur	A	Premier League	0–1
1996	Newcastle United	A	Premier League	0–2

JANUARY 3RD

1903	Preston North End	H	Division 2	3–1
1914	Wolverhampton Wanderers		Division 2	3–1
1920	Manchester City	H	Division 1	2–2
1925	Liverpool	A	Division 1	1–2
1939	Chelsea	A	FA Cup 3rd round	1–2
1942	Portsmouth	H	London League	6–1
1948	Sheffield United	H	Division 1	3–2

1951 Dennis Evans joined from Ellesmere Port Town for £1,500.

1953	Sunderland	A	Division 1	1–3
1959	Leicester City	A	Division 1	3–2
1970	Blackpool	H	FA Cup 3rd round	1–1
1976	Wolverhampton Wanderers	A	FA Cup 3rd round	0–3
1977	Leeds United	H	Division 1	1–1

Alan Hudson's debut in the League for Arsenal.

1981	Everton	A	FA Cup 3rd round	0–2
1983	Liverpool	A	Division 1	1–3
1994	Queen's Park Rangers	H	Premier League	0–0
1998	Port Vale	H	FA Cup 3rd round	0–0

JANUARY 4TH

1890	Windsor Phoenix	H	Friendly	3–1
1896	Loughborough Town	H	Division 2	5–0

Final game for David Howat. He made 56 (2 goals) League and 16 (1 goal) FA Cup appearances.

1897	Blackpool	A	Division 2	1–1
1899	Brighton United	A	United League	1–1
1902	Leicester Fosse	A	Division 2	1–2
1908	Bristol City	A	Division 1	2–1
1908	Ernie Coleman was born in Blidworth, Nottinghamshire.			
1913	Bolton Wanderers	A	Division 1	1–5
1919	Millwall Athletic	H	London Combination	4–1
1930	Sheffield Wednesday	H	Division 1	2–3
1936	Birmingham	H	Division 1	1–1
1941	Reading	A	London War Cup	0–2
1947	Sunderland	A	Division 1	4–1
1958	Northampton Town	A	FA Cup 3rd round	1–3
1964	Wolverhampton Wanderers	H	FA Cup 5th round	2–1
1969	Cardiff City	A	FA Cup 3rd round	0–0
1975	York City	H	FA Cup 3rd round	1–1
1986	Grimsby Town	A	FA Cup 3rd round	4–3
1987	Tottenham Hotspur	A	Division 1	2–1
1992	Wrexham	A	FA Cup 3rd round	1–2
1997	Sunderland	H	FA Cup 3rd round	1–1

JANUARY 5TH

1889	Vulcan	A	Friendly	1–1
1895	Sheppey United	A	Friendly	6–1
1901	Darwen	A	FA Cup Sup	2–0
1907	Middlesbrough	A	Division 1	3–5
1918	Millwall Athletic	H	London Combination	1–0
1924	Chelsea	A	Division 1	0–0
1929	Bolton Wanderers	A	Division 1	2–1
1935	Liverpool	A	Division 1	2–0
1939	Goalkeeper Ted Platt completed his move from Colchester United by signing as a professional.			

1946	West Ham United	A	FA Cup 3rd round 1st leg	0–6

First senior game for Joe Wade.

1952	Aston Villa	H	Division 1	2–1
1957	Stoke City	H	FA Cup 3rd round	4–2

1958 Steve Walford was born in Highgate, London.
1961 John Butler died in London.
1974 Christopher Sebastian Buckley died in Bromsgrove.

1974	Norwich City	A	FA Cup 3rd round	1–0
1980	Cardiff City	A	FA Cup 3rd round	0–0
1985	Hereford United	A	FA Cup 3rd round	1–1
1991	Sunderland	H	FA Cup 3rd round	2–1

JANUARY 6TH

1894	Port Vale	A	Division 2	1–2
1900	Luton Town	H	Division 2	3–1
1906	Sheffield United	H	Division 1	5–1
1912	Aston Villa	H	Division 1	2–2
1917	Luton Town	A	London Combination	4–1
1923	Stoke City	A	Division 1	0–1

1934 The tragic and premature death of Herbert Chapman who had been taken ill a few days earlier came as his team continued to power their way towards retaining the League title. Chapman will always be regarded as the man who laid the foundations for the success of the modern-day Arsenal. He brought numerous innovations both on and off the field to Arsenal and to football in general, whilst establishing the Gunners amongst the elite of the world's clubs.

1934	Sheffield Wednesday	H	Division 1	1–1

1938 Joe Hulme was transferred to Huddersfield Town for £2,000.

1945	Queen's Park Rangers	A	Football League – South	2–3
1951	Carlisle United	H	FA Cup 3rd round	0–0
1962	Bradford City	H	FA Cup 3rd round	3–0
1968	Coventry City	A	Division 1	1–1

1970 The much publicised acquisition of Peter Marinello from Hibernian for £100,000 took place.

1971	Yeovil Town	A	FA Cup 3rd round	3–0

Arsenal were drawn away at Huish Park to play non-league Yeovil Town in the 3rd round of the FA Cup. Although the press had built up the famous 'giant-killers' into thinking they could pull off the greatest cup shock of all time, reality saw the Gunners coast through 3–0. A John Radford header broke the stalemate in the 36th minute and 2 minutes before half-time Ray Kennedy netted from close range. John Radford scored again in the last minute to end any hopes of a shock.

1973	Manchester United	H	Division 1	3–1
1979	Sheffield Wednesday	A	FA Cup 3rd round	1–1
1990	Stoke City	A	FA Cup 3rd round	1–0
1993	Scarborough	A	Coca-Cola Cup 4th round	1–0
1996	Sheffield United	H	FA Cup 3rd round	1–1
1998	West Ham United	a	Coca-Cola Cup 5th round	2–1

JANUARY 7TH

1888	Alexandria United	A	Friendly	

1892	City Ramblers	H	Friendly	3–0
1893	Middlesbrough Ironopolis	H	Friendly	0–2
1895	Leicester Fosse	A	Division 2	1–3
1899	Leicester Fosse	A	Division 2	1–2
1905	Preston North End	A	Division 1	0–3
1911	Sheffield United	A	Division 1	2–3
1922	Queen's Park Rangers	H	FA Cup 1st round	0–0
1928	Sheffield United	A	Division 1	4–6
1933	Sunderland	A	Division 1	2–3
1950	Sheffield Wednesday	H	FA Cup 3rd round	1–0
1950	Malcolm Macdonald was born in Fulham, London.			
1956	Bedford Town	H	FA Cup 3rd round	2–2
1961	Sunderland	A	FA Cup 3rd round	1–2
1967	Tottenham Hotspur	H	Division 1	0–2
1969	Cardiff City	H	FA Cup 3rd round replay	2–0
1975	York City	A	FA Cup 3rd round replay	3–1
1978	Sheffield United	A	FA Cup 3rd round	5–0
1984	Middlesbrough	A	FA Cup 3rd round	2–3
1987	West Ham United bought Stewart Robson for £700,000.			
1988	Charlie Nicholas, one-time darling of the North Bank, was sold to Aberdeen for £400,000.			
1995	Millwall	A	FA Cup 3rd round	0–0

JANUARY 8TH

1887	Erith	H	Friendly	6–1
	This was Royal Arsenal's first fixture and was played at Plumstead Common.			
1898	Newton Heath	H	Division 2	5–1
1910	Sheffield United	A	Division 1	0–2
1916	Croydon Common	H	London Combination	4–2
1921	Queen's Park Rangers	A	FA Cup 1st round	0–2
1927	Sheffield United	A	FA Cup 3rd round	3–2
1938	Bolton Wanderers	H	FA Cup 3rd round	3–1
1944	Chelsea	A	Football League – South	0–2
1949	Tottenham Hotspur	H	FA Cup 3rd round	3–0
1955	Cardiff City	H	FA Cup 3rd round	1–0
1957	Don Roper returned to former club Southampton.			
1962	David Court signed as a professional.			
1966	Liverpool	H	Division 1	0–1
1972	Stoke City	A	Division 1	0–0
1977	Notts County	A	FA Cup 3rd round	1–0
1980	Cardiff City	H	FA Cup 3rd round replay	2–1
1983	Bolton Wanderers	H	FA Cup 3rd round	2–1
1989	West Ham United	A	FA Cup 3rd round	2–2

JANUARY 9TH

1892	Crusaders	H	Friendly	4–1
1897	Loughborough Town	H	United League	5–3
1904	Gainsborough Trinity	H	Division 2	6–0

1909	Newcastle United	A	Division 1	1–3
1915	Merthyr Town	H	FA Cup 1st round	3–0
1926	Wolverhampton Wanderers	A	FA Cup 3rd round	1–1
1932	Darwen	H	FA Cup 3rd round	11–1

Cliff Bastin scored 4 goals and David Jack a hat-trick in Arsenal's record FA Cup win.

1937	Sunderland	A	Division 1	1–1
1943	Fulham	H	Football League – South	7–2
1946	West Ham United	H	FA Cup 3rd round 2nd leg	1–0

Final game for Leslie Jones. Record 46 (3 goals) League and 4 FA Cup appearances. Won a League Championship medal in the 1937–38 season.

First senior appearance of Jimmy Logie who had signed immediately prior to outbreak of war i.e. six years earlier!

1954	Aston Villa	H	FA Cup 3rd round	5–1
1960	Rotherham United	A	FA Cup 3rd round	2–2
1965	Darlington	A	FA Cup 3rd round	2–0
1971	West Ham United	H	Division 1	2–0

Sammy Nelson made his last appearance of the season at home to West Ham United, replacing the injured Bob McNab. Arsenal took the lead in 40th minute when George Graham headed in a Pat Rice cross. The Gunners continued to attack and were rewarded in 80th minute when Ray Kennedy nodded home the simplest of chances. Referee Jack Taylor nearly gave Arsenal a third goal when a Jon Sammels shot hit the frame outside of the goal, but he was persuaded to consult the linesman who advised that the effort should be disallowed and therefore the Gunners had to be content with a 2–0 win.

1979	Sheffield Wednesday	H	FA Cup 3rd round replay	1–1
1988	Millwall	H	FA Cup 3rd round	2–0
1993	Sheffield United	H	Premier League	1–1

JANUARY 10TH

1898	Wellingborough	H	United League	3–1
1900	Bristol City	A	Southern District Combination	3–1
1903	Port Vale	A	Division 2	1–1
1905	Andy Ducat joined from Southend Athletic.			
1914	Bradford City	A	FA Cup 1st round	0–2
1920	Rochdale	H	FA Cup 1st round	4–2
1931	Aston Villa	H	FA Cup 3rd round	2–2
1942	Chelsea	A	London League	5–1
1948	Bradford Park Avenue	H	FA Cup 3rd round	0–1
1953	Doncaster Rovers	H	FA Cup 3rd round	4–0
1959	Bury	A	FA Cup 3rd round	1–0
1970	Manchester United	A	Division 1	1–2
	Debut of Peter Marinello.			
1976	Aston Villa	H	Division 1	0–0
1981	Everton	A	Division 1	2–1
1987	Reading	A	FA Cup 3rd round	3–1
1994	Millwall	A	FA Cup 3rd round	1–0
1996	Newcastle United	H	Coca-Cola Cup 5th round	2–0
1998	Leeds United	H	Premier League	2–1

Once again Leeds tried to bruise their way to a victory but this time, the Gunners with a seemingly new lease of life, battled every inch of the game and were not to be intimidated by the opposition. Chances were few and far between until the 60th minute when Overmars picked up the ball some 40 yards from goal and ran at the centre of the defence to score from the edge of the box with a stunning low shot which gave Martyn no chance. However, the Leeds keeper rescued his team a minute later when he saved from his own player who deflected a Parlour shot. Leeds drew level after 70 minutes when Seaman failed to hold a Wallace cross and the ball landed at the feet of Hasslebaink who tapped into the empty net. However, two minutes later the Gunners went ahead again through Overmars whose blistering pace took him past two defenders into the penalty area where he shot across the goal again giving Martyn no chance to make a save. Arsenal fought with a commitment that matched their opponents and deservedly took the three points that moved them back up to 5th position.

JANUARY 11TH

1890	London Caledonians	N	London Senior Cup	3–1
1893	Sussex Martlets	A	Friendly	2–0
1896	Liverpool	A	Division 2	0–3
1902	Preston North End	H	Division 2	0–0
1904	Queen's Park Rangers	H	London League Premier Division	6–2
1908	Hull City	H	FA Cup 1st round	0–0
1911	John Charles Peart signed as a professional.			
1913	Croydon Common	A	FA Cup 1st round	0–0
1919	Fulham	A	London Combination	1–3
1922	Queen's Park Rangers	A	FA Cup 1st round replay	2–1
1930	Chelsea	H	FA Cup 3rd round	2–0
1936	Bristol Rovers	A	FA Cup 3rd round	5–1
1941	Reading	H	London War Cup	0–1
1947	Chelsea	A	FA Cup 3rd round	1–1
1951	Carlisle United	A	FA Cup 3rd round replay	4–1
1958	Blackpool	H	Division 1	2–3
1964	Bolton Wanderers	A	Division 1	1–1
1969	Sheffield Wednesday	H	Division 1	2–0
1975	Carlisle United	H	Division 1	2–1
1979	Brian Talbot was signed from Ipswich in a club record deal (at the time) of £450,000.			
1989	West Ham United	H	FA Cup 3rd round replay	0–1
1992	Aston Villa	H	Division 1	0–0
1995	Liverpool	A	Coca-Cola Cup 5th round	0–1
1997	Sunderland	A	Premier League	0–1

JANUARY 12TH

1889	Unity	H	Friendly	0–0
1895	Newcastle United	H	Division 2	3–2
1901	Burton Swifts	H	Division 2	3–1
1907	Grimsby Town	A	FA Cup 1st round	1–1
1918	Tottenham Hotspur	A	London Combination	1–4
1924	Luton Town	H	FA Cup 1st round	4–1
1928	Andrew Kennedy sold to Everton for £2,000.			
1929	Stoke City	H	FA Cup 3rd round	2–1
1935	Brighton & Hove Albion	A	FA Cup 3rd round	2–0

1946	West Bromwich Albion	H	Football League – South	2–0
1952	Norwich City	A	FA Cup 3rd round	5–0
1956	Bedford Town	A	FA Cup 3rd round replay	2–1
1957	Portsmouth	H	Division 1	1–1
1974	Norwich City	H	Division 1	2–0
1980	Leeds United	H	Division 1	0–1
1991	Tottenham Hotspur	A	Division 1	0–0
1993	Nottingham Forest	H	Coca-Cola Cup 5th round	2–0

JANUARY 13TH

1891	Frederick Groves was born in Shadwell, London.			
1894	Accrington	H	Friendly	2–0
1900	Port Vale	A	Division 2	1–1
1906	West Ham United	H	FA Cup 1st round	1–1
1912	Bolton Wanderers	A	FA Cup 1st round	0–1
1917	Portsmouth	H	London Combination	1–0
1923	Liverpool	A	FA Cup 1st round	0–0
1926	Wolverhampton Wanderers	H	FA Cup 3rd round replay	1–0

Final match for Harry Woods who played 70 (21 goals) League and 5 (1 goal) FA Cup games.

1934	Luton Town	A	FA Cup 3rd round	1–0
1940	Millwall	H	League South 'A' Division	4–1
1945	Millwall	H	Football League – South	4–1
1945	Peter Simpson was born in Gorleston, Norfolk.			
1951	Middlesbrough	H	Division 1	3–1
1960	Rotherham United	H	FA Cup 3rd round replay	1–1
1962	Bolton Wanderers	H	Division 1	1–2
1968	Sheffield United	H	Division 1	1–1
1970	Rouen	H	European Fairs Cup 3rd round 2nd leg	1–0
1973	Leicester City	H	FA Cup 3rd round	2–2
1975	Graham Rix signed professional forms.			
1979	Nottingham Forest	H	Division 1	2–1

Brian Ernest Talbot made his debut for the Gunners.

1990	Wimbledon	A	Division 1	0–1
1995	John Hartson signed from Luton Town in a deal worth £2,500,000.			
1996	Middlesbrough	A	Premier League	3–2

JANUARY 14TH

1888	Iona Deptford	A	Friendly	3–2
1893	Wolverhampton Wanderers	H	Friendly	1–3
1899	Darwen	H	Division 2	6–0
1905	Middlesbrough	H	Division 1	1–1
1907	Cambridge University	H	Friendly	6–3
1911	Clapton Orient	A	FA Cup 1st round	1–0
1922	Chelsea	H	Division 1	1–0
1925	West Ham United	A	FA Cup 1st round	0–0
1928	West Bromwich Albion	H	FA Cup 3rd round	2–0

| 1931 | Aston Villa | A | FA Cup 3rd round replay | 3–1 |
| 1933 | Walsall | A | FA Cup 3rd round | 0–2 |

This result shocked the nation and is still regarded as one of the greatest FA Cup upsets of all time.

Arsenal were under strength, missing John, Lambert, Coleman, Hapgood and Hulme through injury and illness, and manager Herbert Chapman was forced to play inexperienced reserves Black, Sidey, Warnes and Walsh (none of whom emerged with credit).

After the game an incensed manager refused to allow Tommy Black to return to Highbury citing a rash tackle made by the player that resulted in a penalty and Walsall's second goal as the reason and, indeed, Black was sold to Plymouth within a week. Walsh was transferred to Brentford by the end of the month and Warnes went to Norwich at the end of the season.

1939	Everton	A	Division 1	0–2
1941	Alex Wilson was transferred to St Mirren.			
1950	Huddersfield Town	H	Division 1	1–0
1956	Tottenham Hotspur	H	Division 1	0–1
1961	Manchester City	H	Division 1	5–4
1967	Manchester City	H	Division 1	1–0
1978	Wolverhampton Wanderers	H	Division 1	3–1
1984	Luton Town	A	Division 1	2–1
1989	Everton	A	Division 1	3–1
1995	Everton	H	Premier League	1–1
1995	John Hartson and Chris Kiwomya made their League debuts in the game.			
1998	Port Vale	A	FA Cup 3rd round replay	1–1

Against a team struggling at the wrong end of the first division, the Gunners were taken to a penalty shoot-out after finishing all square after extra time. When Dixon, the first penalty taker, saw his shot saved it needed four successful efforts, a Seaman save and a miss by Vale's Tankard to ease the Gunners into the fourth round of the cup.

JANUARY 15TH

1887	Alexandria United	H	Friendly	11–0
1894	Aston Villa	H	Friendly	1–3
1898	Burton Swifts	A	Division 2	2–1
1906	Cambridge University	H	Friendly	4–2
1910	Watford	H	FA Cup 1st round	3–0
1913	Croydon Common	H	FA Cup 1st round replay	2–1
1916	Chelsea	H	London Combination	0–6
1921	Tottenham Hotspur	A	Division 1	1–2
1927	Derby County	A	Division 1	2–0
1938	Wolverhampton Wanderers	A	Division 1	1–3
1947	Chelsea	H	FA Cup 3rd round replay	1–1
1949	Sheffield United	H	Division 1	5–3
1955	Tottenham Hotspur	A	Division 1	1–0
1966	Blackburn Rovers	A	Division 1	1–2
1969	John Radford made his England international debut in the 1–1 draw against Rumania at Wembley.			

| 1970 | Blackpool | A | FA Cup 3rd round replay | 2–3 |

Terry Neill made his final senior appearance. His record: 241 (8 goals) League, 13 FA Cup, 16 FL Cup and 5 European games. He captained the team during one of the most uninspiring phases in the history of the club and returned in 1976 as manager. Also marked the last outing of Jimmy Robertson who made 46 (7 goals) League, 4 (1 goal) FA Cup, 4 FL Cup and 5 European appearances.

1972	Swindon Town	A	FA Cup 3rd round	2–0
1977	Norwich City	H	Division 1	1–0
1979	Sheffield Wednesday	Leicester	FA Cup 3rd round 2nd replay	2–2
1983	Stoke City	H	Division 1	3–0
1994	Manchester City	A	Premier League	0–0
1997	Sunderland	A	FA Cup 3rd round replay	2–0

JANUARY 16TH

1892	Small Heath	A	FA Cup 1st round	1–5
1897	Millwall	A	FA Cup sup	2–4
1904	Burton United	A	Division 2	1–3
1907	Grimsby Town	H	FA Cup 1st round replay	3–0
1908	Hull City	A	FA Cup 1st round replay	1–4

Last senior game for William Garbutt who made 52 (8 goals) League and 13 (6 goals) FA Cup appearances.

1909	Croydon Common	A	FA Cup 1st round	1–1
1911	Clapton Orient	A	FA Cup 1st round	2–1
1915	Fulham	A	Division 2	1–0
1920	Wally Barnes was born in Brecon, Wales.			
1926	Manchester United	H	Division 1	3–2
1932	Birmingham	H	Division 1	3–0
1937	Chesterfield	A	FA Cup 3rd round	5–1
1943	Clapton Orient	H	Football League – South	6–0
1954	Wolverhampton Wanderers	A	Division 1	2–2
1957	Trevor Ross was born in Ashton-Under-Lyne, Lancs.			
1960	Tottenham Hotspur	A	Division 1	0–3

Final senior appearance of Dennis Evans. He played 189 (10 goals) League and 18 (2 goals) FA Cup games.

| 1965 | Sunderland | A | Division 1 | 2–0 |
| 1971 | Huddersfield Town | A | Division 1 | 1–2 |

Arsenal lost for the first time in 14 League matches to falter in their chase for the championship. The hosts took the lead on the half-hour when Chapman fired the ball past Bob Wilson but the Gunners equalised 7 minutes into the 2nd half when Ray Kennedy deflected a George Graham free kick past Lawson in the Huddersfield goal. Frank McLintock handled the ball seemingly outside of the penalty area after 73 minutes but the referee awarded a penalty kick, which Worthington converted.

| 1988 | Liverpool | A | Division 1 | 0–2 |
| 1993 | Manchester City | A | Premier League | 1–0 |

JANUARY 17TH

| 1891 | Derby County | H | FA Cup 1st round | 1–2 |
| 1896 | Adam Haywood joined from Swadlincote. | | | |

1898	Luton Town	H	United League	0–0
1903	Burnley	H	Division 2	4–0
1914	Hull City	A	Division 2	2–1
1920	Manchester City	A	Division 1	1–4

'Wally' Hardinge made his final appearance for the first team. His record ended: 54 (14 goals) League and 1 FA Cup game.

Also played county cricket for Kent and in a Test match for England.

1922	Bob John was signed from Caerphilly Town.			
1923	Liverpool	H	FA Cup 1st round replay	1–4
1925	Newcastle United	H	FA Cup 1st round replay	0–2
1931	Sunderland	H	Division 1	1–3
1932	Jackie Henderson was born in Glasgow, Scotland.			
1942	Charlton Athletic	H	London League	3–2
1948	Manchester United	A	Division 1	1–1
1953	Wolverhampton Wanderers	H	Division 1	5–3
1959	Everton	H	Division 1	3–1
1968	Huddersfield Town	H	League Cup semi-final 1st leg	3–2
1970	Chelsea	H	Division 1	0–3
1973	Leicester City	A	FA Cup 3rd round replay	2–1
1976	Leicester City	A	Division 1	1–2
1979	Sheffield Wednesday	Leicester	FA Cup 3rd round 3rd replay	3–3
1981	Tottenham Hotspur	A	Division 1	0–2
1993	William 'Bill' Seddon died in Essex.			
1996	Sheffield United	A	FA Cup 3rd round replay	0–1

1997 Paul Read was sold to Wycombe Wanderers for £35,000 without making a senior appearance for the club.

1998	Coventry City	A	Premier League	2–2

One of the most action-packed games of the season with everything except a win for the Gunners. Bergkamp went close to scoring after 5 minutes with a curling free kick that was deflected away from the Coventry goal before Noel Whelan gave the home team the lead when Dion Dublin created an opening for his partner to score. David Seaman then had to produce two world-class saves to deny Coventry going further ahead before Arsenal equalised when, after 50 minutes, the Coventry defence failed to deal with a long clearance and Bergkamp clipped the ball over the goalkeeper. Eight minutes later Anelka put the Gunners in front after a goalmouth scramble and it looked as though they were starting to take control, but Vieira was penalised for handball in the area and after protesting the decision too vigorously, was subsequently red carded. Although Dion Dublin eventually scored from the penalty, the drama was not over. In the 79th minute, Paul Williams was judged to have tripped Bergkamp as he bore down on the Coventry goal and became the second man to be sent off, sparking massive protests from the Coventry team and management who claimed that Bergkamp had dived. TV evidence later proved that Williams had indeed clipped Bergkamp's heel. Although Anelka almost scored in the last few minutes, overall a draw seemed a fair result. However, more bad news was to follow when it was announced that David Seaman had broken his finger in the first half and was to be out for up to a month.

JANUARY 18TH

1890	Old Harrovians	H	Friendly	2–1
1896	Newcastle United	A	Division 2	1–3
1898	Chatham	A	Chatham Charity Cup	1–1
1899	Chatham	A	Chatham Charity Cup	1–1
1902	Burnley	A	Division 2	0–0
1904	Reading	A	Southern Professional Charity Cup	3–1
1906	West Ham United	A	FA Cup 1st round replay	3–2
1908	Manchester City	A	Division 1	0–4
1913	Sheffield United	H	Division 1	1–3
1919	Brentford	H	London Combination	3–3
1930	Burnley	A	Division 1	2–2
1936	Sheffield Wednesday	A	Division 1	2–3
1947	Aston Villa	H	Division 1	0–2
1958	Leicester City	A	Division 1	1–0
1960	Rotherham United	Sheffield Wed		
			FA Cup 3rd round 2nd replay	0–2
1964	Fulham	H	Division 1	2–2

Final senior appearance of John Barnwell.

1969	Newcastle United	A	Division 1	1–2
1975	Middlesbrough	A	Division 1	0–0

1975 Jeff Blockley sold to Leicester City for £100,000.

1977	Birmingham City	A	Division 1	3–3
1978	Manchester City	A	League Cup 5th round	0–0
1983	Sheffield Wednesday	H	Milk Cup 5th round	1–0
1986	Leicester City	A	Division 1	2–2
1987	Coventry City	H	Division 1	0–0
1992	Queen's Park Rangers	A	Division 1	0–0
1995	Millwall	H	FA Cup 3rd round replay	0–2

JANUARY 19TH

1878 Herbert Chapman was born in Kiveton Park on the borders of West Yorkshire and Nottinghamshire.

1889	Clapton	A	London Senior Cup	0–2
1895	Port Vale	A	Division 2	1–0

1898 Bill Harper was born in Tarbrax, Lanarkshire, Scotland.

1901	Barnsley	A	Division 2	0–3
1907	Preston North End	H	Division 1	1–0
1918	Chelsea	H	London Combination	4–1

1921 Robert (Hamilton) Turnbull joined from the Army as an amateur.

1924	Cardiff City	H	Division 1	1–2
1929	Portsmouth	H	Division 1	4–0
1935	Leeds United	H	Division 1	3–0
1946	West Bromwich Albion	A	Football League – South	1–0
1952	Derby County	A	Division 1	2–1
1957	Newcastle United	A	Division 1	1–3
1974	Manchester United	A	Division 1	1–1
1980	Derby County	H	Division 1	2–0
1985	Chelsea	A	Division 1	1–1

1990	Colin Pates was signed from Charlton Athletic for £500,000.			
1991	Everton	H	Division 1	1–0
1997	Everton	H	Premier League	3–1

JANUARY 20TH

1894	Chatham	A	Friendly	4–0
1896	Cambridge University	H	Friendly	7–1
	Debut for Adam Haywood.			
1900	Walsall	H	Division 2	3–1
1906	Notts County	A	Division 1	0–1
1909	Croydon Common	H	FA Cup 1st round replay	2–0
1912	Newcastle United	A	Division 1	2–1
1917	Millwall Athletic	A	London Combination	0–1
1923	Manchester City	H	FA Cup 1st round replay	1–0
1933	Thomas Black was sold to Plymouth Argyle following his part in the defeat at the hands of Walsall some six days earlier.			
	It was Herbert Chapman's punishment for an inauspicious debut.			
1934	Manchester City	A	Division 1	1–2
1940	West Ham United	A	League South 'A' Division	0–3
1945	Brighton & Hove Albion	A	Football League – South	0–3
1947	Chelsea	Tottenham		
			FA Cup 3rd round 2nd replay	0–2
1951	Huddersfield Town	A	Division 1	2–2
1959	Alan Skirton was purchased from Bath City for £5,000.			
1962	Manchester City	A	Division 1	2–3
1968	Tottenham Hotspur	A	Division 1	0–1
1973	Chelsea	A	Division 1	1–0
1982	Stoke City	A	Division 1	1–0
1988	Sheffield Wednesday	A	Littlewoods Cup 5th round	1–0
1990	Tottenham Hotspur	H	Division 1	1–0
1996	Everton	H	Premier League	1–2

JANUARY 21ST

1888	St Luke's	A	Friendly	
1892	Windsor Phoenix	H	Friendly	3–1
1893	Sunderland	A	FA Cup 1st round	0–6
1899	Gainsborough Trinity	A	Division 2	1–0
1905	Wolverhampton Wanderers	A	Division 1	1–4
	Final League game for William Linward. His record: 47 (10 goals) League and 3 FA Cup matches.			
1911	Aston Villa	H	Division 1	2–1
1922	Burnley	H	Division 1	0–0
1925	West Ham United	H	FA Cup 1st round replay	2–2
1925	Alex Forbes was born in Dundee.			
1928	Aston Villa	H	Division 1	0–3
1933	Manchester City	H	Division 1	2–1
1939	Charlton Athletic	H	Division 1	2–0
1950	Bolton Wanderers	H	Division 1	1–1

1956	Portsmouth	A	Division 1	2–5
1961	Tottenham Hotspur	A	Division 1	2–4
1967	Blackpool	A	Division 1	3–0
1978	Nottingham Forest	A	Division 1	0–2
1984	Notts County	H	Division 1	1–1
1987	Nottingham Forest	H	Littlewoods Cup 5th round	2–0
1989	Sheffield Wednesday	H	Division 1	1–1
1995	Coventry City	A	Premier League	1–0

JANUARY 22ND

1887	Eastern Wanderers	H	Friendly	1–0
1898	Millwall Athletic	A	United League	2–2
1906	Oxford University	A	Friendly	4–0
1910	Middlesbrough	H	Division 1	3–0
1916	Brentford	A	London Combination	2–2
1921	Tottenham Hotspur	H	Division 1	3–2
1927	Sheffield United	H	Division 1	1–1

This was the first game ever to host a live radio commentary.

| 1938 | Wolverhampton Wanderers | A | FA Cup 4th round | 2–1 |
| 1944 | Fulham | H | Football League – South | 1–1 |

1948 Harry 'Peter' Goring joined from Cheltenham Town for £1,000.

| 1949 | Aston Villa | A | Division 1 | 0–1 |
| 1966 | Blackburn Rovers | A | FA Cup 3rd round | 0–3 |

Last senior appearance for Joe Baker.

1972	Huddersfield Town	H	Division 1	1–0
1979	Sheffield Wednesday	Leicester	FA Cup 3rd round 4th replay	2–0
1983	Notts County	A	Division 1	0–1
1985	Hereford United	H	FA Cup 3rd round replay	7–2
1986	Aston Villa	A	Milk Cup 5th round	1–1
1994	Oldham Athletic	H	Premier League	1–1

JANUARY 23RD

1892	Grimsby Town	H	Friendly	4–1
1897	Newcastle United	A	Division 2	0–2
1909	Bristol City	H	Division 1	1–1
1915	Stockport County	H	Division 2	3–1
1926	Liverpool	A	Division 1	0–3
1932	Plymouth Argyle	H	FA Cup 4th round	4–2
1937	Wolverhampton Wanderers	H	Division 1	3–0

1939 Alan Skirton was born in Bath, Avon.

1943	Brentford	A	Football League – South	1–0
1954	Sunderland	H	Division 1	2–2
1960	Manchester City	A	Division 1	2–1
1963	Brighton & Hove Albion	A	Friendly	1–2
1965	Leicester City	H	Division 1	4–3
1971	Portsmouth	A	FA Cup 4th round	1–1

Arsenal were drawn against 2nd Division Portsmouth at Fratton Park in the 4th round of the FA Cup and were held to a 1–1 draw by an equaliser from Pompey's Trebilcock with 15 seconds to go. On a very muddy pitch the Gunners took the lead in 34th minute when a John Radford header was handled on the line by a Portsmouth defender and Peter Storey scored from the penalty spot.

1982	Southampton	A	Division 1	1–3

JANUARY 24TH

1891	Millwall Athletic	A	Friendly	1–0
1903	Gainsborough Trinity	A	Division 2	1–0
1914	Barnsley	H	Division 2	1–0
1920	Aston Villa	H	Division 1	0–1
1925	Sheffield United	A	FA Cup 1st round replay	1–2
1931	Chelsea	A	FA Cup 4th round	1–2
1942	West Ham United	A	London League	0–3
1948	Nottingham Forest	A	Friendly	3–2
1953	Charlton Athletic	A	Division 1	2–2
1959	Colchester United	A	FA Cup 4th round	2–2
1978	Manchester City	H	League Cup 5th round replay	1–0
1987	Manchester United	A	Division 1	0–2
1988	Manchester United	H	Division 1	1–2
1995	Southampton	H	Premier Division	1–1
1998	Middlesbrough	A	FA Cup 4th round	2–1

JANUARY 25TH

1890	Foxes	H	Friendly	7–2
1893	Oxford University	A	Friendly	0–1
1896	Leicester Fosse	A	Division 2	0–1
1899	Sevenoaks	A	Friendly	7–1
1902	Newcastle United	H	FA Cup 1st round	0–2
1908	Preston North End	H	Division 1	1–1
1913	Newcastle United	A	Division 1	1–3
1919	West Ham United	A	London Combination	2–1
1930	Birmingham	H	FA Cup 4th round	2–2
1936	Liverpool	A	FA Cup 4th round	2–0
1940	Tottenham Hotspur	A	League South 'A' Division	1–0

Ted Platt made his senior debut.

1941	West Ham United	A	London War Cup	3–1
1958	Swansea Town	A	Friendly	3–2
1960	GB Olympic XI	H	Friendly	4–0

First senior game for Terry Neill.

1961 Beat Oxford City 9–0 in the 4th round of the Youth Cup

1964	West Bromwich Albion	A	FA Cup 4th round	3–3
1969	Charlton Athletic	H	FA Cup 4th round	2–0
1975	Coventry City	A	FA Cup 4th round	1–1

The darling of the North Bank, Charlie George, made his last first-team appearance. In what finished as a slightly turbulent Highbury career, Charlie had notched up 133 (31 goals) League, 22 (11 goals) FA Cup, 8 (2 goals) FL Cup and 16 (5 goals) European games. Often magnificent, always with an attitude that endeared him to the Arsenal faithful.

1986	Rotherham United	H	FA Cup 4th round	5–1
1989	Somerset Cricket Club	A	Friendly	1–0
1993	Leeds United	H	FA Cup 4th round	2–2

JANUARY 26TH

1889	St Luke's	A	Friendly	
1891	Everton	H	Friendly	0–5
1895	Burton Wanderers	H	Division 2	1–1
1901	Lincoln City	A	Division 2	3–3
1907	Newcastle United	A	Division 1	0–1
1918	Brentford	A	London Combination	2–3
1924	Cardiff City	A	Division 1	0–4
1925	West Ham United	Chelsea	FA Cup 1st round 2nd replay	0–1
1929	Mansfield Town	H	FA Cup 4th round	2–0
1935	Leicester City	A	FA Cup 4th round	1–0
1946	Leicester City	A	Football League – South	5–4
1952	Manchester City	H	Division 1	2–2
1957	Newport County	A	FA Cup 4th round	2–0
1963	Tottenham Hotspur	A	Friendly	1–3

1969 James Ramsay died in Sidcup.

1971 The 4th round FA Cup replay at home to Portsmouth was called off less than 2 hours before kick-off due to a waterlogged pitch.

1974	Aston Villa	H	FA Cup 4th round	1–1
1980	Brighton & Hove Albion	H	FA Cup 4th round	2–0
1982	Brighton & Hove Albion	H	Division 1	0–0
1985	York City	A	FA Cup 4th round	0–1

JANUARY 27TH

1894	Sheffield Wednesday	H	FA Cup 1st round	1–2
1900	Bedminster	H	Friendly	3–0
1906	Stoke	H	Division 1	1–2
1912	Sheffield United	H	Division 1	3–1
1917	Watford	H	London Combination	1–1
1923	Manchester City	A	Division 1	0–0
1934	Crystal Palace	H	FA Cup 4th round	7–0

First game for goalkeeper Alex Wilson.

1945	Fulham	H	Football League – South	8–3
1951	Northampton Town	H	FA Cup 4th round	3–2
1968	Shrewsbury Town	A	FA Cup 3rd round	1–1
1973	Newcastle United	H	Division 1	2–2
1977	Bristol City	A	Division 1	0–2
1979	Notts County	H	FA Cup 4th round	2–0
1981	FC Cologne	H	Friendly	1–0
1989	Bermuda National XI	A	Friendly	4–2
1990	Queen's Park Rangers	H	FA Cup 4th round	0–0
1991	Leeds United	H	FA Cup 4th round	0–0

1997 Andy Linighan, the scorer of the last minute winner in the 1993 FA Cup final against Sheffield Wednesday, was sold to Crystal Palace for a fee of approximately £100,000.

JANUARY 28TH

1888	Champion Hill	H	Friendly	6–0
1893	Chatham	A	Friendly	1–3
1899	Derby County	H	FA Cup 1st round	0–6
1905	Bury	H	Division 1	2–1
1911	Sunderland	A	Division 1	2–2
1922	Bradford Park Avenue	A	FA Cup 2nd round	3–2
1928	Everton	H	FA Cup 4th round	4–3
1931	Grimsby Town	H	Division 1	9–1

Arsenal's biggest League win at Highbury.

1939	Aston Villa	A	Division 1	3–1
1950	Swansea Town	H	FA Cup 4th round	2–1
1956	Aston Villa	H	FA Cup 4th round	4–1
1959	Colchester United	H	FA Cup 4th round replay	4–0
1961	Charlton Athletic	A	Friendly	2–4
1967	Bristol Rovers	A	FA Cup 3rd round	3–0
1978	Wolverhampton Wanderers	H	FA Cup 4th round	2–1
1984	Stoke City	A	Division 1	0–1
1998	Chelsea	H	Coca-Cola Cup semi-final 1st leg	2–1

JANUARY 29TH

1887	Erith	A	Friendly	3–2
1894	Blackpool	H	Friendly	5–2
1898	Burnley	A	FA Cup 1st round	1–3
1900	Chatham	H	Southern District Combination	4–0

1906 Goalkeeper Hugh Laughlan McDonald joined from Beith for the start of three spells with the club.

1910	Bolton Wanderers	H	Division 1	2–0
1916	Fulham	H	Friendly	2–0
1921	Sunderland	H	Division 1	1–2
1927	Port Vale	A	FA Cup 4th round	2–2
1930	Birmingham	A	FA Cup 4th round replay	1–0
1938	Sunderland	A	Division 1	1–1
1944	Clapton Orient	H	Football League – South	1–0
1949	Derby County	A	FA Cup 4th round	0–1
1955	Wolverhampton Wanderers	A	FA Cup 4th round	0–1

Final senior game for Arthur Milton. His record: 75 (18 goals) League and 9 (3 goals) FA Cup.

1960	West Ham United	H	Friendly	0–1
1964	West Bromwich Albion	H	FA Cup 4th round replay	2–0
1966	Stoke City	A	Division 1	3–1
1972	Sheffield United	A	Division 1	5–0
1975	Coventry City	H	FA Cup 4th round replay	3–0
1977	Coventry City	H	FA Cup 4th round	3–1

Peter Storey made his final senior appearance for the Gunners. His record finished: 391 (9 goals) League, 51 (4 goals) FA Cup, 37 (2 goals) FL Cup and 22 (2 goals) European games. The hard man of the Fairs Cup and Double winning teams had much more to his game than he was often given credit for and fully merited the 19 full England caps he was awarded.

| 1983 | Leeds United | H | FA Cup 4th round | 1–1 |

1988 Lee Dixon, after an undistinguished start to his career in the lower divisions with Burnley, Chester City, and Bury was signed by George Graham from Stoke City for a fee of £400,000.

| 1992 | Liverpool | A | Division 1 | 0–2 |
| 1997 | West Ham United | A | Premier League | 2–1 |

JANUARY 30TH

1892	Burton Wanderers	H	Friendly	3–1
1893	Sherwood Foresters	A	Friendly	3–0
1897	Ilkeston Town	H	Friendly	7–0
1899	Millwall	H	Friendly	2–4
1904	Manchester United	A	Division 2	0–1
1909	Preston North End	A	Division 1	0–0
1915	Chelsea	A	FA Cup 2nd round	0–1
1926	Blackburn Rovers	H	FA Cup 4th round	3–1
1932	Manchester City	H	Division 1	4–0
1935	West Bromwich Albion	A	Division 1	3–0
1937	Manchester United	H	FA Cup 4th round	5–0
1943	Reading	A	Football League – South	5–4
1954	Norwich City	H	FA Cup 4th round	1–2
1963	Oxford United	H	FA Cup 3rd round	5–1
1965	Peterborough United	A	FA Cup 4th round	1–2
1968	Shrewsbury Town	H	FA Cup 3rd round replay	2–0
1971	Liverpool	A	Division 1	0–2

Another League defeat left the Gunners 5 points behind Leeds United with a game in hand. Liverpool took the lead as early as 3rd minute through Toshack and completed the victory 5 minutes after the interval when Smith fired home a free kick.

| 1974 | Aston Villa | A | FA Cup 4th round replay | 0–2 |
| 1982 | Leeds United | H | Division 1 | 1–0 |

1984 Tony Adams signed his first professional contract with the club.
1987 Tommy Caton was sold to Oxford United for £180,000.

| 1988 | Brighton & Hove Albion | A | FA Cup 4th round | 2–1 |
| 1991 | Leeds United | A | FA Cup 4th round replay | 1–1 |

JANUARY 31ST

| 1891 | Old Westminsters | A | London Senior Cup | 4–5 |

1893 Steven Dunn was born in Darlaston, Staffordshire.

1903	Burton United	H	Division 2	3–0
1914	Everton	H	Friendly	1–2
1920	Bristol City	A	FA Cup 2nd round	0–1
1925	Chelsea	H	Friendly	0–1
1931	Birmingham	H	Division 1	1–1
1934	Tottenham Hotspur	H	Division 1	1–3
1942	Watford	H	London League	11–0
1948	Preston North End	H	Division 1	3–0
1953	Bury	H	FA Cup 4th round	6–2

1959	Tottenham Hotspur	A	Division 1	4–1
1962	Manchester United	A	FA Cup 4th round	0–1
1970	Coventry City	A	Division 1	0–2
1976	Sheffield United	H	Division 1	1–0
1981	Coventry City	H	Division 1	2–2
1987	Plymouth Argyle	H	FA Cup 4th round	6–1
1990	Queen's Park Rangers	A	FA Cup 4th round replay	0–2
1993	Liverpool	H	Premier Division	0–1
1994	Bolton Wanderers	A	FA Cup 3rd round	2–2
1998	Southampton	H	Premier League	3–0

With a new-found team spirit Arsenal poured forward in search of the victory that would give them an outside chance of challenging for the Premiership title. Chance after chance fell for the Gunners but it seemed as though a goal would not materialise and Alex Manninger was required to make a couple of crucial saves in the first half that received acclaim from the Highbury crowd. The second half continued as the first with shots flying in at the Southampton goal until the 62nd minute when Bergkamp sprung the offside trap and opened the scoring. Parlour then hit the woodwork twice in as many minutes before Tony Adams scored a header from a Petit corner. A couple of minutes later Arsenal scored their 3rd goal when Anelka tapped in at the far post after some great work by Bergkamp. Overmars also hit the post in the final minute for what was to be Arsenal's 27th attempt on goal. After 23 games the Gunners were in 5th position with 41 points.

FEBRUARY 1ST

1890	Great Marlow	H	London Charity Cup	4–1
1896	Burnley	A	FA Cup 1st round	1–6
1902	Chesterfield	A	Division 2	3–1
1908	Tottenham Hotspur	A	Friendly	1–0
1913	Liverpool	H	FA Cup 2nd round	1–4
1919	Tottenham Hotspur	H	London Combination	2–3
1930	Bolton Wanderers	A	Division 1	0–0
1933	Bolton Wanderers	A	Division 1	4–0
1935	Robert Davidson arrived from St Johnstone for £4,000.			
1936	Stoke City	H	Division 1	1–0
1939	Wolverhampton Wanderers	H	Division 1	0–0
1941	Clapton Orient	A	London War Cup	3–3
1947	Manchester United	H	Division 1	6–2
1956	Tommy Lawton moved on to Kettering Town as player-manager for £1,000. He played only 35 (13 goals) League and 2 (1 goal) FA Cup games for the Gunners.			
1958	Manchester United	H	Division 1	4–5
1964	Manchester United	A	Division 1	1–3
1969	Nottingham Forest	H	Division 1	1–1
1971	Portsmouth	H	FA Cup 4th round replay	3–2

The Gunners scraped through 3–2 in their FA Cup 4th round replay on a very wet Highbury surface. Piper gave the visitors a shock lead in 6th minute but Arsenal equalised 7 minutes later through Charlie George, who made his first start since the opening day of the League season. In 34th minute Peter Simpson put the Gunners ahead when he volleyed home a George Armstrong corner. Portsmouth fought back after the break and were rewarded with an equaliser in 57th minute by Ley. With 5 minutes remaining John Radford was fouled in the penalty area and Peter Storey made Pompey suffer the ultimate price with the winning goal from the penalty spot.

1975	Liverpool	H	Division 1	2–0
1986	Luton Town	H	Division 1	2–1
1988	Kevin Campbell signed his first professional forms for the club.			
1992	Manchester United	H	Division 1	1–1
1995	AC Milan	H	European Super Cup 1st leg	0–0
1997	Leeds United	A	Premier League	0–0

FEBRUARY 2ND

1889	Ilford	H	Friendly	1–2
1895	Bolton Wanderers	A	FA Cup 1st round	0–1
1907	Bristol City	H	FA Cup 2nd round	2–1
1918	Crystal Palace	A	London Combination	4–1
1927	Port Vale	H	FA Cup 4th round replay	1–0

Manager Herbert Chapman relegated first-team trainer George Hardy to the reserves following comments from the bench voiced during this match. It then allowed the promotion of Tom Whittaker to the job.

1929	Manchester City	H	Division 1	0–0
1935	Sheffield Wednesday	H	Division 1	4–1
1938	Leicester City	H	Division 1	3–1
1946	Birmingham City	H	Football League – South	0–3
1952	Barnsley	H	FA Cup 4th round	4–0
1957	Sheffield Wednesday	H	Division 1	6–3
1968	Bobby Gould signed from Coventry City for £90,000.			
1974	Burnley	H	Division 1	1–1
1982	Wolverhampton Wanderers	H	Division 1	2–1
1983	Leeds United	H	FA Cup 4th round replay	2–1
1984	Martin Keown signed as professional for the club he supported as a boy.			
1985	Coventry City	H	Division 1	2–1
1991	Chelsea	A	Division 1	1–2

FEBRUARY 3RD

1894	Lincoln City	A	Division 2	0–3
1899	Bob John was born in Barry Dock, South Wales.			
1900	Middlesbrough	A	Division 2	0–1
1902	Queen's Park Rangers	A	London League Premier Division	2–2
1906	Watford	H	FA Cup 2nd round	3–0
1917	Clapton Orient	A	London Combination	2–2
1923	Nottingham Forest	A	Division 1	1–2
1926	Burnley	H	Division 1	1–2
1934	Everton	H	Division 1	1–2
1937	Derby County	A	Division 1	4–5
1942	John Sneddon was born in Bonnybridge, Scotland.			
1945	Reading	A	Football League Cup – South	3–1
1951	Newcastle United	A	Division 1	0–0

| 1954 | George Swindin was granted a free transfer to Peterborough United where he became player-manager. | | | |

| 1962 | West Bromwich Albion | H | Division 1 | 0–1 |
| 1968 | Manchester City | A | Division 1 | 1–1 |

Bobby Gould's debut.

1973	Bradford City	H	FA Cup 4th round	2–0
1979	Manchester United	A	Division 1	2–0
1993	Leeds United	A	FA Cup 4th round replay	3–2
1996	Coventry City	H	Premier League	1–1

FEBRUARY 4TH

1888	Tottenham Hotspur	H	Friendly	6–2
1892	Sheffield United	H	Friendly	1–4
1893	Casuals	A	Friendly	4–2
1899	Glossop North End	A	Division 2	0–2
1905	Bristol City	H	FA Cup 1st round	0–0

Final appearance of William Gooing. Record: 94 (45 goals) League and 12 (3 goals) FA Cup.

1911	Swindon Town	A	FA Cup 2nd round	0–1
1922	Newcastle United	H	Division 1	2–1
1928	Derby County	H	Division 1	3–4
1933	Everton	A	Division 1	1–1
1939	Sunderland	H	Division 1	2–0
1950	Birmingham City	A	Division 1	1–2
1956	Sunderland	H	Division 1	3–1
1961	Newcastle United	A	Division 1	3–3

Last game for Tommy Docherty. Record: 83 (1 goal) League and 7 FA Cup.

| 1967 | Chelsea | H | Division 1 | 2–1 |

| 1970 | Kevin Campbell was born in Lambeth, London. | | | |

1975	England XI	H	Friendly	0–2
1978	Aston Villa	H	Division 1	0–1
1984	Queen's Park Rangers	H	Division 1	0–2
1986	Aston Villa	H	Milk Cup 5th round replay	1–2
1989	West Ham United	H	Division 1	2–1

| 1993 | Martin Keown rejoined Arsenal from Everton in a deal worth over £2,000,000. | | | |

| 1995 | Sheffield Wednesday | A | Premier League | 1–3 |

Kevin Campbell's final League game. He reached 166 (46 goals) League, 19 (2 goals) FA Cup, 24 (6 goals) FL Cup and 17 (5 goals) European appearances.

| 1997 | Leeds United | H | FA Cup 4th round | 0–1 |

Last game for John Hartson who had scored a total of 24 goals in 53 League, 3 FA Cup, 6 FL Cup and 9 European games.

Hartson left, after consultation with manager Wenger, because it was deemed that an offer made by West Ham would not only be good business for the club but beneficial to the player's career also.

FEBRUARY 5TH

1887	Millwall Rovers	A	Friendly	0–4
1898	Manchester City	H	Division 2	2–2
1910	Everton	A	FA Cup 2nd round	0–5

1916	Watford	H	London Combination	1–1
1921	Sunderland	A	Division 1	1–5

Final appearance for Frederick Pagnam. His record: 50 (26 goals) League and 3 (1 goal) FA Cup games.

1926	Joe Hulme signed from Blackburn Rovers for £3,500.			
1927	Liverpool	A	Division 1	0–3
1931	Leicester City	A	Division 1	7–2
1938	Derby County	H	Division 1	3–0
1944	Brentford	A	Football League – South	1–4
1949	Sunderland	H	Division 1	5–0
1955	Preston North End	H	Division 1	2–0
1960	Brian Marwood was born in Seaham Harbour, Durham.			
1966	Burnley	H	Division 1	1–1
1972	Reading	A	FA Cup 4th round	2–1
1974	Leeds United	A	Division 1	1–3
1977	Sunderland	H	Division 1	0–0
1983	Brighton & Hove Albion	H	Division 1	3–1

FEBRUARY 6TH

1892	Cambridge University	H	Friendly	2–1
1893	Royal Lancaster Regiment	H	Friendly	2–0
1894	Rotherham Town	A	Division 2	1–1
1899	Kettering Town	H	United League	4–2
1904	Fulham	H	FA Cup 1st round	1–0
1909	Millwall Athletic	H	FA Cup 2nd round	1–1
1915	Leeds City	H	Division 2	2–0
1926	Leeds United	A	Division 1	2–4

Debut for Joe Hulme.

1932	Everton	A	Division 1	3–1
1937	Manchester United	H	Division 1	1–1
1943	Crystal Palace	H	Football League – South	9–0
1954	Manchester City	A	Division 1	0–0
1960	Blackburn Rovers	H	Division 1	5–2
1965	Chelsea	A	Division 1	1–2
1968	Huddersfield Town	A	League Cup semi-final 2nd leg	3–1

Arsenal booked their trip to Wembley with an aggregate victory of 6–3.

1971	Manchester City	H	Division 1	1–0

After losing their previous two League games, Arsenal were desperate for victory at home to Manchester City. With Leeds United losing at Liverpool it was imperative that the Gunners won and they finally achieved the breakthrough with only 4 minutes left. Peter Simpson carried the ball from almost the halfway line and shot from 35 yards but City keeper Corrigan could only parry the ball to John Radford who scored a priceless goal and gave Arsenal a 1–0 victory.

1982	Sunderland	A	Division 1	0–0

FEBRUARY 7TH

1891	St Bartholomew's Hospital	H	Friendly	5–4

1900	Portsmouth	A	Southern District Combination	1–3
1903	Sheffield United	H	FA Cup 1st round	1–3
1914	Bury	A	Division 2	1–1
1920	Oldham Athletic	H	Division 1	3–2
1925	Blackburn Rovers	A	Division 1	0–1
1931	Sheffield United	A	Division 1	1–1
1942	Aldershot	A	London League	0–1
1948	Stoke City	A	Division 1	0–0

1951 Eddie Kelly was born in Glasgow.

1953	Tottenham Hotspur	H	Division 1	4–0

Apart from the obvious delight in beating Spurs a couple of milestones were achieved during the game. The first goal scored by Cliff Holton was the 100th goal in all League and Cup derby games between the two clubs, and the 4th goal scored by Jimmy Logie was the 100th goal scored in all League games.

1959	Manchester City	A	Division 1	0–0
1970	Stoke City	H	Division 1	0–0

1970 Frank Moss died in Preston.

1976	Norwich City	A	Division 1	1–3
1978	Liverpool	A	League Cup semi-final 1st leg	1–2
1981	Stoke City	A	Division 1	1–1
1988	Everton	A	Littlewoods Cup semi-final 1st leg	1–0

A spectacular goal from Perry Groves decided the game and gave Arsenal a valuable away goal.

1993	Crystal Palace	A	Coca-Cola Cup semi-final 1st leg	3–1

Arsenal were always too good for a poor Crystal Palace side that included Eddie McGoldrick as sweeper, and effectively won the tie in this first leg.

FEBRUARY 8TH

1890	Chiswick Park	H	Friendly	1–1
1896	Royal Ordnance	H	Friendly	6–0
1897	Luton Town	H	Friendly	5–1
1902	Gainsborough Trinity	H	Division 2	5–0

First game for Thomas Tindal Fitchie.

1904	Brentford	H	London League Premier Division	3–2
1905	Bristol City	A	FA Cup 1st round replay	0–1
1908	Aston Villa	H	Division 1	0–1
1913	Oldham Athletic	H	Division 1	0–0
1919	Chelsea	A	London Combination	2–1
1930	Everton	H	Division 1	4–0
1936	Blackburn Rovers	A	Division 1	1–0

Final senior game for Frank Moss, regular goalkeeper during the championship-winning seasons of 1932–33, 1933–34 and 1934–35. He made 143 (1 goal) League and 16 FA Cup appearances.

1940	Watford	H	League South 'A' Division	2–2
1941	Clapton Orient	H	London War Cup	15–2

Leslie Compton scored a staggering 10 goals in this game, Dennis, his brother also netted twice.

1947	Blackpool	H	Division 1	1–1
1960	Peterborough United	A	Friendly	1–1

1964	Burnley	H	Division 1	3–2
1975	Wolverhampton Wanderers	A	Division 1	0–1
1979	Brian McDermott graduated from apprentice to full professional.			
1987	Tottenham Hotspur	H	Littlewoods Cup semi-final 1st leg	0–1
1992	Notts County	A	Division 1	1–0
1995	AC Milan	A	European Super Cup 2nd leg	0–2
1998	Chelsea	H	Premier League	2–0

A frantic start to the game saw both physios on the pitch in the early stages of what turned out to be as physical a game as the confrontation at Stamford Bridge had been earlier in the season. In the 4th minute a bad backpass saw Anelka charge through to see his shot parried by the keeper only for Stephen Hughes to smash home the rebound from the edge of the area. Steve Bould then appeared to haul back Vialli, who was through on goal, but was let off with a yellow card. Manninger continued to impress with a couple of fine saves before Tony Adams knocked down a free kick for Stephen Hughes to score with a diving header from close range to seal the Gunners 2–0 victory. Arsenal remained in 5th position.

FEBRUARY 9TH

1889	Gravesend	A	Kent Senior Cup	3–3
1893	Cambridge University	A	Friendly	2–4
1895	Rotherham Town	H	Division 2	1–1
1898	Maidstone United	A	Friendly	3–0
1901	Blackburn Rovers	H	FA Cup 1st round	2–0
1903	Millwall	H	Southern Professional Charity Cup	2–3
1907	Liverpool	A	Division 1	0–4
1918	Fulham	H	London Combination	0–3
1924	Sheffield United	A	Division 1	1–3
1929	Huddersfield Town	A	Division 1	1–0
1935	Birmingham	A	Division 1	0–3
1946	Tottenham Hotspur	H	Football League – South	1–1
1952	Tottenham Hotspur	A	Division 1	2–1
1957	Manchester United	A	Division 1	2–6
1961	Tommy Docherty transferred to Chelsea as player-coach.			
1963	Leicester City	A	Division 1	0–2
1980	Aston Villa	H	Division 1	3–1
1984	Paul Mariner was signed by Don Howe for Arsenal from Ipswich Town at a price of £150,000.			
1983	Leeds United	A	FA Cup 4th round 2nd replay	1–1
1994	Bolton Wanderers	H	FA Cup 4th round	1–3

FEBRUARY 10TH

1894	Crewe Alexandra	H	Division 2	3–2
1900	Chesterfield	H	Division 2	2–0
1906	Wolverhampton Wanderers	H	Division 1	2–1
1909	Millwall Athletic	A	FA Cup 2nd round replay	0–1
1912	Bolton Wanderers	H	Division 1	3–0
1917	Fulham	H	London Combination	3–2

1922	John Mackie joined from Forth River (Belfast).			
1923	Nottingham Forest	H	Division 1	2–0
1927	Leicester City	A	Division 1	1–2
1927	Ben Marden was born in Fulham, London.			
1934	Middlesbrough	A	Division 1	2–0
1940	Brentford	H	League South 'C' Division	3–1
1945	Clapton Orient	H	Football League Cup – South	5–0
1948	Jimmy Rimmer was born in Southport, Lancashire.			
1951	Manchester United	A	FA Cup 5th round	0–1
1962	Birmingham City	A	Division 1	0–1

Mel Charles's last game, his final record: 60 (26 goals) League and 4 (2 goals) FA Cup appearances.

1968	Newcastle United	H	Division 1	0–0
1973	Liverpool	A	Division 1	2–0
1979	Middlesbrough	H	Division 1	0–0
1984	Gus Caesar graduated to professional status.			
1993	Wimbledon	H	Premier League	0–1
1996	Nottingham Forest	A	Premier League	1–0

FEBRUARY 11TH

1888	Millwall Rovers	H	Friendly	3–3

First game to be played at The Manor Ground (Plumstead).

1893	Small Heath	H	Friendly	3–1
1895	Luton Town	A	Friendly	2–1
1899	Walsall	H	Division 2	0–0
1905	Blackburn Rovers	H	Division 1	2–0

Debut of Andy Ducat.

1911	Bradford City	H	Division 1	0–0
1920	Aston Villa	A	Division 1	1–2
1922	Newcastle United	A	Division 1	1–3
1928	West Ham United	A	Division 1	2–2
1933	Blackpool	H	Division 1	1–1

Final senior game for Horace Cope. His record: 65 League and 11 FA Cup appearances.

1950	Burnley	H	FA Cup 5th round	2–0
1956	Aston Villa	A	Division 1	1–1
1961	Cardiff City	H	Division 1	2–3

Final senior appearance of Len Wills who played 195 (4 goals) League and 13 FA Cup games.

1967	Leicester City	A	Division 1	1–2
1978	Leicester City	A	Division 1	1–1
1984	Liverpool	A	Division 1	1–2
1988	David Hillier was taken on to the professional staff.			
1989	Millwall	A	Division 1	2–1
1992	Norwich City	H	Division 1	1–1
1995	Leicester City	H	Premier League	1–1

FEBRUARY 12TH

1887	Alexandria United	A	Friendly	6–0
1894	Walsall Town Swifts	A	Division 2	2–1

1898	Grimsby Town	A	Division 2	4–1
1910	Blackburn Rovers	H	Division 1	0–1
1910	Andy Ducat made his England international debut against Ireland in the 1–1 draw in Belfast			
1916	Brentford	A	London Combination	1–2
1921	Oldham Athletic	A	Division 1	1–1
1927	Leeds United	H	Division 1	1–0
1937	Laurie Scott signed from Bradford City in a part exchange deal with Ernest Tucket.			
1938	Preston North End	H	FA Cup 5th round	0–1
1944	Watford	A	Football League – South	2–0
1949	Swindon Town	A	Friendly	4–1
1955	Burnley	A	Division 1	0–3
1966	Southampton	A	Friendly	3–1
	Last appearance in an Arsenal shirt for Joe Baker.			
1969	West Bromwich Albion	A	FA Cup 5th round	0–1
1972	Derby County	H	Division 1	2–0
1977	Manchester City	A	Division 1	0–1
1985	Liverpool	A	Division 1	0–3

FEBRUARY 13TH

1892	Chatham	A	Friendly	3–2
1893	Third Lanark	H	Friendly	2–1
1897	Leicester Fosse	A	Division 2	3–6
1899	Glossop North End	H	Division 2	3–0
1904	Bradford City	A	Division 2	0–1
1909	Manchester City	A	Division 1	2–2
1915	Clapton Orient	A	Division 2	0–1
1926	Newcastle United	H	Division 1	3–0
1932	Portsmouth	A	FA Cup 5th round	2–0
1937	Sheffield Wednesday	A	Division 1	0–0
1943	Tottenham Hotspur	H	Football League – South	1–0
1954	Cardiff City	H	Division 1	1–1
1956	Liam Brady was born in Dublin.			
1960	Blackpool	A	Division 1	1–2
1965	Leeds United	H	Division 1	1–2
	Final appearance of Terry Anderson in Arsenal colours.			
1971	Arsenal were due to play Manchester City at Maine Road in 5th round of the FA Cup but the match was postponed.			
1979	Queen's Park Rangers	A	Division 1	2–1
1982	Notts County	H	Division 1	1–0
1988	Luton Town	H	Division 1	2–1
	Debut for Lee Dixon.			
1991	Leeds United	A	FA Cup 4th round 2nd replay	2–1
1993	Nottingham Forest	H	FA Cup 5th round	2–0
1994	Norwich City	A	Premier League	1–1

FEBRUARY 14TH

1891	Crusaders	H	London Charity Cup	1–0
1903	Glossop North End	H	Division 2	0–0
1912	Bryn Jones was born in Merthyr Tydfil, Wales.			

1914	Huddersfield Town	H	Division 2	0–1
1920	Oldham Athletic	A	Division 1	0–3
1925	Huddersfield Town	H	Division 1	0–5

1927 Daniel Lewis made his Welsh international debut against England in the 3–3 draw in Wrexham.

1931	Derby County	H	Division 1	6–3
1942	Millwall	H	London League	10–0
1948	Burnley	H	Division 1	3–0
1953	Burnley	A	FA Cup 5th round	2–0
1959	Sheffield United	H	FA Cup 5th round	2–2
1970	Everton	A	Division 1	2–2

Last senior appearance of Bobby Gould. Record: 65 (16 goals) League, 7 (3 goals) FA Cup, 9 (3 goals) FL Cup and 2 (1 goal) European games.

1978	Liverpool	H	League Cup semi-final 2nd leg	0–0
1987	Sheffield Wednesday	A	Division 1	1–1
1989	France	H	Friendly	2–0

1995 Glenn Helder, previously with Ajax and Sparta, was signed for £2,300,000 from Vitesse Arnhem.

1996	Aston Villa	H	Coca-Cola Cup semi-final 1st leg	2–2

1997 John Hartson was transferred to West Ham United for a basic fee of £3,200,000 but with the provision that the sum payable would escalate up to a maximum £5,000,000 depending on certain criteria.

FEBRUARY 15TH

1890	Chatham	A	Kent Senior Cup	5–0
1896	Port Vale	A	Division 2	2–0
1897	Glasgow Celtic	H	Friendly	4–5
1899	Gravesend	A	Friendly	2–3
1902	Middlesbrough	A	Division 2	0–1
1908	Liverpool	A	Division 1	1–4
1913	Chelsea	A	Division 1	1–1
1919	Clapton Orient	H	London Combination	4–0
1930	Middlesbrough	A	FA Cup 5th round	2–0

1934 Jimmy Bloomfield was born in Kensington, London.

1936	Newcastle United	A	FA Cup 5th round	3–3
1941	Brighton & Hove Albion	A	Football League War Cup	4–1
1958	Barnsley	A	Friendly	6–0
1958	Eintracht Frankfurt	H	Friendly	1–0
1964	Liverpool	H	FA Cup 5th round	0–1

1968 Eddie Kelly upgraded from apprentice to full professional.

1969	Burnley	H	Division 1	2–0
1975	Leicester City	H	FA Cup 5th round	0–0
1977	Middlesbrough	A	Division 1	0–3
1981	St Mirren	A	Provan Jewellers Challenge Cup	3–2
1983	Manchester United	H	Milk Cup semi-final 1st leg	2–4
1986	Luton Town	A	FA Cup 5th round	2–2
1992	Sheffield Wednesday	H	Division 1	7–1
1997	Tottenham Hotspur	A	Premier League	0–0
1998	Crystal Palace	H	FA Cup 5th round	0–0

FEBRUARY 16TH

1889	Millwall Rovers	H	Friendly	won
1895	Chatham	A	Friendly	6–0
1901	Stockport County	A	Division 2	1–3
1907	Bristol City	H	Division 1	1–2

1907 Tim Coleman made his only appearance for England against Ireland in the 1–0 victory at Goodison Park, Everton.

1918	Queen's Park Rangers	A	London Combination	3–0
1924	Aston Villa	H	Division 1	0–1
1929	Swindon Town	A	FA Cup 5th round	0–0
1935	Reading	A	FA Cup 5th round	1–0
1938	Manchester City	A	Division 1	2–1
1946	Tottenham Hotspur	A	Football League – South	0–2
1952	Preston North End	H	Division 1	3–3

1955 Arthur Milton was sold to Bristol City for £4,000.

1957	Preston North End	A	FA Cup 5th round	3–3
1960	Ipswich Town	A	Friendly	0–4
1963	Bolton Wanderers	H	Division 1	3–2
1974	Tottenham Hotspur	H	Division 1	0–1
1980	Bolton Wanderers	A	FA Cup 5th round	1–1
1982	Middlesbrough	H	Division 1	1–0
1991	Leeds United	H	FA Cup 4th round 3rd replay	0–0

FEBRUARY 17TH

1894	Lincoln City	H	Division 2	4–0
1900	Gainsborough Trinity	A	Division 2	1–1
1902	Queen's Park Rangers	H	London League Premier Division	3–0
1906	Blackburn Rovers	H	Division 1	3–2

Hugh McDonald's debut.

1906 Jimmy Ashcroft became the first ever Arsenal player to play for England in the 5–0 victory over Ireland in Belfast.

1912	Bradford City	A	Division 1	1–1
1917	Chelsea	H	London Combination	3–0
1923	Chelsea	A	Division 1	0–0
1932	Grimsby Town	H	Division 1	4–0
1934	Derby County	H	FA Cup 5th round	1–0

1936 Joe Haverty was born in Dublin.

1945	Portsmouth	A	Football League Cup – South	4–2
1951	West Bromwich Albion	H	Division 1	0–2
1962	Dundee	H	Friendly	2–2
1968	Swansea Town	A	FA Cup 4th round	1–0
1971	Manchester City	A	FA Cup 5th round	2–1

Arsenal faced a tough trip to Maine Road to play Manchester City in 5th round of FA Cup. Charlie George scored both of the Gunners' goals in 17th and 51st minutes to set up a 2–1 win. His 1st was an 18-yard free kick and his 2nd was a cool finish slotting the ball past City keeper Corrigan after picking up the ball just inside the opposition's half. City pulled a goal back through Bell 5 minutes from time but Arsenal thoroughly deserved the victory.

| 1973 | Leicester City | H | Division 1 | 1–0 |
| 1990 | Sheffield Wednesday | A | Division 1 | 0–1 |

FEBRUARY 18TH

1888	Erith	H	Friendly	2–1
1893	Millwall Athletic	H	Friendly	5–0
1899	Burton Swifts	A	Division 2	2–1
1905	Corinthians	A	Friendly	1–2
1911	Blackburn Rovers	A	Division 1	0–1
1922	Leicester City	H	FA Cup 3rd round	3–0
1928	Aston Villa	H	FA Cup 5th round	4–1
1939	Chelsea	H	Division 1	1–0
1950	Derby County	H	Division 1	1–0
1953	Derby County	H	Division 1	6–2
1956	Charlton Athletic	A	FA Cup 5th round	2–0
1958	Bolton Wanderers	H	Division 1	1–2

Last game for Derek Tapscott. His record: 119 (62 goals) League and 13 (6 goals) FA Cup appearances.

1959	Sheffield United	A	FA Cup 5th round replay	0–3
1961	West Bromwich Albion	A	Division 1	3–2

League debut of David Bacuzzi, son of former Fulham and England international Joe Bacuzzi.

1964	Ipswich Town	A	Division 1	2–1
1965				

Terry Anderson was transferred to Norwich City having made 26 senior appearances for Arsenal in which he scored 7 goals. After a career in the lower divisions he later became a publican in Norfolk but, in January 1980, was found drowned after a training run in Yarmouth.

1967	Bolton Wanderers	A	FA Cup 4th round	0–0
1969	Ipswich Town	H	Division 1	0–2
1970	Manchester City	A	Division 1	1–1
1976	Derby County	A	Division 1	0–2
1978	Walsall	H	FA Cup 5th round	4–1
1984	Aston Villa	H	Division 1	1–1

Debut for Paul Mariner.

1987 Tony Adams made his international debut for England in the 4–2 victory over Spain in Madrid. He also became the first player to be born after England won the World Cup in 1966 to play for England at full international level.

1989	Queen's Park Rangers	A	Division 1	0–0
1998	Chelsea	A	Coca-Cola Cup semi-final 2nd leg	1–3

FEBRUARY 19TH

1898	Millwall Athletic	H	United League	2–2
1900	Derby County	H	Friendly	0–1
1901	Chesterfield	A	Division 2	1–0
1905	Herbie Roberts was born in Oswestry, Shropshire.			
1910	Fulham	H	Friendly	2–2
1916	Reading	H	London Combination	4–1

This was the infamous game when full-back Robert Benson, who had been engaged on munitions work to assist the war effort and who thus had not played football for almost 12 months, chose to help out Arsenal when they were a man short.

During the match Benson felt unwell, had to retire from the field and died later in the dressing-room.

Benson's record for Arsenal: played 52 (7 goals) League and 2 FA Cup matches.

1921	Oldham Athletic	H	Division 1	2–2
1927	Liverpool	H	FA Cup 5th round	2–0
1930	Derby County	A	Division 1	1–4
1936	Newcastle United	H	FA Cup 5th round replay	3–0
1938	Chelsea	H	Division 1	2–0
1944	Luton Town	H	Football League Cup – South	7–1

1948 Alex Forbes signed from Sheffield United for £12,500.

1949	Wolverhampton Wanderers	A	Division 1	3–1
1955	Leicester City	H	Division 1	1–1
1957	Preston North End	H	FA Cup 5th round replay	2–1
1966	Chelsea	A	Division 1	0–0
1972	Ipswich Town	A	Division 1	1–0
1975	Leicester City	A	FA Cup 5th round replay	1–1
1977	West Ham United	H	Division 1	2–3
1980	Bolton Wanderers	H	FA Cup 5th round replay	3–0
1983	Middlesbrough	A	FA Cup 5th round	1–1
1994	Everton	A	Premier League	1–1
1997	Manchester United	H	Premier League	1–2

FEBRUARY 20TH

1892	Burton Swifts	H	Friendly	3–1
1897	Burton Swifts	H	Division 2	3–0
1898	Chatham	H	Chatham Charity Cup	3–3
1899	Chatham	H	Chatham Charity Cup	3–3
1904	Manchester City	H	FA Cup 2nd round	0–2
1909	Liverpool	H	Division 1	5–0
1915	Blackpool	A	Division 2	2–0
1922	Burnley	A	Division 1	0–1
1926	Aston Villa	A	FA Cup 5th round	1–1
1929	Swindon Town	H	FA Cup 5th round replay	1–0
1932	Blackpool	H	Division 1	2–0
1935	Stoke City	H	Division 1	2–0

Debut for Robert Davidson.

1937	Burnley	A	FA Cup 5th round	7–1
1943	Queen's Park Rangers	A	Football League – South	2–3
1954	Portuguese de Desportos	H	Friendly	7–1
1960	Everton	H	Division 1	2–1
1965	Fulham	H	Division 1	2–0
1971	Ipswich Town	H	Division 1	3–2

Arsenal looked to be coasting to victory at home to Ipswich Town when they took a 3–0 half-time lead through goals by Charlie George, John Radford and Frank McLintock. George headed in a Radford free kick after 15 minutes and the Gunners increased the gap when Radford fired home a Ray Kennedy cross. Shortly before half-time McLintock scored with a header from a George Armstrong corner but Ipswich rallied in the second half. Former Gunner Jimmy Robertson scored directly from a corner with 20 minutes to go and the same player reduced the arrears 10 minutes later to set up a nervous finish to the match which resulted in a 3–2 home win.

1982	Manchester United	A	Division 1	0–0
1988	Manchester United	H	FA Cup 5th round	2–1
1993	Oldham Athletic	A	Premier League	1–0
1998	Death of George Male.			

FEBRUARY 21ST

1891	Casuals	H	London Senior Cup	3–2
1898	Luton Town	H	United League	2–2
1903	West Ham United	H	London League Premier Division	0–1
1914	Lincoln City	A	Division 2	2–5
1920	Manchester United	H	Division 1	0–3
1931	Manchester United	H	Division 1	4–1
1934	Blackburn Rovers	H	Division 1	2–1
1939	Grimsby Town	A	Division 1	1–2
1942	Clapton Orient	A	London League	3–1
1953	Blackpool	A	Division 1	2–3
1956	Everton	H	Division 1	3–2
1959	West Bromwich Albion	A	Division 1	1–1
1961	Vienna Sports Club	H	Friendly	1–0
1962	Rhys Wilmot was born in Newport, Gwent.			
1964	Laurie Brown was sold to Tottenham Hotspur for £40,000.			
1970	Derby County	A	Division 1	2–3
1976	Birmingham City	H	Division 1	1–0
1981	Nottingham Forest	A	Division 1	1–3
1987	Barnsley	H	FA Cup 5th round	2–0
1989	Coventry City	A	Division 1	0–1
1990	Southend United	A	Paul Clark Testimonial	4–2

Final senior appearance of Niall Quinn who had played 67 (14 goals) League, 10 (2 goals) FA Cup and 16 (4 goals) FL Cup games.
Lost the battle for a first-team spot to Alan Smith and had to move on to get his career going again.

| 1995 | George Graham was relieved of his duties as Arsenal manager following allegations that he received improper payments from an overseas agent in respect of the deals that brought Pal Lyderson and John Jensen to the club. | | | |

During his time in charge, Graham had been arguably the most successful Arsenal manager of all time, steering the club to two League Championships, an FA Cup win, two FL Cup wins and a European Cup Winners Cup final victory.

| 1995 | Nottingham Forest | H | Premier League | 1–0 |

Debut for Glenn Helder.

| 1996 | Aston Villa | A | Coca-Cola Cup semi-final 2nd leg | 0–0 |
| 1998 | Crystal Palace | H | Premier League | 1–0 |

Another rearguard performance from Palace who clearly came to defend (sometimes with all 11 players behind the ball) seeking a draw. Tactics Arsenal, without 7 first-team regulars, found difficult to break down. Giles Grimandi scored a rare goal with a volley from an acute angle in the 49th minute to give Arsenal the 3 points that took them back into 2nd place.

FEBRUARY 22ND

| 1890 | 2nd Scots Guards | H | London Charity Cup | 3–0 |

1896	East Stirlingshire	H	Friendly	5–0
1902	Bristol City	H	Division 2	2–0
1904	West Ham United	A	London League Premier Division	4–2
1908	Middlesbrough	H	Division 1	4–1

Final appearance JG 'Tim' Coleman. Record 172 (79 goals) League and 24 (5 goals) FA Cup games.

1919	Queen's Park Rangers	H	London Combination	1–3
1930	Grimsby Town	A	Division 1	1–1

1932 Leslie Compton engaged as a professional.

1933	Derby County	A	Division 1	2–2
1936	Portsmouth	H	Division 1	2–3
1941	Brighton & Hove Albion	H	Football League War Cup	3–1
1947	Stoke City	A	Division 1	1–3

1947 John Radford was born in Hemsworth, Yorkshire.

1958	Tottenham Hotspur	H	Division 1	4–4

1962 Mel Charles left for Cardiff City in a £28,500 deal.

1964	Tottenham Hotspur	A	Division 1	1–3
1967	Bolton Wanderers	H	FA Cup 4th round replay	3–0

1968 Charlie George was awarded a professional contract.

1975	Derby County	A	Division 1	1–2
1992	Tottenham Hotspur	A	Division 1	1–1

FEBRUARY 23RD

1889	Ilford Rovers	A	Friendly	0–1
1895	Burton Swifts	H	Division 2	3–0
1901	West Bromwich Albion	H	FA Cup 2nd round	0–1

1903 John Mackie was born in Monkstown, Co Antrim.

1907	Bristol Rovers	H	FA Cup 3rd round	1–0
1918	Clapton Orient	H	London Combination	7–1
1929	West Ham United	A	Division 1	4–3
1935	Manchester City	A	Division 1	1–1
1946	Brentford	A	Football League – South	3–6
1952	Leyton Orient	A	FA Cup 5th round	3–0
1957	Everton	H	Division 1	2–0
1963	Tottenham Hotspur	H	Division 1	2–3
1965	Tottenham Hotspur	H	Division 1	3–1

When Joe Baker scored the 2nd goal in the game, it was Arsenal's 100th time they had netted against Spurs.

1974	Birmingham City	A	Division 1	1–3
1980	Bolton Wanderers	H	Division 1	2–0
1983	Manchester United	A	Milk Cup semi-final 2nd leg	1–2
1985	Manchester United	H	Division 1	0–1

1989 Rhys Wilmot was sold to Plymouth Argyle for £100,000.

1991	Crystal Palace	H	Division 1	4–0
1997	Wimbledon	H	Premier Division	0–1

FEBRUARY 24TH

1892 Woolwich Arsenal called a meeting at Anderton's Hotel, Fleet Street of local football clubs with the proposal that the possible members elect clubs to form a Southern version of the

Football League. Chatham, Chiswick Park, Crouch End, Ilford, Luton, Marlow, Millwall, Old St Mark's, Reading, Swindon, West Herts (Watford) and Woolwich Arsenal were all duly elected. Tottenham Hotspur with just one vote did not gain recognition! However, the London FA threatened to ban the clubs if they took part and the venture failed.

1894	Middlesbrough Ironopolis	A	Division 2	6–3
1896	Newton Heath	H	Friendly	6–1
1900	Bolton Wanderers	H	Division 2	0–1
1902	Millwall	A	London League Premier Division	1–2
1906	Sunderland	H	FA Cup 3rd round	5–0
1912	Middlesbrough	A	Division 1	2–0
1917	Southampton	A	London Combination	2–0
1923	Athenian League	A	Friendly	11–1
1923	Chelsea	H	Division 1	3–1
1926	Aston Villa	H	FA Cup 5th round replay	2–0
1934	Newcastle United	A	Division 1	1–0
1937	Charlton Athletic	H	Division 1	1–1
1940	Millwall	H	League South 'C' Division	4–1
1945	Reading	H	Football League Cup – South	3–0
1951	Charlton Athletic	A	Division 1	2–5

Jack Kelsey's senior debut.

1954	Preston North End	A	Division 1	1–0
1959	Leeds United	H	Division 1	1–0

Final senior appearance of 'Peter' Goring who played 220 (51 goals) League and 20 (2 goals) FA Cup games before being given a free transfer that took him to Boston.

1962	Blackpool	A	Division 1	1–0

League debut given to George Armstrong.

1968	Manchester United	H	Division 1	0–2
1973	Carlisle United	A	FA Cup 5th round	2–1
1975	Leicester City	A	FA Cup 5th round 2nd replay	1–0
1976	Liverpool	H	Division 1	1–0
1979	Wolverhampton Wanderers	H	Division 1	0–1
1981	Manchester City	H	Division 1	2–0
1988	Everton	H	Littlewoods Cup semi-final 2nd leg	3–1

Arsenal won 4–1 on aggregate after a memorable night at Highbury.

1993	Leeds United	H	Premier League	0–0
1996	West Ham United	A	Premier League	1–0

FEBRUARY 25TH

1886	Wally Hardinge was born in Greenwich, London.			
1888	Forest Gate Alliance	H	Friendly	1–1
1892	Windsor Phoenix	A	Friendly	5–0
1893	Walsall Town Swifts	H	Friendly	2–0
1895	Liverpool	A	Friendly	4–3
1897	Tottenham Hotspur	A	United League	2–2
1899	Port Vale	H	Division 2	1–0
1905	Sheffield Wednesday	H	Division 1	3–0
1911	Nottingham Forest	H	Division 1	3–2

1922	Liverpool	A	Division 1	0–4
1924	Sheffield United	H	Division 1	1–3
1928	Leicester City	A	Division 1	2–3
1933	Blackburn Rovers	H	Division 1	8–0
1939	Preston North End	A	Division 1	1–2

Last match for Wilf Copping who had made 166 League and 19 FA Cup appearances.

1950	Everton	A	Division 1	1–0
1956	Newcastle United	A	Division 1	0–2
1961	Leicester City	H	Division 1	1–3
1967	Newcastle United	A	Division 1	1–2
1978	West Ham United	A	Division 1	2–2
1984	Nottingham Forest	A	Division 1	1–0
1986	Shamrock Rovers	A	Friendly	0–1
1987	Oxford United	A	Division 1	0–0
1989	Luton Town	H	Division 1	2–0
1995	Crystal Palace	A	Premier League	3–0
1998	Crystal Palace	A	FA Cup 5th round replay	2–1

FEBRUARY 26TH

1887	2nd Rifle Brigade	H	Friendly	0–0
1898	Newton Heath	A	Division 2	1–5
1900	Chatham	A	Southern District Combination	2–1
1910	Sunderland	H	Division 1	1–2
1916	Clapton Orient	A	London Combination	1–1
1921	Preston North End	A	Division 1	1–0

1921 Alex Graham made his international debut for Scotland in the 2–0 victory over Ireland in Belfast.

1927	Burnley	H	Division 1	6–2
1938	Portsmouth	A	Division 1	0–0
1944	Queen's Park Rangers	A	Football League Cup – South	1–1
1949	Bolton Wanderers	H	Division 1	5–0
1955	Sheffield Wednesday	H	Division 1	3–2

1966 Joe Baker sold to Nottingham Forest for a fee of £65,000. He amassed 93 goals in 144 League, 4 goals in 10 FA Cup and 3 goals in 2 European games for the Gunners.

1972	Derby County	A	FA Cup 5th round	2–2
1977	Middlesbrough	A	FA Cup 5th round	1–4
1979	Nottingham Forest	A	FA Cup 5th round	1–0
1983	West Bromwich Albion	A	Division 1	0–0

1986 Tony Woodcock won his 42nd and last cap for England (18 of them whilst at Arsenal) in the 2–1 victory over Israel in Ramat Gan. He scored 16 international goals in his career.

1994	Blackburn Rovers	H	Premier League	1–0

FEBRUARY 27TH

1892	Derby County	H	Friendly	3–4
1893	Notts Greenhalgh	H	Friendly	1–3
1897	Millwall Athletic	H	United League	3–1
1899	Clapton	A	Friendly	3–0
1904	Barnsley	H	Division 2	3–0
1905	Queen's Park	H	Friendly	6–1

1909	Bury	A	Division 1	1–1
1915	Derby County	H	Division 2	1–2
1926	Cardiff City	A	Division 1	0–0

1926 Final senior game for Andrew Neil. His record: 54 (10 goals) League and 3 FA Cup matches.

1926 William Harper made his Scottish international debut in the 4–0 defeat against Ireland in Glasgow.

1932	Huddersfield Town	A	FA Cup 6th round	1–0
1937	Grimsby Town	A	Division 1	3–1
1943	Aldershot	H	Football League – South	0–1
1954	Tottenham Hotspur	H	Division 1	0–3
1960	Newcastle United	H	Division 1	1–0
1965	Burnley	A	Division 1	1–2
1971	Derby County	A	Division 1	0–2

1971 Arsenal lost 2–0 to Derby County at the Baseball Ground to leave them 7 points behind Leeds United with 2 games in hand. After 31 minutes McFarland scored from close range to give Derby the lead and Hector completed the scoring in 49th minute. Arsenal threw everything at their opponents for the last half-hour to no avail.

1982	Swansea City	H	Division 1	0–2

1986 Albert Edward 'Pat' Beasley died in Taunton, Somerset.

1988	Charlton Athletic	H	Division 1	4–0
1990	Charlton Athletic	A	Division 1	0–0
1991	Shrewsbury Town	A	FA Cup 5th round	1–0

FEBRUARY 28TH

1891	Clapton	H	London Senior Cup	3–2
1903	Stockport County	H	Division 2	3–1

1903 Final appearance of Fergus Hunt. His record: 72 (30 goals) League and 9 (5 goals) FA Cup matches.

1908 JG 'Tim' Coleman sold to Everton for £700.

1914	Blackpool	H	Division 2	2–1
1920	Manchester United	A	Division 1	1–0
1925	Tottenham Hotspur	A	Division 1	0–2
1931	West Ham United	A	Division 1	4–2
1942	Queen's Park Rangers	A	London League	1–0
1948	Aston Villa	A	Division 1	2–4
1953	Blackpool	H	FA Cup 6th round	1–2
1959	Manchester United	H	Division 1	3–2

1964 John Radford joined the professional ranks at Highbury.

1970	Sunderland	H	Division 1	3–1

1970 Final senior match for David Court. Played 175 (17 goals) League, 10 FA Cup, 11 (1 goal) FL Cup and 8 European games.

1973	West Bromwich Albion	A	Division 1	0–1
1976	Middlesbrough	A	Division 1	1–0
1978	Norwich City	H	Division 1	0–0
1981	Middlesbrough	H	Division 1	2–2

1981 Last senior game for Steve Walford. His final record read 77 (3 goals) League, 10 FA Cup, 5 (1 goal) FL Cup and 5 European matches. Was a dependable deputy centre-back whenever called on to replace O'Leary or Young but an absolute disaster when called on to play at full-back, witness his performance in the 1978–79 League Cup shock defeat at Swindon.

| 1983 | Middlesbrough | H | FA Cup 5th round replay | 3–2 |
| 1989 | Millwall | H | Division 1 | 0–0 |

FEBRUARY 29TH

1896	Loughborough Town	A	Division 2	1–2
1904	Burnley	H	Division 2	4–0
1908	Sheffield United	A	Division 1	2–2
1924	James Ramsay joined from Kilmarnock in a move worth £1,775.			
1936	Barnsley	H	FA Cup 6th round	4–1
1964	Stoke City	H	Division 1	1–1
1972	Derby County	H	FA Cup 5th round replay	0–0
1992	Barnet	A	Barry Fry Testimonial	6–0

Pal Lydersen made his debut.

MARCH 1ST

1890	Birmingham St George's	H	Friendly	1–4
1894	London Caledonians	H	Friendly	1–0
1897	Reading	H	Friendly	6–2
1902	Blackpool	A	Division 2	3–1
1913	Bradford City	H	Division 1	1–1
1919	Millwall Athletic	A	London Combination	3–0
1924	Liverpool	H	Division 1	3–1

Debut of James Ramsay.

1930	West Ham United	A	FA Cup 6th round	3–0
1935	Alf Kirchen signed from Norwich City for £6,000.			
1941	Watford	A	Football League War Cup	4–0
1944	David Court was born in Mitcham, Surrey.			
1947	Chelsea	H	Division 1	1–2
1952	Burnley	A	Division 1	1–0
1958	Birmingham City	A	Division 1	1–4
1969	Sheffield Wednesday	A	Division 1	5–0
1975	Everton	H	Division 1	0–2
1977	Everton	A	Division 1	1–2
1980	Stoke City	A	Division 1	3–2
1986	Newcastle United	A	Division 1	0–1
1987	Tottenham Hotspur	A	Littlewoods Cup semi-final 2nd leg	2–1

With the Gunners trailing by an aggregate score of 2–0 at half-time, the Tottenham announcer saw fit to advise the patrons of White Hart Lane how to obtain their tickets for the final at Wembley. He need not have bothered as second half goals from Anderson and Quinn earned Arsenal a replay, which, on the toss of a coin, gave Spurs the home advantage.

| 1993 | Chelsea | A | Premier League | 0–1 |
| 1997 | Everton | A | Premier League | 2–0 |

MARCH 2ND

| 1889 | London Caledonians | H | Friendly | 1–2 |
| 1895 | Bury | A | Division 2 | 0–2 |

1896	Casuals	H	Friendly	4–1
1901	Grimsby Town	A	Division 2	0–1
1907	Sheffield United	H	Division 1	0–1
1910	Nottingham Forest	A	Division 1	1–1
1912	Manchester City	H	Division 1	2–0
1918	Millwall Athletic	A	London Combination	3–0

1923 Henry White was sold to Blackpool.

| 1924 | Cardiff City | A | FA Cup 2nd round | 0–1 |

1926 Tom Parker was recruited from Southampton for £3,250.

| 1929 | Aston Villa | A | FA Cup 6th round | 0–1 |

Last senior outing for Sidney Hoar, played 100 (16 goals) League and 17 (2 goals) FA Cup games.

1932	Bolton Wanderers	A	Division 1	0–1
1935	Sheffield Wednesday	A	FA Cup 6th round	1–2
1940	Fulham	A	League South 'C' Division	1–1
1946	Fulham	A	Friendly	1–2
1953	Sheffield Wednesday	A	Division 1	4–1
1955	Tottenham Hotspur	A	Friendly	4–1
1957	West Bromwich Albion	A	FA Cup 6th round	2–2

1958 David O'Leary was born in Stoke Newington, North London.

| 1963 | West Ham United | A | Division 1 | 4–0 |

League debut made by Terry Anderson.

| 1968 | Leeds United | | Wembley League Cup final | 0–1 |

Arsenal's first visit to Wembley since 1952 was lost to another controversial goal. Leeds centre-half Jack Charlton appeared to impede goalkeeper Jim Furnell's attempt to get to a ball delivered from a corner and full-back Terry Cooper took advantage to score.

| 1971 | Wolverhampton Wanderers | A | Division 1 | 3–0 |

An excellent display at Molyneux by Arsenal gave them a 3–0 win over Wolverhampton Wanderers. The Gunners had the best possible start with a goal in the 1st minute when George Armstrong nodded in from a Jon Sammels corner. After half an hour John Radford netted from a Frank McLintock pass and the scoring was completed in 55th minute when Ray Kennedy fired home after some good approach work by Charlie George.

| 1974 | Southampton | H | Division 1 | 1–0 |

1977 Peter Storey was transferred to Fulham for £11,000 whilst Willie Young arrived from Tottenham Hotspur for £80,000.

1985	West Ham United	H	Division 1	2–1
1994	Torino	A	Cup Winners Cup quarter-final 1st leg	0–0
1995	Auxerre	H	Cup Winners Cup quarter-final 1st leg	1–1
1996	Queen's Park Rangers	A	Premier League	1–1
1998	West Ham United	A	Premier League	0–0

West Ham had won all but 1 of their home League games to set up a potentially difficult match for the Gunners. In what proved to be a very physical confrontation with few chances, Manninger enhanced his growing reputation with some excellent saves that included a brilliant reflex stop from ex-Gunner John Hartson. This was Arsenal's 4th clean sheet in a row and the point moved them back into 2nd spot and a realistic chance of a Champions League place.

MARCH 3RD

1888	Grange Institute	H	Friendly	2–1
1892	Borough Road College	H	Friendly	4–1
1894	Crewe Alexandra	A	Division 2	0–0
1900	Loughborough Town	A	Division 2	3–2
1906	Birmingham	H	Division 1	5–0
1917	Clapton Orient	H	London Combination	3–1
1923	Middlesbrough	A	Division 1	0–2
1928	Stoke City	H	FA Cup 6th round	4–1
1934	Aston Villa	H	FA Cup 6th round	1–2
1939	Wilf Copping rejoined Leeds United for £3,500.			
1945	Clapton Orient	A	Football League Cup – South	3–1
1951	Manchester United	H	Division 1	1–3
1956	Birmingham City	H	FA Cup 6th round	1–3
1962	Blackburn Rovers	H	Division 1	0–0
1967	Manchester United	H	Division 1	1–1
1973	Sheffield United	H	Division 1	3–2
1979	Southampton	A	Division 1	0–2
1984	Sunderland	A	Division 1	2–2
1986	Luton Town	H	FA Cup 5th round replay	0–0
1990	Queen's Park Rangers	A	Division 1	0–2
1991	Liverpool	A	Division 1	1–0
1993	Norwich City	A	Premier League	1–1

MARCH 4TH

1893	Middlesbrough	A	Friendly	0–2
1899	Small Heath	A	Division 2	1–4
1901	Southern League XI	H	Friendly	2–1
1905	Sunderland	A	Division 1	1–1
1910	George Grant joined from Invicta FC as an amateur.			
1911	Manchester City	A	Division 1	1–1
1916	Tottenham Hotspur	H	London Combination	0–3
1922	Preston North End	H	FA Cup 4th round	1–1
1932	Ernest 'Tim' Coleman signed from Grimsby Town for £7,500.			
1933	Liverpool	H	Division 1	0–1

Chapman introduced a radical change to the Arsenal strip by incorporating white sleeves onto the red jersey. The idea came from cartoonist Tom Webster who had played golf in a white shirt with a sleeveless sweater over the top and liked the effect.

1936	Derby County	A	Division 1	4–0
1939	Bolton Wanderers	H	Division 1	3–1
1944	Reading	H	Football League Cup – South	2–3
1950	Leeds United	H	FA Cup 6th round	1–0
1961	Aston Villa	A	Division 1	2–2
1972	Manchester City	A	Division 1	0–2
1978	Manchester City	H	Division 1	3–0
1987	Tottenham Hotspur	A	Littlewoods Cup semi-final replay	2–1

Spurs again opened the scoring and again were beaten, this time by late goals from substitute Ian Allinson and David Rocastle. Arsenal, not Spurs, took up the ticket allocation from Wembley!

MARCH 5TH

1892	Wolverhampton Wanderers	H	Friendly	1–4
1894	Luton Town	H	Friendly	2–0
1898	Small Heath	H	Division 2	4–2
1900	Southampton	H	Southern District Combination	1–0
1904	Lincoln City	A	Division 2	2–0
1910	Millwall Athletic	A	Friendly	3–3

Last senior game for Charlie Satterthwaite who made 129 (45 goals) League and 12 (3 goals) FA Cup appearances.

1921	Nottingham Forest	H	Friendly	2–1
1927	Wolverhampton Wanderers	H	FA Cup 6th round	2–1
1932	Leicester City	H	Division 1	2–1
1938	Stoke City	H	Division 1	4–0
1949	Burnley	A	Division 1	1–1
1955	Charlton Athletic	A	Division 1	1–1
1957	West Bromwich Albion	H	FA Cup 6th round replay	1–2
1960	Preston North End	A	Division 1	3–0
1966	Blackpool	H	Division 1	0–0

1966 Gus Caesar was born in Tottenham, London.

1977	Ipswich Town	H	Division 1	1–4

Willie Young's Arsenal debut and instantly forgettable.

1980	Gothenburg	H	Cup Winners Cup quarter-final 1st leg	5–1
1983	Nottingham Forest	H	Division 1	0–0
1986	Luton Town	A	FA Cup 5th round 2nd replay	0–3
1992	Shelbourne	A	Challenge Match	1–1
1994	Ipswich Town	A	Premier League	5–1
1995	West Ham United	H	Premier League	0–1
1996	Manchester City	H	Premier League	3–1

MARCH 6TH

1895	Eastbourne	A	Friendly	5–1
1897	Casuals	A	Friendly	3–5
1898	Chatham	A	Chatham Charity Cup	1–2
1899	Chatham	A	Chatham Charity Cup	1–2

1905 Thomas Fitchie and Robert Templeton became the first Arsenal players to represent Scotland against Wales in Wrexham. Wales won 3–1.

1908	Sheffield United	H	Division 1	3–0
1909	Sheffield United	H	Division 1	3–0
1911	Oldham Athletic	A	Division 1	0–3
1915	Lincoln City	A	Division 2	0–1
1920	Sheffield United	A	Division 1	0–2
1926	Swansea Town	A	FA Cup 6th round	1–2

Last game for Dr James Paterson. He played 70 (1 goal) League and 7 (1 goal) FA Cup matches.

1935	Tottenham Hotspur	A	Division 1	6–0

Alf Kirchen's debut.

1937	West Bromwich Albion	A	FA Cup 6th round	1–3

1943	Brighton & Hove Albion	A	Football League Cup – South	5–1
1948	Wolverhampton Wanderers	H	Division 1	5–2

Alex Forbes made his debut.

1954	Burnley	A	Division 1	1–2
1956	Preston North End	H	Division 1	3–2
1965	Sheffield United	H	Division 1	1–1

1965 John Snedden was sold to Charlton Athletic for a fee of £15,000.

1971	Leicester City	A	FA Cup 6th round	0–0

Arsenal were drawn away for the fourth match running in the FA Cup against 2nd Division Leicester City. As the fixtures piled up the last result the Gunners needed was a draw but had to accept a 0–0 scoreline in a match where Leicester seldom threatened the Arsenal goal.

1982	Manchester City	A	Division 1	0–0
1988	Tottenham Hotspur	H	Division 1	2–1

1991 Ray Parlour signed his first professional contract with Arsenal.

1993	Ipswich Town	A	FA Cup 6th round	4–2

1997 Nicolas Anelka was signed by Arsène Wenger from French club Paris St-Germain after much wrangling about whether or not a transfer fee was required. Anelka, at seventeen, had been too young to sign a professional contract with PSG and it was claimed, therefore, by the Gunners that he was free to move under the Bosman ruling. The matter was resolved by Arsenal making a payment in the region of £500,000 to PSG as a gesture of goodwill.

MARCH 7TH

1891	St Bartholomew's Hospital	N	London Senior Cup	6–0
1896	Notts County	H	Division 2	2–0
1903	Blackpool	A	Division 2	0–0
1904	Millwall	A	London League Premier Division	0–3
1908	Chelsea	H	Division 1	0–0
1910	Everton	A	Division 1	0–1
1914	Nottingham Forest	A	Division 2	0–0

1920 Reg Lewis was born in Billston, Staffordshire.

1921 Frederick Pagnam was sold to Cardiff City for £3,000.

1925	Bolton Wanderers	H	Division 1	1–0
1927	West Ham United	A	Division 1	0–7
1928	Liverpool	H	Division 1	6–3
1931	Huddersfield Town	H	Division 1	0–0

Final first-team match for Alf Baker who retired at end of season and became a scout for Arsenal. Baker had compiled 310 League and 41 FA Cup games for Arsenal scoring a total of 26 goals. He appeared in both the 1927 and 1930 FA Cup final teams.

1936	Huddersfield Town	H	Division 1	1–1
1942	Reading	A	London League	4–1
1953	Cardiff City	H	Division 1	0–1
1959	Wolverhampton Wanderers	A	Division 1	1–6
1962	Bohemians	A	Friendly	8–3
1964	Nottingham Forest	A	Division 1	0–2

Last senior game for Vic Groves who had played 185 (31 goals) League, 16 (6 goals) FA Cup and 2 European games.

1973   Ray Parlour was born in Romford, Essex.

1981   Leicester City   A   Division 1   0–1
Final appearance of David Price. His record: 126 (16 goals) League, 26 (1 goal) FA Cup, 11 FL Cup and 12 (2 goals) European competitions.
Injuries to Richie Powling and John Matthews cleared the way for Price to claim a regular first-team place. He had to endure criticism from fans and pundits alike, but made the most of his limited ability to play a holding role in midfield and ended up with an FA Cup winners medal in 1979.

1987   Chelsea   A   Division 1   0–1
1990   Nottingham Forest   H   Division 1   3–0

MARCH 8TH

1890	Old Westminsters	N	London Senior Cup	0–1
1902	Stockport County	H	Division 2	3–0
1913	Manchester City	A	Division 1	1–0
1919	Fulham	H	London Combination	5–0
1922	Preston North End	A	FA Cup 4th round replay	1–2
1930	West Ham United	A	Division 1	2–3
1932	Bill Seddon was sold to Grimsby Town for £2,500.			
1934	Leicester City	A	Division 1	1–4
1941	Watford	H	Football League War Cup	5–0
1950	Middlesbrough	H	Division 1	1–1
1952	Luton Town	A	FA Cup 6th round	3–2
1958	Chelsea	H	Division 1	5–4
1966	Tottenham Hotspur	H	Division 1	1–1
1972	Ajax	A	European Cup 3rd round 1st leg	1–2
1975	West Ham United	H	FA Cup 6th round	0–2
1977	West Bromwich Albion	H	Division 1	1–2
1980	Watford	A	FA Cup 6th round	2–1
1986	Aston Villa	A	Division 1	4–1
1995	Blackburn Rovers	A	Premier League	1–3
1997	Nottingham Forest	H	Premier League	2–0
1998	West Ham United	H	FA Cup 6th round	1–1

Arsenal were reduced to 10 men with the dismissal of Dennis Bergkamp for a foul on Steve Lomas. Nevertheless they took the lead before half-time with a goal from Nicolas Anelka and held on until old boy, John Hartson, squared matters. Fittingly, in a game in which Alex Manninger had been superb, the Gunners won the penalty shoot-out after a miss by Abou.

MARCH 9TH

1889	Tottenham Hotspur	A	Friendly	1–0
1895	Leicester Fosse	H	Division 2	3–3
1899	Casuals	A	Friendly	3–1
1901	Lincoln City	H	Division 2	0–0
1903	Manchester United	A	Division 2	0–3
1907	Barnsley	A	FA Cup 4th round	2–1
1912	Oldham Athletic	A	Division 1	0–0
1918	Tottenham Hotspur	H	London Combination	4–1

| 1929 | Liverpool | A | Division 1 | 4–2 |
| 1935 | Sunderland | H | Division 1 | 0–0 |

The attendance figure 73,295 was the highest ever recorded for an Arsenal home match and, unless the club chooses to relocate, is unlikely to ever be broken at Highbury.

1940	Southampton	A	League South 'C' Division	2–3
1946	Chelsea	H	Football League – South	1–2
1957	Luton Town	H	Division 1	1–3
1963	Liverpool	H	Division 1	2–2
1966	Valencia	A	Friendly	0–0
1968	Birmingham City	H	FA Cup 5th round	1–1
1971	FC Köln	H	European Fairs Cup 4th round 1st leg	2–1

Cologne, from West Germany, were the visitors to Highbury for the 1st leg of the 4th round of the Fairs Cup. Arsenal took the lead in 26th minute when John Radford took a long throw to Charlie George, whose volley was saved by Cologne goalkeeper Manglitz, but the ball broke to Frank McLintock who scored from the rebound. On the stroke of half-time the Germans scored a bizarre goal when Thielen netted directly from a corner. Arsenal took a 2–1 lead into the 2nd leg when Peter Storey scored from a Radford pass. After the match the Cologne manager, Ernet Oerwirk, stated that Arsenal did not make the best of their chances and that his team would win the 2nd leg 1–0.

| 1985 | Sunderland | A | Division 1 | 0–0 |
| 1991 | Cambridge United | H | FA Cup 6th round | 2–1 |

MARCH 10TH

1888	Brixton Rangers	A	Friendly	9–3
1892	Casuals	H	Friendly	3–1
1894	Middlesbrough Ironopolis	H	Division 2	1–0
1897	Reading	A	Friendly	2–0
1900	Newton Heath	H	Division 2	2–1
1904	David Neave joined from Arbroath.			
1906	Manchester United	A	FA Cup 4th round	3–2
1909	Hastings	A	Friendly	3–1
1917	West Ham United	A	London Combination	3–2
1922	Samson Haden joined from Castleford Town as an amateur.			
1923	Middlesbrough	H	Division 1	3–0
1928	Bolton Wanderers	A	Division 1	1–1
1928	Arthur Milton was born in Bristol, Avon.			
1934	Aston Villa	H	Division 1	3–2
1937	Liverpool	H	Division 1	1–0
1945	Portsmouth	H	Football League Cup – South	2–4
1951	Aston Villa	H	Division 1	2–1
1951	First League game for Arthur Milton.			
1956	Charlton Athletic	A	Division 1	0–2
1962	Dundee	A	Friendly	1–0
1964	John Barnwell sold to Nottingham Forest for £30,000. He made in excess of 150 senior appearances for the club.			
1973	Ipswich Town	A	Division 1	2–1
1979	Bristol City	H	Division 1	2–0
1979	League debut (as substitute) for Brian McDermott.			

1984	Ipswich Town	H	Division 1	4–1
1987	Liverpool	H	Division 1	0–1
1990	Manchester City	A	Division 1	1–1
1992	Oldham Athletic	H	Division 1	2–1
1993	Crystal Palace	H	Coca-Cola Cup semi-final 2nd leg	2–0

Arsenal won 5–1 on aggregate.

MARCH 11TH

1893	Dumbarton	H	Friendly	3–1
1899	Tottenham Hotspur	H	United League	2–1
1903	Ashford United	A	Chatham Charity Cup	2–0
1905	Stoke	A	Division 1	0–2
1911	Everton	H	Division 1	1–0

League debut of John Peart.

1916	Millwall Athletic	A	London Combination	0–2
1922	Manchester United	A	Division 1	0–1
1931	Leeds United	A	Division 1	2–1
1933	Leicester City	A	Division 1	1–1
1936	Manchester City	A	Division 1	0–1
1939	Leeds United	A	Division 1	2–4
1944	Luton Town	A	Football League Cup – South	1–1
1950	Charlton Athletic	A	Division 1	1–1
1961	Blackburn Rovers	H	Division 1	0–0
1967	Birmingham City	A	FA Cup 5th round	0–1
1970	Dinamo Bacau	A	European Fairs Cup 4th round 1st leg	2–0
1972	Newcastle United	A	Division 1	0–2

Brendon Batson became the first black footballer to appear for Arsenal. Although he subsequently had a distinguished career with West Bromwich Albion, he failed to make the grade with the Gunners and managed only a total of 10 League games. He has spent the last few years working for the PFA.

1978	Wrexham	A	FA Cup 6th round	3–2
1980	Bristol City	H	Division 1	0–0

1981 Peter Nicholas signed from Crystal Palace for £400,000.

1986	Ipswich Town	A	Division 1	2–1
1989	Nottingham Forest	H	Division 1	1–3
1998	Wimbledon	A	Premier League	1–0

After the initial League game at Selhurst Park had been abandoned just after half-time due to floodlight failure, the start of this match was delayed for over half an hour due to a security alert at the ground. Arsenal began in a positive mood and after 15 minutes Wreh had the ball in the net only for it to be disallowed for offside. However, Wreh who looked lively on his first start for the Gunners scored 6 minutes later when Overmars provided an excellent ball for him to stab home. Arsenal continued to press forward with Bergkamp going close on a couple of occasions only to be thwarted by Sullivan in the Wimbledon goal. The second half brought the inevitable onslaught from Wimbledon and Manninger produced a heroic display to keep them out. With the Dons committing themselves to attack they were left vulnerable at the back and only some brilliant defending by Chris Perry prevented Bergkamp from adding to Arsenal's tally. At the final whistle the Arsenal players celebrated with their fans, and it was evident that they now believed they had a real chance of catching Manchester United in the title race.

MARCH 12TH

1887	Millwall Rovers	H	Friendly	3–0
1892	Great Marlow	H	Friendly	5–2
1894	Sheffield United	A	Friendly	2–0
1898	Darwen	A	Division 2	4–1
1900	Loughborough Town	H	Division 2	12–0

Arsenal's record victory in senior competitions; took place at the Manor Ground.

1904	Stockport County	H	Division 2	5–2
1910	Manchester United	H	Division 1	0–0
1921	Burnley	A	Division 1	0–1
1924	Aston Villa	A	Division 1	1–2
1927	Sheffield Wednesday	A	Division 1	2–4
1930	Manchester United	H	Division 1	4–2
1932	Manchester City	Aston Villa		
			FA Cup semi-final	1–0

Sixth FA Cup semi-final appearance in which Cliff Bastin scored the only goal of the game.

1938	Middlesbrough	A	Division 1	1–2
1949	Preston North End	H	Division 1	0–0
1955	Aston Villa	H	Division 1	2–0
1960	Leyton Orient	H	Friendly	0–2
1963	Sheffield Wednesday	H	FA Cup 4th round	2–0
1966	Everton	H	Division 1	0–1
1968	Birmingham City	A	FA Cup 5th round replay	1–2
1974	Barcelona	H	George Armstrong Testimonial	1–3

1975 Alan Ball captained England against West Germany at Wembley. Malcolm McDonald scored one of the 2 goals in the 2–0 victory.

1977	Queen's Park Rangers	A	Division 1	1–2

1981 David Price was sold to Crystal Palace for £80,000.

1983	Aston Villa	H	FA Cup 6th round	2–0
1988	Nottingham Forest	H	FA Cup 6th round	1–2

1992 Andy Cole, who had been unable to establish himself in the first team, was allowed to move to Bristol City, with whom he had completed a successful loan spell, for a fee of £500,000 and an agreed 40 per cent share of any subsequent sale. Exactly one year to the day, Cole left the West Country club to join Newcastle United in a deal that netted Arsenal about another £400,000.

MARCH 13TH

1893	Aston Villa	H	Friendly	0–1
1895	Bromley & District	A	Friendly	4–1
1897	Burton Swifts	A	Division 2	2–1
1899	Loughborough Town	H	Division 2	3–1
1909	Aston Villa	A	Division 1	1–2
1915	Birmingham	H	Division 2	1–0
1920	Sheffield United	H	Division 1	3–0

1924 Andrew Neil was signed from Brighton and Hove Albion for £3,000.

1926	Everton	A	Division 1	3–2

1926 Andrew Neil returned to Brighton and Hove Albion.

1929	Birmingham	A	Division 1	1–1

1937	Leeds United	A	Division 1	4–3
1943	Watford	H	Football League Cup – South	4–1
1946	Birmingham City	A	Football League – South	1–0
1948	Everton	A	Division 1	2–0
1952	Charlton Athletic	H	Division 1	2–1
1954	Charlton Athletic	H	Division 1	3–3
1957	Tottenham Hotspur	A	Division 1	3–1
1965	Nottingham Forest	A	Division 1	0–3

1970 Jimmy Robertson was transferred to Ipswich Town for £50,000.

1971	Crystal Palace	A	Division 1	2–0

Arsenal kept up the pressure at the top of the table with a 2–0 win against Crystal Palace at Selhurst Park. In 28th minute George Graham rose high to head in a Frank McLintock cross to put the Gunners in front. After 18 minutes of the 2nd half Jon Sammels came on as substitute for Charlie George and it was Sammels who score the second goal 11 minutes from time.

1972	Derby County	Leicester	FA Cup 5th round 2nd replay	1–0
1976	Coventry City	A	Division 1	1–1
1982	Ipswich Town	H	Division 1	1–0
1985	Aston Villa	A	Division 1	0–0
1993	Coventry City	A	Premier League	2–0

MARCH 14TH

1891	Old Harrovians	H	Friendly	5–1
1892	Third Lanark	H	Friendly	0–1

1894 Henry Woods was born in St Helens, Lancashire.

1896	Darwen	A	Division 2	1–1
1903	Chesterfield	A	Division 2	2–2
1904	Bristol City	H	Division 2	2–0
1908	Nottingham Forest	A	Division 1	0–1

1912 Cliff Bastin was born in Exeter, Devon.

1914	Fulham	H	Division 2	2–0
1925	Notts County	A	Division 1	1–2
1928	Sunderland	A	Division 1	1–5
1931	Aston Villa	A	Division 1	1–5

1933 Ray Bowden joined from Plymouth Argyle in a £4,500 deal.

1934 Edward Joseph 'Ted' Drake was signed from Southampton for a fee of £6,500.

1936	Preston North End	A	Division 1	0–1
1942	Brighton & Hove Albion	H	London League	4–2
1953	Newcastle United	A	Division 1	2–2
1959	Blackburn Rovers	H	Division 1	1–1

1963 Tony Burns joined from Tunbridge Wells.

1964	Chelsea	H	Division 1	2–4

Final League game for Dave Bacuzzi, but the League debut of Peter Simpson.

1970	Liverpool	H	Division 1	2–1

1979 Nicolas Anelka was born in Versailles, France.

1987	Watford	H	FA Cup 6th round	1–3
1992	West Ham United	A	Division 1	2–0
1998	Manchester United	A	Premier League	1–0

Arsenal arrived for the morning kick-off knowing that a victory would give them a huge psychological advantage over their title rivals and it showed from the kick-off as an unusually quiet crowd watched as Arsenal took control. In the 7th minute Overmars skipped by the inexperienced Curtis to chip the ball inches past the post. On the 15-minute mark Overmars again had a snap shot which Schmeichel needed 2 attempts to save. Alex Manninger, who had not conceded a goal in a League game, produced an excellent save from Sheringham. A few moments later Overmars appeared to be brought down in the penalty area, but the referee declined to award a spot kick thus protecting the run of over 18 months that had elapsed since any English opponent had been awarded a penalty at Old Trafford. Ironically, Manchester United later appealed for a penalty against Petit when the ball hit him in the chest which the referee also dismissed, much to the annoyance of the home support. In the second half Nicolas Anelka was introduced as substitute for Wreh, who had run himself into the ground, and his pace immediately caused problems. With just over 10 minutes to go Bergkamp found Anelka who flicked the ball onto Overmars who this time made no mistake as he placed the ball into the far side of the goal. Whilst the home fans fell silent, the visitors supporters made merry. In the final moments of the game Schmeichel came up for a corner as United tried in vain to grab an equaliser but pulled a hamstring in a frantic attempt to return to his goal. The Gunners held out for a magnificent win, that brought them within touching distance of their title rivals with the destiny of the Championship now in their own hands. This result must have made the long journey home for the United fans seem like an eternity!

MARCH 15TH

1890	Ilford	A	Friendly	4–1
1897	Southampton St Mary's	H	Friendly	2–1
1902	Newton Heath	A	Division 2	1–0
1911	Aston Villa	H	Division 1	1–1
1913	West Bromwich Albion	H	Division 1	1–0
1919	Brentford	A	London Combination	0–2
1924	Nottingham Forest	A	Division 1	1–2

Debut for Andrew Neil.

1930	Birmingham	H	Division 1	1–0
1941	West Ham United	A	Football League War Cup	1–0
1947	Preston North End	H	Division 1	4–1
1952	Fulham	A	Division 1	0–0
1955	Glasgow Rangers	H	Friendly	3–3
1958	Manchester City	A	Division 1	4–2
1960	Leicester City	H	Division 1	1–1
1969	Swindon Town		Wembley League Cup final	1–3

On a pitch that had been ruined by an earlier Horse of the Year show and turned into a mudheap by excessive watering and rainfall, Arsenal with 8 players still suffering the after-effects of a bout of flu could not find the energy to stay with their third division opponents as the game was taken to extra time. The score at 90 minutes had stood at one goal each thanks to an horrendous mix up between goalkeeper Wilson and centre-half Ure that presented the aptly named Smart with an open goal and an equaliser just before full time from Gould. However, with Arsenal literally on their knees in extra time Rogers scored twice to take the Cup to the West Country.

1971	Leicester City	H	FA Cup 6th round replay	1–0

In front of 57,443 spectators Arsenal beat Leicester City 1–0 in their 6th Road FA Cup replay at Highbury. In a hard fought match Charlie George headed the only goal from a George Armstrong corner seconds before half-time. This victory took the Gunners to their first FA Cup semi-final for 19 years.

1975	Birmingham City	H	Division 1	1–1
1976	Jack McClelland died in Ireland at the age of 35 years.			
1980	Manchester City	A	Division 1	3–0
1983	Birmingham City	A	Division 1	1–2
1986	West Ham United	H	Division 1	1–0
1990	Niall Quinn was sold to Manchester City for a fee of £700,000.			
1994	Torino	H	Cup Winners Cup quarter-final 2nd leg	1–0
1997	Southampton	A	Premier Division	2–0

MARCH 16TH

1889	South Eastern Rangers	H	Friendly	1–2
1895	Gainsborough Trinity	A	Friendly	2–0
1896	Tottenham Hotspur	H	Friendly	1–3
1901	Newton Heath	A	Division 2	0–1
1907	Manchester United	H	Division 1	4–0
1912	West Bromwich Albion	H	Division 1	0–2
1918	Chelsea	A	London Combination	2–4
1929	Cardiff City	H	Division 1	2–1
1935	Everton	A	Division 1	2–0

Frank Moss, Arsenal's most celebrated goalkeeper of the 1930s, suffered a double dislocation of his collar bone that effectively brought his career to an end. He returned to the pitch to play the balance of the game on the wing from where he scored a spectacular goal on the run. The victory and results elsewhere virtually sealed the destiny of the League Championship which returned to Highbury for a third consecutive season (and the fourth time in five years).

1936	George Marks joined from Salisbury Corinthians.			
1940	West Ham United	H	League South 'C' Division	2–3
1946	Chelsea	A	Football League – South	2–1
1956	Doug Lishman was transferred to Nottingham Forest for £8,000.			
1957	Aston Villa	A	Division 1	0–0
1961	Bill Dodgin sold to Fulham for £7,000.			
1963	Liverpool	H	FA Cup 5th round	1–2
1968	Wolverhampton Wanderers	H	Division 1	0–2
1974	Ipswich Town	A	Division 1	2–2
1976	Newcastle United	H	Division 1	0–0
1982	West Bromwich Albion	H	Division 1	2–2
1985	Leicester City	H	Division 1	2–0
1995	Auxerre	A	Cup Winners Cup quarter-final 2nd leg	1–0

Another spectacular goal from Ian Wright saw the Gunners into the semi-final against Sampdoria.

| 1996 | Wimbledon | A | Premier League | 3–0 |

MARCH 17TH

| 1888 | Ascham | A | Friendly | 5–0 |
| 1894 | Millwall Athletic | H | Friendly | 2–2 |

1900	Sheffield Wednesday	A	Division 2	1–3

Last appearance for Roger Ord. His record: 89 League and 10 FA Cup games.

1906	Derby County	H	Division 1	1–0
1909	Middlesbrough	H	Division 1	1–1
1917	Crystal Palace	A	London Combination	0–1
1923	Oldham Athletic	H	Division 1	2–0

1923 Robert John made his Welsh international debut against Scotland in the 2–0 defeat at Paisley

1926	Sheffield United	H	Division 1	4–0
1928	Blackburn Rovers	H	Division 1	3–2
1945	Millwall	Chelsea	Football League Cup – South semi-final	0–1

1949 Pat Rice was born in Belfast.

1951	Derby County	A	Division 1	2–4
1956	Manchester United	H	Division 1	1–1
1962	Cardiff City	H	Division 1	1–1

1964 Lee Dixon was born in Manchester.

1973	Chelsea	A	FA Cup 6th round	2–2
1979	Ipswich Town	A	Division 1	0–2
1981	Orient	A	Friendly	1–0

Debut of Peter Nicholas.

1984	Manchester United	A	Division 1	0–4
1987	Nottingham Forest	H	Division 1	0–0
1990	Chelsea	H	Division 1	0–1
1991	Leeds United	H	Division 1	2–0
1998	West Ham United	A	FA Cup 6th round replay	1–1

Arsenal were reduced to ten men after the first half sending-off of Dennis Bergkamp. Despite opening the scoring through Anelka, once again a penalty shoot-out victory was required to progress (4–3 pens).

MARCH 18TH

1893	Middlesbrough Ironopolis	H	Friendly	3–0
1899	Blackpool	H	Division 2	6–0
1903	Brighton & Hove Albion	A	Friendly	3–1
1905	Derby County	H	Division 1	0–0
1911	Sheffield Wednesday	A	Division 1	0–0
1916	Brentford	H	London Combination	5–2
1922	Aston Villa	A	Division 1	0–2
1933	Wolverhampton Wanderers	H	Division 1	1–2

Ray Bowden's first game.

1939	Liverpool	H	Division 1	2–0
1944	Queen's Park Rangers	H	Football League Cup – South	1–4
1950	Chelsea	Tottenham	FA Cup semi-final	2–2

Eighth FA Cup semi-final appearance again saw Arsenal two-nil down before goals by Freddie Cox and Leslie Compton ensured a replay.

1961	Manchester United	A	Division 1	1–1
1967	West Bromwich Albion	A	Division 1	1–0

1970	Dinamo Bacau	H	European Fairs Cup 4th round 2nd leg	7–1
1972	Orient	A	FA Cup 6th round	1–0
1975	Newcastle United	H	Division 1	3–0
1978	Bristol City	H	Division 1	4–1

MARCH 19TH

1892	71st Highland Light Infantry	H	Friendly	3–2
1898	Loughborough Town	H	Division 2	4–0
1900	Queen's Park Rangers	H	Southern District Combination	5–1
1904	Chesterfield	A	Division 2	0–1
1910	Bradford City	A	Division 1	1–0
1921	Burnley	H	Division 1	1–1
1927	Everton	H	Division 1	1–2
1932	Newcastle United	H	Division 1	1–0
1938	Grimsby Town	H	Division 1	5–1
1949	Newcastle United	A	Division 1	2–3
1953	Preston North End	H	Division 1	1–1
1955	Sunderland	A	Division 1	1–0
1958	Leeds United	A	Division 1	0–2
1960	Burnley	A	Division 1	2–3
1966	Manchester United	A	Division 1	1–2

Last League game for Billy McCullough. He played 253 (4 goals) League, 11 FA Cup and 4 (1 goal) European matches.

1979	Southampton	A	FA Cup 6th round	1–1
1980	Gothenburg	A	Cup Winners Cup quarter-final 2nd leg	0–0
1983	Luton Town	H	Division 1	4–1
1985	Ipswich Town	H	Division 1	1–1
1988	Newcastle United	H	Division 1	1–1
1992	Death of Jack Kelsey.			
1994	Southampton	A	Premier League	4–0

Anders Limpar made his final appearance. The Swedish international played 96 (17 goals) League, 7 (2 goals) FA Cup, 9 FL Cup and 3 (1 goal) European games in his brief but glittering spell at the club. He was one of the most inspirational players in the 1990–91 Championship-winning season even though frequently substituted towards the end of matches.

| 1995 | Newcastle United | A | Premier League | 0–1 |

MARCH 20TH

1895	Home Park	A	Friendly	2–1
1897	Luton Town	A	United League	2–5
1909	Nottingham Forest	H	Division 1	1–2
1915	Grimsby Town	A	Division 2	0–1
1920	Middlesbrough	A	Division 1	0–1
1926	Manchester City	H	Division 1	1–0

Final game for Jock Rutherford veteran of 222 (25 goals) League and 10 (2 goals) FA Cup matches.

| 1937 | Birmingham | H | Division 1 | 1–1 |

Final senior appearance of Bob John. Gunners legend John amassed 421 (12 goals)

League and 46 (1 goal) FA Cup games during a career that saw the Welshman pick up 3 League Championship and 1 FA Cup winners medals.

1943	West Ham United	A	Football League Cup – South	3–1
1948	Chelsea	H	Division 1	0–2
1954	Sheffield Wednesday	A	Division 1	1–2
1957	Manchester City	A	Division 1	3–2

1968 Paul Merson was born in Harlesden, London.

1971	Blackpool	H	Division 1	1–0

Blackpool keeper Ramsbottom fumbled 9 minutes into the 2nd half. George Graham crossed the ball, which hit the goalkeeper's chest and ended up at the feet of Storey who lobbed in the winning goal.

1973	Chelsea	H	FA Cup 6th round replay	2–1
1976	West Ham United	H	Division 1	6–1
1982	Coventry City	A	Division 1	0–1
1984	Windsor & Eton	A	Friendly	3–0

Martin Keown's first senior game, Brian McDermott's last. The latter played 61 (12 goals) League, 1 FA Cup, 4 FL Cup and 6 (1 goal) European matches.

1991	Nottingham Forest	H	Division 1	1–1
1993	Southampton	H	Premier League	4–3
1996	Manchester United	A	Premier League	0–1

MARCH 21ST

1891	Sheffield United	H	Friendly	1–1
1895	Weymouth Athletic	A	Friendly	5–0
1896	Crewe Alexandra	H	Division 2	7–0

1896 Caesar Jenkyns became the first ever Arsenal player to be recognised at international level when he was capped by Wales in the 4–0 defeat by Scotland in Dundee.

1898	Bristol City	H	Friendly	3–1
1903	Doncaster Rovers	H	Division 2	3–0

1903 Thomas Shanks became the first Arsenal player to win an international cap for Ireland when he played in the 2–0 victory over Scotland in Glasgow.

1904	Queen's Park Rangers	A	London League Premier Division	1–3

Final appearance Frederick Coles. Record: 78 (2 goals) League and 8 FA Cup.
First appearance David Neave.

1906	Everton	A	Division 1	1–0
1908	Manchester United	H	Division 1	1–0
1913	Manchester United	A	Division 1	0–2
1925	Everton	H	Division 1	3–1
1931	Sheffield Wednesday	H	Division 1	2–0
1936	Grimsby Town	Huddersfield		
			FA Cup semi-final	1–0

Seventh FA Cup semi-final appearance which was won (as on the previous occasion) with a goal by Bastin.

1942	Clapton Orient	H	London War Cup	4–1
1953	West Bromwich Albion	H	Division 1	2–2
1955	Hibernian	A	Friendly	2–2
1959	Newcastle United	A	Division 1	0–1
1964	West Ham United	A	Division 1	1–1

John Radford's League debut.

1966	Martin Hayes was born in Walthamstow, London.			
1970	Southampton	A	Division 1	2–0
1978	Birmingham City	A	Division 1	1–1
1979	Southampton	H	FAC Cup 6th round replay	2–0
1981	Nottingham Forest	A	Division 1	1–1
1987	Watford	A	Division 1	0–2
1989	Charlton Athletic	H	Division 1	2–2

MARCH 22ND

1890	Thanet Wanderers	N	Kent Senior Cup	3–0
1892	Preston North End	H	Friendly	3–3
1897	Newton Heath	A	Division 2	1–1
1899	Blackpool	A	Division 2	1–1
1902	Glossop North End	H	Division 2	4–0
1913	Everton	A	Division 1	0–3
1919	West Ham United	H	London Combination	3–2
1922	Liverpool	H	Division 1	1–0
1924	Nottingham Forest	H	Division 1	1–0
1930	Hull City	Leeds	FA Cup semi-final	2–2

Arsenal's 5th appearance in a semi-final begun a sequence of reoccurring events. The Gunners were two goals down before rousing themselves and earning a replay with goals from Jack and, 8 minutes before full time, Bastin.

1940	Charlton Athletic	A	League South 'C' Division	2–1
1941	Millwall	A	London War Cup	6–1
1947	Leeds United	A	Division 1	1–1
1950	Chelsea	Tottenham		
			FA Cup semi-final replay	1–0

Freddie Cox scored in the 14th minute of extra time to steer the Gunners to a Wembley meeting with Liverpool.

1952	Middlesbrough	H	Division 1	3–1
1958	Sheffield Wednesday	H	Division 1	1–0
1969	Queen's Park Rangers	A	Division 1	1–0
1972	Ajax	H	European Cup 3rd round 2nd leg	0–1
1975	Burnley	A	Division 1	3–3
1980	Crystal Palace	H	Division 1	1–1
1983	Ipswich Town	H	Division 1	2–2
1986	Coventry City	H	Division 1	3–0
1992	Leeds United	H	Division 1	1–1
1994	Neil Heaney moved to Southampton for £300,000.			
1994	Manchester United	H	Premier League	2–2
1995	Manchester United	A	Premier League	0–3

MARCH 23RD

1889	2nd Rifle Brigade	H	Friendly	2–0
1894	Northwich Victoria	H	Division 2	6–0
1895	Crewe Alexandra	A	Division 2	0–0
1896	Sheffield United	H	Friendly	3–1
1901	Glossop	H	Division 2	2–0
1903	Brentford	A	London League Premier Division	1–0

Final senior game for Alexander Main. His record: 63 (14 goals) League and 6 FA Cup matches.

1907	Sheffield Wednesday	Birmingham	FA Cup semi-final	1–3

Second consecutive appearance in a semi-final by Arsenal again ended in defeat.

1912	Sunderland	A	Division 1	0–1
1918	Brentford	H	London Combination	1–3
1925	West Ham United	H	Division 1	1–2

Last game as a player for Tom Whittaker. He made 64 (2 goals) League and 6 FA Cup matches. A solid, if unspectacular, career as a footballer was surpassed by his time as trainer, assistant manager and secretary manager when he became known as 'Mr Arsenal'.

1929	Sheffield United	A	Division 1	2–2
1935	Grimsby Town	H	Division 1	1–1
1940	Chelsea	H	League South 'C' Division	3–0
1946	Millwall	A	Football League – South	1–1
1951	Portsmouth	H	Division 1	0–1
1954	Hull City	A	Friendly	3–1
1957	Wolverhampton Wanderers	H	Division 1	0–0
1963	Blackburn Rovers	H	Division 1	3–1
1968	Fulham	A	Division 1	3–1
1971	FC Köln	A	European Fairs Cup 4th round 2nd leg	0–1

Arsenal travelled to Cologne to play in the 2nd leg of the 4th round of the Fairs Cup and were controversially beaten 1–0. They were therefore eliminated on the away goals rule after a 2–2 aggregate scoreline. Cologne forward, Kapellmann fell over Bob McNab's leg in the penalty area after 4 minutes and the referee awarded the kick. The decision was bitterly disputed by the Arsenal players but the referee would not change his mind and Biskup converted the kick. Arsenal went out of the competition they won the previous season but were still on course for the League and Cup Double.

1974	Manchester City	H	Division 1	2–0
1977	Stoke City	A	Division 1	1–1
1985	Everton	A	Division 1	0–2

1988 Kenny Sansom made his 80th and last appearance for England in the 3–1 defeat by Holland in the European Championship game in Dusseldorf, Germany. 77 caps were won during his time at Highbury and he managed to score 1 international goal.

1991	Norwich City	A	Division 1	0–0
1996	Newcastle United	H	Premier League	2–0

MARCH 24TH

1888	2nd Rifle Brigade	H	Friendly	
1894	Notts County	H	Division 2	1–2
1900	Lincoln City	H	Division 2	2–1
1906	Sheffield Wednesday	A	Division 1	2–4
1913	Aston Villa	A	Division 1	1–4
1917	Portsmouth	H	London Combination	2–1
1923	Oldham Athletic	A	Division 1	0–0
1928	Blackburn Rovers	Leicester	FA Cup semi-final	0–1

For the second time Arsenal managed to reach a semi-final in consecutive years. Their defeat made their record only one success in four attempts at this stage of the competition.

| 1934 | Wolverhampton Wanderers | H | Division 1 | 3–2 |

Ted Drake made his debut for the Gunners.

| 1945 | Crystal Palace | H | Football League – South | 1–0 |
| 1951 | Wolverhampton Wanderers | H | Division 1 | 2–1 |

Dave Bowen's first-team debut.

1956	Sheffield United	A	Division 1	2–0
1962	Chelsea	A	Division 1	3–2
1964	Sheffield Wednesday	H	Division 1	1–1
1969	Tottenham Hotspur	H	Division 1	1–0
1973	Manchester City	A	Division 1	2–1
1979	Manchester City	H	Division 1	1–1
1984	Wolverhampton Wanderers	H	Division 1	4–1
1990	Derby County	A	Division 1	3–1

Kwame Ampadu made his League debut as substitute.

1993	Manchester United	A	Premier League	0–0
1994	Anders Limpar was sold to Everton for £1,600,000.			
1997	Liverpool	H	Premier League	1–2

MARCH 25TH

1893	Millwall Athletic	A	Friendly	1–0
1895	Millwall Athletic	H	Friendly	1–1
1899	Grimsby Town	H	Division 2	1–1
1905	Burnley	H	Friendly	3–0
1910	Newcastle United	A	Division 1	1–1
1911	Bristol City	H	Division 1	3–0
1911	John Milne was born in Stirling, Scotland.			
1916	Reading	A	London Combination	1–1
1922	Aston Villa	H	Division 1	2–0
1932	Derby County	H	Division 1	2–1
1933	Newcastle United	A	Division 1	1–2
1936	Everton	H	Division 1	1–1
1939	Leicester City	A	Division 1	2–0
1940	Charlton Athletic	H	League South 'C' Division	1–1
1944	Reading	A	Football League Cup – South	1–5
1950	Fulham	A	Division 1	2–2
1961	West Ham United	H	Division 1	0–0
1966	Pat Rice was upgraded from apprentice to full professional.			
1967	Sheffield United	H	Division 1	2–0
1972	Leeds United	A	Division 1	0–3
1975	Luton Town	A	Division 1	0–2
1978	West Bromwich Albion	H	Division 1	4–0
1988	Brian Marwood signed from Sheffield Wednesday for £600,000.			
1989	Southampton	A	Division 1	3–1

MARCH 26TH

1887	2nd Rifle Brigade	A	Friendly	0–1
1892	Everton	H	Friendly	2–2
1894	St Mirren	H	Friendly	1–3
1896	Tottenham Hotspur	A	Friendly	3–1
1898	Gainsborough Trinity	A	Division 2	0–1
1900	Reading	H	Southern District Combination	1–1
1900	Harold Peel was born in Bradford, Yorkshire.			
1904	Bolton Wanderers	H	Division 2	3–0
1910	Sheffield Wednesday	H	Division 1	0–1
1921	Sheffield United	H	Division 1	2–6

Last senior game for Frederick Groves. Played 50 (6 goals) League and 3 (1 goal) FA Cup matches.

| 1921 | Ted Platt was born in Romford. | | | |
| 1927 | Southampton | Chelsea | FA Cup semi-final | 2–1 |

Goals by Hulme and Buchan ensured the Gunners first success in their third semi-final appearance and took them to their first FA Cup final against Cardiff City at Wembley.

| 1930 | Hull City | Aston Villa | | |
| | | | FA Cup semi-final replay | 1–0 |

David Jack's goal from a right-footed volley gave the Gunners victory and a visit to Wembley to face Huddersfield Town.

1932	West Ham United	A	Division 1	1–1
1937	Stoke City	H	Division 1	0–0
1938	West Bromwich Albion	A	Division 1	0–0
1948	Middlesbrough	H	Division 1	7–0
1951	Portsmouth	A	Division 1	1–1
1955	Bolton Wanderers	H	Division 1	3–0
1960	Leeds United	H	Division 1	1–1
1963	Everton	H	Division 1	4–3
1966	Newcastle United	H	Division 1	1–3
1973	Crystal Palace	H	Division 1	1–0
1977	Chelsea	A		
			Benefit Match (Houseman/Gillham Children's fund)	0–3
1979	Bolton Wanderers	A	Division 1	2–4
1983	Everton	A	Division 1	3–2
1987	Alan 'Smudger' Smith was signed from Leicester City for £850,000 and then promptly loaned back to them for the remainder of the season.			
1988	Derby County	A	Division 1	0–0
1994	Liverpool	H	Premier League	1–0

MARCH 27TH

1891	71st Highland Light Infantry	H	Friendly	3–1
1897	Nottingham Forest	H	Friendly	1–0
1907	Bolton Wanderers	A	Division 1	0–3
1909	Sunderland	A	Division 1	0–1
1912	Everton	A	Division 1	0–1
1915	Huddersfield Town	H	Division 2	0–3
1920	Middlesbrough	H	Division 1	2–1

1926	Bury	A	Division 1	2–2
1937	Middlesbrough	A	Division 1	1–1
1943	Brighton & Hove Albion	H	Football League Cup – South	5–0
1948	Blackpool	A	Division 1	0–3
1954	Manchester United	H	Division 1	3–1
1959	Jim Fotheringham sold to Hearts for £6,500.			
1965	West Ham United	A	Division 1	1–2
1967	Liverpool	A	Division 1	0–0
1971	Stoke City	Sheffield Wed		
		FA Cup semi-final		2–2

Arsenal's tenth FA Cup semi-final appearance and a game that evoked memories of Arsenal's previous exploits at the same stage of this competition. Hillsborough, Sheffield was the venue against Stoke City, who were bidding for their first ever FA Cup final appearance. Arsenal attacked steadily from the kick-off but after 22 minutes, following a Stoke corner, the ball struck Smith and was deflected into the Arsenal goal. Worse was to happen in 29th minute when an extremely poor back-pass from Charlie George to goalkeeper Bob Wilson was intercepted by Stoke centre forward Ritchie, who slotted the ball into the net. It appeared that the Double dream was over until early in the 2nd half when Peter Storey sent a rasping drive past Banks in the City goal to reduce the arrears. There were chances at either end until the Gunners won a corner deep into injury time, which was taken by George Armstrong. The corner was headed by Frank McLintock past the helpless Banks but was punched off the line by the diving Mahoney. Storey slotted home the penalty kick to give Arsenal the chance of a very unlikely replay.

1976	Leeds United	A	Division 1	0–3
1978	Chelsea	A	Division 1	0–0
1982	Aston Villa	H	Division 1	4–3
1997	Steve Morrow, best known for his winning goal in the 1993 Coca-Cola Cup final against Sheffield Wednesday and subsequent accident at the hands of Tony Adams, was transferred to QPR for a fee of £500,000.			

MARCH 28TH

1891	Old Harrovians	H	Friendly	5–0
1896	Millwall Athletic	A	Friendly	3–1
1898	Rushden	A	United League	3–2
1902	West Ham United	A	London League Premier Division	2–0
1903	Lincoln City	A	Division 2	2–2
	Last game for Duncan McNichol. Played 101 (1 goal) League and 11 FA Cup matches.			
1908	Blackburn Rovers	A	Division 1	1–1
1910	Chelsea	A	Division 1	1–0
1914	Birmingham	A	Division 2	0–2
1921	West Bromwich Albion	H	Division 1	2–1
1925	Sunderland	A	Division 1	0–2
1928	Portsmouth	H	Division 1	0–2
1931	Middlesbrough	A	Division 1	5–2
1932	Derby County	A	Division 1	1–1
1936	Wolverhampton Wanderers	A	Division 1	2–2
1942	West Ham United	A	London War Cup	4–0
1953	Middlesbrough	A	Division 1	0–2

1959	West Ham United	H	Division 1	1–2
1964	Sheffield United	H	Division 1	1–3
1967	Liverpool	H	Division 1	1–1
1970	Wolverhampton Wanderers	H	Division 1	2–2
1972	Southampton	H	Division 1	1–0
1980	Everton	A	Division 1	1–0
1981	Liverpool	H	Division 1	1–0
1987	Everton	H	Division 1	0–1
1992	Wimbledon	A	Division 1	3–1

1993   A benefit day was held at Highbury for boxer and lifelong Arsenal fan Michael Watson, who was injured in championship fight with Chris Eubank. Arsenal Ladies beat Doncaster Belles 2–1 to win the ladies championship for the first time. An Old Arsenal XI beat an Old Spurs XI 7–2 in front of an estimated 20,000 fans.

1998   Sheffield Wednesday   H   Premier League   1–0

David Seaman resumed in goal in place of Manninger (who was elected the 'Carling Player of the Month' in recognition of his heroic performances as the England goalkeeper's understudy), in what was a pretty one-sided affair. Wreh hit the bar early on and it was no surprise when Bergkamp volleyed home an Overmars cross after 35 minutes. The move was almost repeated 5 minutes later but this time Bergkamp headed over from 10 yards out. The second half petered out with the Gunners in full control, however towards the end Bergkamp almost scored with an audacious shot from all of 40 yards which just went wide. Arsenal still remained in 2nd place but had games in hand over Manchester United. They had now won 7 out of their last 9 games and drawn 2. More importantly they had not conceded a goal in their last 7 games.

MARCH 29TH

1890	Clapton	A	Friendly	0–2
1897	Small Heath	H	Division 2	2–3
1902	Doncaster Rovers	A	Division 2	0–1
1907	Sheffield Wednesday	H	Division 1	1–0
1913	Sheffield Wednesday	H	Division 1	2–5
1918	West Ham United	A	London Combination	1–4
1919	Tottenham Hotspur	A	London Combination	1–0
1921	West Bromwich Albion	A	Division 1	4–3
1929	Blackburn Rovers	H	Division 1	1–0
1930	Blackburn Rovers	H	Division 1	4–0
1937	Stoke City	A	Division 1	0–0
1941	West Ham United	H	Football League War Cup	2–1
1947	Leicester City	H	Friendly	3–1
1948	Middlesbrough	A	Division 1	1–1
1950	Aston Villa	H	Division 1	1–3
1958	Portsmouth	A	Division 1	4–5
1966	Ipswich Town	A	Friendly	2–3
1968	West Ham United	A	Division 1	1–1
1969	Southampton	H	Division 1	0–0

1973   Marc Overmars was born in Ernst, Holland.

1975   Stoke City   H   Division 1   1–1

Final senior appearance for Bob McNab who played 278 (4 goals) League, 39 FA Cup,

27 (2 goals) FL Cup and 21 European games. Left-back in the first Double winning team, he also won a European Fairs Cup medal the previous season.

Frank Stapleton, however, launched his first-team career in this match.

1982	Tottenham Hotspur	A	Division 1	2–2
1986	Tottenham Hotspur	A	Division 1	0–1
1994	Paris St–Germain	A	Cup Winners Cup semi-final 2nd leg	1–1

MARCH 30TH

1888	Millwall Rovers	H	Friendly	3–0
1889	Royal Artillery	H	Friendly	9–0
1891	Heart of Midlothian	H	Friendly	1–5
1894	Joseph Toner was born in Castlewellan, County Down.			
1895	Newton Heath	H	Division 2	3–2
1901	Middlesbrough	A	Division 2	1–1
1907	Blackburn Rovers	H	Division 1	2–0
1912	West Ham United	H	Friendly	3–0

Alexander Graham's first-team debut.

1918	Crystal Palace	H	London Combination	3–0
1929	Bury	H	Division 1	7–1
1934	Derby County	H	Division 1	1–0
1935	Aston Villa	A	Division 1	3–1
1940	Tottenham Hotspur	A	League South 'C' Division	1–1
1946	Millwall	H	Football League – South	4–0
1954	Bristol City	A	Friendly	1–3
1957	Bolton Wanderers	A	Division 1	1–2
1963	Ipswich Town	A	Division 1	1–1
1964	Sheffield Wednesday	A	Division 1	4–0
1970	Crystal Palace	H	Division 1	2–0
1974	Stoke City	A	Division 1	0–0
1985	Stoke City	A	Division 1	0–2

Final senior appearance of Raphael Meade, remembered more for his off-the-field exploits than for his performances on the field of play. Lots of speed, but not much control. Played 41 (14 goals) League, 3 FA Cup, 4 (1 goal) FL Cup and 3 (1 goal) European games.

| 1988 | Oxford United | A | Division 1 | 0–0 |

Debut of Brian Marwood.

| 1991 | Derby County | A | Division 1 | 2–0 |

MARCH 31ST

1890	Mr WH Loraine's XI	H	Friendly	3–1
1891	Nottingham Forest	H	Friendly	0–5
1892	Notts County	H	Friendly	2–4
1893	Middlesbrough	H	Friendly	4–1
1894	Small Heath	H	Division 2	1–4
1899	Wellingborough	H	United League	3–0
1900	Small Heath	A	Division 2	1–3
1902	West Bromwich Albion	H	Division 2	2–1
1906	Newcastle United	Stoke	FA Cup semi-final	0–2

Arsenal's first appearance in a major cup competition semi-final.

1917	Chelsea	A	London Combination	0–2
1919	Fulham	H	London Victory Cup	1–4
1923	Aston Villa	H	Division 1	2–0
1928	Birmingham	H	Division 1	2–2
1934	Stoke City	A	Division 1	1–1
1945	Reading	H	Football League – South	0–2
1951	Sunderland	A	Division 1	2–0

1955 Jack Kelsey made his international debut for Wales in the 0–0 draw with Ireland in Wrexham in a World Cup qualifying game.

1956	Luton Town	H	Division 1	3–0

1959 Mel Charles signed from Swansea Town for £42,750 and the services of David Dodson and Paul Davies.

1961	Fulham	A	Division 1	2–2

Last League game for Joe Haverty. His record: 114 (25 goals) League and 8 (1 goal) FA Cup matches.

1962	Aston Villa	H	Division 1	4–5
1969	Liverpool	A	Division 1	1–1
1970	Ipswich Town	A	Division 1	1–2
1971	Stoke City	Aston Villa		
			FA Cup semi-final replay	2–0

In the FA Cup semi-final replay against Stoke City at Villa Park, Birmingham, Arsenal gained a much tighter grip on the match than they had done on the previous Saturday to gain a last gasp draw. George Graham headed the Gunners in front after 13 minutes from George Armstrong's corner. In 47th minute John Radford crossed low and hard and Graham stepped over the ball for the onrushing Ray Kennedy to score from close range. A 2–0 victory took Arsenal to the FA Cup final for the first time in 19 years.

1973	Derby County	H	Division 1	0–1

Final appearance of Frank McLintock. The inspirational captain of the team that won the European Fairs Cup in 1970 and the League Championship and FA Cup Double the following season (when he was also awarded the title of 'Footballer of the Year').
His final record: 314 (26 goals) League, 36 (1 goal) FA Cup, 34 (4 goals) FL Cup and 19 (1 goal) European games.

1975	Sheffield United	H	Division 1	1–0
1979	Wolverhampton	Aston Vill		
	Wanderers		FA Cup semi-final	2–0

Fourteenth FA Cup semi-final appearance. Steve Gatting deputised for an injured Liam Brady, Stapleton and Sunderland got the goals.

1981	Birmingham City	H	Division 1	2–1
1984	Coventry City	A	Division 1	4–1
1986	Watford	H	Division 1	0–2
1990	Everton	H	Division 1	1–0
1992	Nottingham Forest	H	Division 1	3–3
1998	Bolton Wanderers	A	Premier League	1–0

The Gunners arrived at the Reebok Stadium for what was to be a potentially difficult game against relegation-threatened Bolton. The first 15 minutes saw Bolton have a couple of half chances and a lot of possession without looking too dangerous. Anelka, just prior to half-time, was unlucky not to put the Gunners ahead with a near-post effort. Then, shortly after the break, Wreh picked up a loose ball on the edge of the area an unleashed a venomous shot that seemed to gain pace as it hit the net, setting off with his now famous cartwheel celebrations. Bolton with their heads down looked vulnerable and both Anelka and Wreh missed opportunities to put the game beyond doubt. On the hour Keown, who had been battling all night with Nathan Blake, was sent off for a second bookable offence; thus, not for the first time this season Arsenal were reduced to 10 men. Seaman produced the save of the game 10 minutes later from Thomson, which ensured another clean sheet (his 150th shut-out for Arsenal) to set a new premiership record for not conceding a goal as the Gunners continued their excellent run.

APRIL 1ST

Year	Opponent	H/A	Competition	Score
1889	2nd Rifle Brigade		Friendly	6–1
	Debut of David Howat.			
1893	Accrington	H	Friendly	3–1
1895	Blackburn Rovers	H	Friendly	2–2
1897	Kent	A	Friendly	3–0
1898	Loughborough Town	H	United League	4–1
1899	Newton Heath	A	Division 2	2–2
1901	Millwall	H	Friendly	1–1
1902	Blackburn Rovers	H	Friendly	2–0
1904	Preston North End	A	Division 2	0–0
1905	Small Heath	H	Division 1	1–1
1907	Aston Villa	H	Division 1	3–1
1909	Sheffield United	H	Division 1	1–0
1911	Newcastle United	A	Division 1	1–0
1916	Clapton Orient	H	London Combination	2–1
1918	West Ham United	H	London Combination	1–3
1922	Middlesbrough	H	Division 1	2–2
1925	Aston Villa	A	Division 1	1–0
1933	Aston Villa	H	Division 1	5–0
1933	Joe Hulme made his 9th and last appearance for England in the 1–2 defeat by Scotland in Glasgow. He scored 4 international goals.			
1936	Bolton Wanderers	H	Division 1	1–1
1939	Middlesbrough	H	Division 1	1–2
1944	Aldershot	A	Football League – South	3–0
1949	Sammy Nelson was born in Belfast, N. Ireland.			
1950	Manchester City	H	Division 1	4–1
1955	Alfred Baker died.			
1961	Bolton Wanderers	A	Division 1	1–1
1966	Sammy Nelson joined from Belfast.			
1967	Stoke City	A	Division 1	2–2
1972	Nottingham Forest	H	Division 1	3–0
1978	Manchester United	H	Division 1	3–1
1986	Watford	A	Division 1	0–3
1995	Norwich City	H	Premier League	5–1

APRIL 2ND

Year	Opponent	H/A	Competition	Score
1892	Chatham	H	Friendly	5–3
1894	Nottingham Forest	H	Friendly	1–3
1896	Stockton	H	Friendly	2–0
1898	Burnley	H	Division 2	1–1

1900	Millwall	H	Southern District Combination	0–1
1904	Burnley	A	Division 2	0–1
1906	Nottingham Forest	H	Division 1	3–1
1910	Bristol City	A	Division 1	1–0
1915	Hull City	A	Division 2	0–1

Last League game for George Grant. Played 54 (4 goals) League and 3 FA Cup matches.

1920	Bolton Wanderers	A	Friendly	2–4
1921	Sheffield United	A	Division 1	1–1
1923	Blackburn Rovers	H	Division 1	1–1
1924	Liverpool	A	Division 1	0–0
1926	Aston Villa	A	Division 1	0–3
1927	Huddersfield Town	H	Division 1	0–2

Billy Milne's final senior game. He had made 114 (1 goal) League and 10 (2 goals) FA Cup appearances.

He retired and was appointed assistant trainer at Arsenal.

1927 Joe Hulme made his England international in the 2–1 victory against Scotland in Glasgow.

1929	Newcastle United	H	Division 1	1–2
1930	Liverpool	H	Division 1	0–1
1932	Chelsea	H	Division 1	1–1
1934	Derby County	A	Division 1	4–2
1938	Charlton Athletic	H	Division 1	2–2
1945	Brentford	A	Football League – South	1–3
1949	Birmingham City	A	Division 1	1–1
1955	Huddersfield Town	A	Division 1	1–0
1956	Huddersfield Town	H	Division 1	2–0
1960	West Ham United	A	Division 1	0–0

1974 Jimmy Rimmer's move from Manchester United was sealed with a £40,000 fee paid by the Gunners.

1977	Leicester City	H	Division 1	3–0
1980	Norwich City	A	Division 1	1–2
1983	Southampton	H	Division 1	0–0
1988	Chelsea	A	Division 1	1–1
1989	Manchester United	A	Division 1	1–1
1994	Swindon Town	H	Premier League	1–1

APRIL 3RD

1893	Grimsby Town	H	Friendly	3–5
1896	Dundee	H	Friendly	3–1
1897	Newton Heath	H	Division 2	0–2
1899	Manchester City	H	Division 2	0–1

1899 David Jack was born in Bolton, Lancashire.

| 1909 | Chelsea | H | Division 1 | 0–0 |
| 1915 | Bristol City | A | Division 2 | 1–1 |

Last game for Thomas Winship. He played 55 (7 goals) League and 1 FA Cup matches.

| 1920 | Burnley | A | Division 1 | 1–2 |
| 1926 | Blackburn Rovers | H | Division 1 | 4–2 |

League debut of Tom Parker.

| 1931 | Portsmouth | A | Division 1 | 1–1 |

1937	West Bromwich Albion	H	Division 1	2–0
1940	Southend United	A	League South 'A' Division	5–0
1943	Watford	A	Football League Cup – South	1–1
1946	Death of Alf Common.			
1948	Blackburn Rovers	H	Division 1	2–0
1953	Chelsea	A	Division 1	1–1
1954	Bolton Wanderers	A	Division 1	1–3
1956	Huddersfield Town	A	Division 1	1–0
1957	Reading	A	Southern Floodlight Challenge Cup	1–2
1961	Fulham	H	Division 1	4–2
1965	West Bromwich Albion	H	Division 1	1–1
1966	Remi Garde born in L'Arbesle, France.			
1971	Chelsea	H	Division 1	2–0

The highest attendance of the season at Highbury, 62,087 witnessed Arsenal defeat Chelsea 2–0. Two second-half goals from Ray Kennedy sealed the win. Two minutes after the interval George Armstrong crossed low, Charlie George dummied the ball and Kennedy shot home. Arsenal made sure of victory in 76th minute, while the Chelsea defence waited for the offside flag George passed square to Kennedy, who finished with a firm shot.

1976	Tottenham Hotspur	H	Division 1	0–2
1979	Coventry City	H	Division 1	1–1
1982	Wolverhampton Wanderers	A	Division 1	1–1
1983	Jimmy Bloomfield died at Chingford, Essex.			
1991	Aston Villa	H	Division 1	5–0

APRIL 4TH

1891	Old Carthusians	N	London Charity Cup	1–1
1896	Grimsby Town	A	Division 2	1–1
1898	Kettering Town	A	United League	2–1
1899	Millwall	A	Friendly	0–0
1903	Small Heath	H	Division 2	6–1
1904	Glossop North End	H	Division 2	2–1
1912	Archibald Gray transferred to Fulham for £250.			
1914	Bristol City	H	Division 2	1–1
1925	Cardiff City	H	Division 1	1–1
1929	Mike Tiddy was born in Helston, Cornwall.			
1931	Chelsea	H	Division 1	2–1
1936	Brentford	H	Division 1	1–1
1942	Clapton Orient	A	London War Cup	2–1
1947	Huddersfield Town	H	Division 1	1–2
1953	Liverpool	H	Division 1	5–3
1959	Nottingham Forest	A	Division 1	1–1
1964	Blackpool	A	Division 1	1–0
1970	West Ham United	H	Division 1	2–1
1972	Leicester City	A	Division 1	0–0
1981	Brighton & Hove Albion	A	Division 1	1–0
1983	Tottenham Hotspur	A	Division 1	0–5
1988	Norwich City	H	Division 1	2–0
1992	Coventry City	A	Division 1	1–0

1993	Tottenham Hotspur	Wembley	FA Cup semi-final	1–0

Arsenal's 18th FA Cup semi-final appearance. Tony Adams champagne moment!

1994	Sheffield United	A	Premier League	1–1

APRIL 5TH

1890	Old Westminsters	N	London Charity Cup	3–1
1901	Nottingham Forest	II	Friendly	1–1
1902	Lincoln City	H	Division 2	2–0
1905	Everton	A	Division 1	0–1
1912	Manchester United	H	Division 1	2–1
1913	Blackburn Rovers	A	Division 1	1–1
1915	Barnsley	H	Division 2	1–0
1919	Chelsea	H	London Combination	2–1
1920	West Bromwich Albion	H	Division 1	1–0
1922	Manchester United	H	Division 1	3–1
1924	Burnley	H	Division 1	2–0
1926	Aston Villa	H	Division 1	2–0
1930	Newcastle United	A	Division 1	1–1
1941	Tottenham Hotspur	H	Football League War Cup	2–1
1947	Bolton Wanderers	A	Division 1	3–1
1952	Chelsea	Tottenham	FA Cup semi-final	1–1

Ninth FA Cup semi-final appearance. Freddie Cox scored for the Gunners as he had two years previously against the same opponents at the same venue at the same stage of the competition.

1960	West Ham United	H	Southern Floodlight Challenge Cup	1–3
1966	West Bromwich Albion	H	Division 1	1–1
1969	Sunderland	A	Division 1	0–0
1975	John Hartson was born in Swansea, Wales.			
1980	Southampton	H	Division 1	1–1
1986	Manchester City	A	Division 1	1–0
1987	Liverpool	Wembley	Littlewoods Cup final	2–1

George Graham's team secured a major prize in his first season in charge at the club and finally buried the hoodoo that had plagued Arsenal in the League (Littlewoods sponsored on this occasion) Cup. The goals were scored by Charlie Nicholas but the enduring memory is of Perry Groves skinning the Liverpool full-back to supply the cross that led to Charlie's winner. The ginger winger's celebrations were pretty special too!

1997	Chelsea	A	Premier League	3–0

Final senior appearance of Ian Selley. With a career blighted by injury he did well to clock up 39 League, 3 FA Cup, 6 FL Cup and 10 European matches. The highlight of Selley's career with Arsenal surely being the 1994 European Cup Winners Cup final victory against the much fancied Parma when he did his bit to bring the trophy back to Highbury.

1998	Wolverhampton Wanderers	Villa Park	FA Cup semi-final	1–0

Nineteenth appearance in the FA Cup semi-final, the first won by a goal from a Liberian (Chris Wreh) who scored after 13 minutes. A very one-sided game saw Wolves manage only 2 efforts on goal whereas the Gunners had 12. Ray Parlour received a yellow card which meant that he would have been suspended had the FA Cup final gone to a replay.

APRIL 6TH

1889	Old St Paul's	A	Friendly	1–0
1895	Crewe Alexandra	H	Division 2	7–0
1896	Newcastle United	H	Division 2	2–1
1901	Burnley	H	Division 2	3–1
1907	Sunderland	A	Division 1	3–2
1912	Sheffield Wednesday	A	Division 1	0–3
1917	Tottenham Hotspur	A	London Combination	0–0
1918	Fulham	A	London Combination	1–2
1920	West Bromwich Albion	A	Division 1	0–1

Senior debut for Tom Whittaker.

1927	Newcastle United	A	Division 1	1–6
1928	Cardiff City	H	Division 1	3–0
1929	Aston Villa	A	Division 1	2–4

Final senior game for 'Billy' Blyth who completed 314 (45 goals) League and 29 (6 goals) FA Cup matches for Arsenal.

1931	Portsmouth	H	Division 1	1–1
1932	Sunderland	A	Division 1	0–2

First senior game for Ted 'Pat' Beasley.

1935	Chelsea	H	Division 1	2–2
1940	Brentford	A	League South 'C' Division	4–2
1942	West Ham United	H	London War Cup	1–4
1946	Southampton	H	Football League – South	1–1
1953	Chelsea	H	Division 1	2–0
1954	Aston Villa	H	Division 1	1–1
1957	Leeds United	H	Division 1	1–0
1959	West Ham United	A	Southern Floodlight Challenge Cup	2–0

Mel Charles made his first senior start.

1963	Nottingham Forest	H	Division 1	0–0
1965	Birmingham City	H	Division 1	3–0

Tommy Baldwin's first-team debut.

1968	Everton	A	Division 1	0–2
1971	Coventry City	H	Division 1	1–0

On a frustrating night at Highbury the Gunners played Coventry City and Ray Kennedy scored his 25th goal of the season in 52nd minute to settle the match. George Graham lobbed towards the bye-line to George Armstrong who half volleyed a pass to Kennedy. He controlled the ball with one foot while scoring with the other. This was another game in hand on leaders Leeds United that Arsenal won to close the gap at the top.

1974	West Ham United	H	Division 1	0–0
1985	Norwich City	H	Division 1	2–0
1991	Sheffield United	A	Division 1	2–0
1993	Middlesbrough	A	Premier League	0–1
1995	Sampdoria	H	Cup Winners Cup semi-final 1st leg	3–2

A result that many pundits predicted would not be good enough to see Arsenal progress to the final. How wrong they were!

1996	Leeds United	H	Premier League	2–1

APRIL 7TH

1888	Alexandria United	A	Friendly	3–1

1890	1st Lincolnshire Regiment	H	Friendly	2–1
1894	Millwall Athletic	A	Friendly	4–1
1897	Loughborough Town	A	United League	0–4
1900	New Brighton Tower	H	Division 2	5–0
1902	Portsmouth	A	Southern Professional Charity Cup	2–1
1906	Manchester City	A	Division 1	2–1
1917	Southampton	H	London Combination	2–2
1923	Aston Villa	A	Division 1	1–1
1928	Tottenham Hotspur	A	Division 1	0–2
1934	Huddersfield Town	H	Division 1	3–1
1939	Blackpool	A	Division 1	0–1
1945	Fulham	A	Friendly	3–0
1947	Huddersfield Town	A	Division 1	0–0
1951	Liverpool	H	Division 1	1–2
1952	Chelsea	Tottenham	FA Cup semi-final replay	3–0

Freddie Cox continued scoring in semi-finals when he bagged a brace which complemented a goal from Doug Lishman.

1956	Burnley	A	Division 1	1–0
1958	Wolverhampton Wanderers	H	Division 1	0–3
1962	Nottingham Forest	A	Division 1	1–0
1967	Charlton Athletic	A	Friendly	0–0

First senior appearance of Pat Rice.

| 1969 | Wolverhampton Wanderers | H | Division 1 | 3–1 |
| 1973 | Sunderland | Sheffield Wed | FA Cup semi-final | 1–2 |

Twelfth FA Cup semi-final appearance. Arsenal started the game as overwhelming favourites against second division opposition but the odds had been calculated without the 'Jeff Blockley' factor. Charlie George scored the consolation goal.

| 1979 | Liverpool | A | Division 1 | 0–3 |

Steve Brignall established a record that was to stand for the best part of two decades when he made a brief appearance as a substitute towards the end of this game. As it was the only time he tasted first-team action, his became the shortest ever senior Arsenal career until this dubious distinction was passed to Jehad Muntasser in 1997.

| 1980 | Tottenham Hotspur | A | Division 1 | 2–1 |

League debut for Paul Davis in a game in which he played a starring role. Coming only a couple of days before the first leg of the European Cup Winners Cup semi-final against Juventus, Arsenal sought to rearrange this fixture but got no encouragement from their neighbours. The Gunners were, therefore, forced to beat Spurs with half a team of reserves.

| 1984 | Stoke City | H | Division 1 | 3–1 |

APRIL 8TH

1891	Old Carthusians	N	London Charity Cup	2–2
1893	Crusaders	A	Friendly	2–0
1895	Millwall Athletic	A	Friendly	0–0

1896	Gravesend	A	Friendly	4–0
1897	Grimsby Town	A	Division 2	1–3
1898	Tottenham Hotspur	A	United League	0–0
1899	New Brighton Tower	H	Division 2	4–0
1901	Blackpool	H	Division 2	3–1
1905	Manchester City	A	Division 1	0–1
1911	Tottenham Hotspur	H	Division 1	2–0
1912	Preston North End	H	Division 1	4–1
1916	Tottenham Hotspur	A	London Combination	2–3
1922	Middlesbrough	A	Division 1	2–4

Last senior game for Angus McKinnon. His record: 211 (4 goals) League and 6 FA Cup matches.

1933	Middlesbrough	A	Division 1	4–3
1939	Birmingham	A	Division 1	2–1

Final match for Alex Wilson who had played 82 League and 7 FA Cup games.

1940	West Ham United	A	League South 'C' Division	1–2
1944	Crystal Palace	H	Football League – South	5–2
1950	Blackpool	A	Division 1	1–2
1955	Cardiff City	H	Division 1	2–0
1958	Wolverhampton Wanderers	A	Division 1	2–1
1961	Blackpool	H	Division 1	1–0

1961 Brian McDermott was born in Slough, Berkshire.

1963	Wolverhampton Wanderers	A	Division 1	0–1
1969	Leicester City	A	Division 1	0–0
1970	Ajax	H	European Fairs Cup semi-final 1st leg	3–0

Two goals from Charlie George (one from a penalty) and a strike from Sammels secured a convincing lead to defend in Amsterdam.

1972	Wolverhampton Wanderers	H	Division 1	2–1
1975	Coventry City	H	Division 1	2–0
1978	Orient	Chelsea	FA Cup semi-final	3–0

Thirteenth FA Cup semi-final appearance. Macdonald scored twice and Rix netted the other goal.

1981	Kent County FA XI	Gillingham		
			Centenary	2–2
1986	Nottingham Forest	H	Division 1	1–1

Last senior outing for Paul Mariner. He had accumulated 60 (14 goals) League, 6 FA Cup and 4 (1 goal) FL Cup games.

If the suspicion had been that Mariner, at the tailend of his career, had come for the money he quickly won over the fans with his whole-hearted effort and overall contribution to the team. However, as part of the clique of senior players who had formed themselves into a 'team within a team' he did not survive the clean sweep by the new broom (George Graham) and in August 1986 was given a free transfer to Portsmouth.

1987	West Ham United	A	Division 1	1–3
1989	Everton	H	Division 1	2–0
1992	Norwich City	A	Division 1	3–1

| 1995 | Queen's Park Rangers | A | Premier League | 1–3 |
| 1996 | Sheffield Wednesday | A | Premier League | 0–1 |

APRIL 9TH

1892	South Shore	H	Friendly	1–1
1894	Sheffield United	H	Friendly	0–1
1898	Darwen	H	Division 2	3–1
1900	Queen's Park Rangers	A	Southern District Combination	0–3
1904	Preston North End	H	Division 2	0–0
1906	Tottenham Hotspur	A	Southern Professional Charity Cup	0–0
1909	Exeter City	H	Friendly	2–3
1910	Bury	H	Division 1	0–0
1917	Tottenham Hotspur	H	London Combination	3–2
1921	Bradford Park Avenue	H	Division 1	2–1

1924 Arthur Shaw was born in Limehouse, London.

1927	Sunderland	A	Division 1	1–5
1928	Cardiff City	A	Division 1	2–2
1930	Middlesbrough	A	Division 1	1–1
1932	Liverpool	A	Division 1	1–2
1938	Leeds United	A	Division 1	1–0

1943 Death of James Ashcroft who between 1900–08 made over 300 first-team appearances in goal for Arsenal.

1949	Middlesbrough	H	Division 1	1–1
1955	Blackpool	H	Division 1	3–0
1960	Chelsea	H	Division 1	1–4
1977	West Bromwich Albion	A	Division 1	2–0
1980	Juventus	H	Cup Winners Cup semi-final 1st leg	1–1

David O'Leary was cynically put out of the game by an horrendous tackle from Roberto Bettaga and Marco Tardelli was sent off for an assault on Liam Brady as the Italians forced a draw. Bettaga did his best to make amends for his behaviour by putting through his own goal.

1983	Coventry City	H	Division 1	2–1
1984	Everton	A	Division 1	0–0
1988	Southampton	A	Division 1	2–4

Steve Williams final senior appearance. His record finished 95 (4 goals) League, 11 FA Cup and 15 FL Cup games.

Quite often brilliant but also often petulant, as when he made the rash challenge that led to a last-minute penalty and elimination from the FA Cup at York in 1985.

| 1991 | Southampton | A | Division 1 | 1–1 |

APRIL 10TH

1897	Reserves	H	Friendly	1–2
1903	Chesterfield	H	Division 2	3–0
1907	Everton	A	Division 1	1–2
1909	Blackburn Rovers	A	Division 1	3–1
1914	Stockport County	A	Division 2	0–2
1915	Bury	H	Division 2	3–1
1920	Burnley	H	Division 1	2–0
1926	Sunderland	A	Division 1	1–2

1936	West Bromwich Albion	H	Division 1	4–0
1937	Manchester City	A	Division 1	0–2
1939	Blackpool	H	Division 1	2–1
1943	West Ham United	H	Football League Cup – South	3–1
1944	Brighton & Hove Albion	H	Football League – South	3–1
1948	Huddersfield Town	A	Division 1	1–1

This result confirmed Arsenal as League Champions for the sixth time.

1950	Stoke City	H	Division 1	6–0
1954	Liverpool	H	Division 1	3–0

Final appearance for Joe Mercer. He had played 247 (2 goals) League and 26 FA Cup games for Arsenal.

Inspirational captain and driving force who led his team to League Championship victories in 1947–48 and 1952–53, as well as winning the FA Cup in 1950.

In the same game Derek Tapscott made his League debut.

1968	Southampton	A	Division 1	0–2
1971	Southampton	A	Division 1	2–1

After a 2–1 win against Southampton at the Dell, Arsenal were in touching distance of League leaders Leeds United being 3 points behind with 2 games in hand. The hosts had been unbeaten at home for the previous 5 months but fell behind in 34th minute when John Radford scored. The Gunners' joy was short-lived as Paine equalised for Southampton 2 minutes later. The winning goal was scored in 55th minute when a long throw by Radford was flicked on by George Graham to leave skipper Frank McLintock to slot the ball home.

1976	Everton	A	Division 1	0–0
1979	Tottenham Hotspur	H	Division 1	1–0
1982	Brighton & Hove Albion	A	Division 1	1–2
1993	Ipswich Town	A	Premier League	2–1

APRIL 11TH

1891	Old Carthusians	N	London Charity Cup	1–2
1896	Millwall Athletic	H	Friendly	2–2
1898	Burton Swifts	H	Division 2	3–0
1903	Leicester Fosse	A	Division 2	2–0
1908	Birmingham	A	Division 1	2–1
1910	Aston Villa	H	Division 1	1–0
1914	Leeds City	A	Division 2	0–0
1925	Preston North End	A	Division 1	0–2
1931	Grimsby Town	A	Division 1	1–0
1936	Middlesbrough	A	Division 1	2–2

Last senior appearance 'Tiger' Hill. Record: 76 (4 goals) League and 2 FA Cup.

1942	Brighton & Hove Albion	A	London War Cup	3–0
1952	Blackpool	A	Division 1	0–0
1953	Manchester City	A	Division 1	4–2
1955	Cardiff City	A	Division 1	2–1
1959	Chelsea	H	Division 1	1–1

1959 Tommy Docherty made his 25th and last appearance for Scotland in the 1–0 defeat by England at Wembley. Three of these caps were won during his time at Arsenal.

1962	Fulham	A	Division 1	2–5
1964	Blackburn Rovers	H	Division 1	0–0

1966	West Bromwich Albion	A	Division 1	4–4
1972	Crystal Palace	A	Division 1	2–2
1977	Tottenham Hotspur	H	Division 1	1–0
1978	Queen's Park Rangers	A	Division 1	1–2
1981	Leeds United	H	Division 1	0–0
1987	Charlton Athletic	H	Division 1	2–1
1990	Aston Villa	H	Division 1	0–1
1992	Crystal Palace	H	Division 1	4–1
1998	Newcastle United	H	Premier League	3–1

The Toon Army came to Highbury in a dress rehearsal for the FA Cup final, even though there was lot more at stake for the Gunners. Arsenal pressurised Newcastle who looked as though they were playing for a point and nothing more. Anelka had 3 early chances, one of which hit the post from a very tight angle and it came as no surprise when the young Frenchman scored on 40 minutes after a good ball from Petit from the edge of the box. Ray Parlour who had been in outstanding form all season darted in between Pearce and Batty to provide a cross for Anelka to nod home his 2nd goal after 65 minutes to put the game almost out of Newcastle's reach. Six minutes later the ball fell to Vieira 35 yards out, he took one step forward (about 5 yards in his case) and unleashed such a powerful shot it hit the net before Shay Given reacted. On 78 minutes, a lapse in concentration in the Arsenal defence let in Gunners fan Warren Barton to score for the Magpies. Arsenal had conceded their first goal in 9 games. With a couple of minutes to go Anelka was substituted to one of the loudest standing ovations of the season. It had taken a while for Anelka to gain acceptance from the Highbury regulars but it appeared that Arsène Wenger's belief in his talents had been vindicated.

APRIL 12TH

1890	Great Marlow	H	Friendly	3–1
1894	Westerham & District XI	A	Friendly	6–3
1895	Walsall Town Swifts	H	Division 2	6–1
1902	West Bromwich Albion	A	Division 2	1–2
1905	West Norwood	A	Friendly	7–0
1909	Sheffield Wednesday	H	Division 1	2–0
1913	Derby County	H	Division 1	1–2
1919	Clapton Orient	A	London Combination	2–2
1924	Sunderland	H	Division 1	2–0
1930	Sheffield United	H	Division 1	8–1
1941	Tottenham Hotspur	A	Football League War Cup	1–1
1947	Middlesbrough	H	Division 1	4–0
1948	Arsenal acquired the services of Arthur Shaw from Brentford.			
1952	Bolton Wanderers	A	Division 1	1–2
1958	Newcastle United	A	Division 1	3–3
1963	West Bromwich Albion	H	Division 1	3–2
1969	Leeds United	H	Division 1	1–2
1975	Leeds United	H	Division 1	1–2
1980	Liverpool	Hillsborough		
			FA Cup semi-final	0–0

Fifteenth FA Cup semi-final appearance. The tie needed three replays before being settled in Arsenal's favour.

| 1982 | Tottenham Hotspur | H | Division 1 | 1–3 |

1986	Everton	H	Division 1	0–1
1988	West Ham United	A	Division 1	1–0
1993	Aston Villa	H	Premier League	0–1
1994	Paris St-Germain	H	Cup Winners Cup semi-final	1–0

Kevin Campbell scored the all-important goal but the game will be remembered for the booking of Ian Wright which meant he was suspended for the final.

1995	Liverpool	H	Premier League	0–1
1997	Leicester City	H	Premier League	2–0

APRIL 13TH

1895	Dumbarton	H	Friendly	5–1
1896	Everton	H	Friendly	2–0
1898	Southampton	A	United League	0–3
1900	Burnley	H	Friendly	2–0
1901	Port Vale	A	Division 2	0–1
1903	Leicester Fosse	H	Division 2	0–0
1906	Aston Villa	H	Division 1	2–1
1907	Birmingham	H	Division 1	2–1
1912	Bury	H	Division 1	1–0
1914	Stockport County	H	Division 2	4–0
1918	Millwall Athletic	H	National War Fund	4–3
1925	West Bromwich Albion	A	Division 1	0–2
1929	Leicester City	H	Division 1	1–1
1935	Wolverhampton Wanderers	A	Division 1	1–1
1936	West Bromwich Albion	A	Division 1	0–1
1940	Portsmouth	H	League South 'C' Division	3–2
1946	Southampton	A	Football League – South	1–1
1957	Sunderland	A	Division 1	0–1

John Barnwell's League debut.

1962	Peter Simpson signed a full professional contract.			
1963	Sheffield United	A	Division 1	3–3
1968	Leicester City	H	Division 1	2–1
1971	Nottingham Forest	A	Division 1	3–0

Arsenal ran out convincing 3–0 winners against Nottingham Forest at the City ground in front of their largest attendance of the season 40,727. Frank McLintock opened the scoring in 18th minute by heading in a George Armstrong corner. The ball bobbled about the goal line and Ray Kennedy slammed the ball into the goal but the linesman had already awarded the goal for McLintock's effort. Kennedy himself headed the 2nd goal in 38th minute and the third was added by Charlie George from a Bob McNab pass 5 minutes from the end. Arsenal were 2 points behind leaders Leeds United with 2 games in hand.

1974	Chelsea	A	Division 1	3–1
1976	Wolverhampton Wanderers	H	Division 1	2–1
1985	Nottingham Forest	H	Division 1	1–1
1998	Blackburn Rovers	A	Premier League	4–1

Arsenal went to Ewood Park knowing that victory was a must if they were to take over top spot in the title race. If anyone had any doubts about how committed they were they had their answer in the first 15 minutes when the Gunners scored 3 goals. After 80 seconds Bergkamp ran on to a pass from Anelka to shoot powerfully home for his 20th goal of the season. Five minutes later it was Bergkamp the provider for Ray Parlour to shoot home from inside the box for the second. In the 15th minute Bergkamp had a powerful shot fumbled by the goalkeeper and Parlour hammered in the rebound to set off delirious scenes for the travelling Arsenal fans. On the half-hour Blackburn had their first effort when Gallacher headed straight at Seaman when it might have been easier to score. In the 42nd minute Winterburn launched a ball to Anelka who ran from his own half and outpaced the defence to score a fabulous goal as he dummied the keeper twice before slotting home. At half-time a snowstorm hit Ewood Park and the second half had to be played with an orange ball. Blackburn scored a late consolation goal through Gallacher but the game was never in doubt. Arsenal took over top spot with 66 points from 32 games and had to win their next 4 games (3 were to be played at home) to make sure of the championship.

APRIL 14TH

1894	Burton Swifts	H	Division 2	0–2
1900	Grimsby Town	A	Division 2	0–1
1903	Northampton Town	A	Friendly	1–1
1906	Bury	H	Division 1	4–0
1908	Bolton Wanderers	H	Division 1	1–1
1911	Liverpool	H	Division 1	0–0
1917	Clapton Orient	A	London Combination	3–1
1919	Arthur Hutchins was signed from Croydon Common for £50 and goalkeeper Ernie Williamson also joined from the same club in a £150 deal.			
1923	Preston North End	H	Division 1	1–1
1925	West Bromwich Albion	H	Division 1	2–0
1928	Huddersfield Town	H	Division 1	0–0
1933	Sheffield Wednesday	H	Division 1	4–2
1934	Liverpool	A	Division 1	3–2
1934	Frank Moss made his international debut for England in the 3–0 victory over Scotland at Wembley. Cliff Bastin scored one of England's goals in the game.			
1936	Another legendary goalkeeper, George Swindin, was signed to the Arsenal ranks. He joined from Bradford City for £4,000.			
1941	Chelsea	A	South Regional League	1–3
1945	Charlton Athletic	A	Football League – South	0–5
1951	Fulham	A	Division 1	2–3
1952	Blackpool	H	Division 1	4–1
1956	Birmingham City	H	Division 1	1–0
1958	Geoff Strong signed a contract to turn professional. He had joined the club at the end of the previous year as an amateur from Stanley United at the cost of £100 to Arsenal.			
1959	Birmingham City	A	Division 1	1–4
1962	Wolverhampton Wanderers	H	Division 1	3–1
1964	Watford	A	George Catleugh Testimonial	0–1
	Final appearance of John McClelland who kept goal in 46 League and 3 FA Cup games.			
1967	Dunfermline Athletic	H	Friendly	2–1
1969	Chelsea	A	Division 1	1–2
1973	Tottenham Hotspur	H	Division 1	1–1

1979	West Bromwich Albion	A	Division 1	1–1
1987	Newcastle United	H	Division 1	0–1
1990	Crystal Palace	A	Division 1	1–1
1991	Tottenham Hotspur	Wembley	FA Cup semi-final	1–3

Arsenal's seventeenth and most forgettable FA Cup semi-final.

APRIL 15TH

1892	Small Heath	H	Friendly	1–2
1893	Casuals	H	Friendly	3–0
1895	Small Heath	H	Friendly	3–4
1899	Lincoln City	A	Division 2	0–2

1899 Jock Robson was born in Innerleithen, Scotland

1903	Sheppey United	H	Chatham Charity Cup	3–0
1905	Notts County	H	Division 1	1–2

Final game for Thomas Briercliffe, having represented the club in 122 (33 goals) League and 11 (1 goal) FA Cup matches.

1907	Stoke	A	Division 1	0–2
1911	Middlesbrough	A	Division 1	1–1
1916	Millwall Athletic	H	London Combination	0–0
1922	Tottenham Hotspur	A	Division 1	0–2
1927	Aston Villa	H	Division 1	2–1
1933	Portsmouth	H	Division 1	2–0

1934 David Herd was born in Hamilton, Scotland.

1938	Brentford	H	Division 1	0–2
1939	Manchester United	H	Division 1	2–1
1949	Blackpool	A	Division 1	1–1
1950	Newcastle United	H	Division 1	4–2

Last League match for Archie Macaulay. His record: 103 (1 goal) League and 4 FA Cup appearances.

1953	Bolton Wanderers	H	Division 1	4–1

Bill Dodgin made League debut.

1960	Fulham	H	Division 1	2–0
1961	Chelsea	A	Division 1	1–3
1963	West Bromwich Albion	A	Division 1	2–1
1968	Southampton	H	Division 1	0–3
1970	Ajax	A	European Fairs Cup semi-final 2nd leg.	0–1

Arsenal won the tie on a 3–1 aggregate score to reach their first European final.

1972	Stoke City	Aston Villa		
			FA Cup semi-final	1–1

Eleventh FA Cup semi-final appearance. Bob Wilson was injured and replaced in goal by John Radford. A goal by Geordie Armstrong and a strong rearguard action forced a replay.

1974	Wolverhampton Wanderers	A	Division 1	1–3
1978	Newcastle United	H	Division 1	2–1
1984	Heart of Midlothian	A	Friendly	2–3
1988	Watford	H	Division 1	0–1
1989	Newcastle United	H	Division 1	1–0
1995	Ipswich Town	H	Premier League	4–1
1996	Tottenham Hotspur	H	Premier League	0–0

APRIL 16TH

1892	Crewe Alexandra	H	Friendly	2–1
1894	Luton Town	A	Friendly	3–3
1897	Newcastle United	H	Division 2	5–1
1898	Luton Town	A	United League	1–2
1900	Archie Cross joined from Dartford.			
1900	Grimsby Town	H	Division 2	2–0
1904	Grimsby Town	A	Division 2	2–2
1906	Newcastle United	A	Division 1	1–1
1910	Tottenham Hotspur	A	Division 1	1–1
1921	Bradford Park Avenue	A	Division 1	1–0
1923	Clapton Orient	A	Friendly	1–2
1927	West Bromwich Albion	H	Division 1	4–1
1932	Sheffield Wednesday	H	Division 1	3–1
1938	Birmingham	H	Division 1	0–0
1949	Everton	A	Division 1	0–0
1952	Newcastle United	H	Division 1	1–1
1954	Portsmouth	H	Division 1	3–0
1955	Wolverhampton Wanderers	A	Division 1	1–3
1960	Birmingham City	A	Division 1	0–3
1962	Manchester United	A	Division 1	3–2
1965	Blackpool	A	Division 1	1–1
1966	West Ham United	A	Division 1	1–2
1977	Liverpool	A	Division 1	0–2
1979	Chelsea	H	Division 1	5–2
1980	Liverpool	Aston Villa		
			FA Cup semi-final replay	1–1

Arsenal's scorer was Alan Sunderland.

| 1983 | Manchester United | Aston Villa | | |
| | | | FA Cup semi-final | 1–2 |

Sixteenth FA Cup semi-final appearance. Arsenal took the lead through Tony Woodcock but lost after Stewart Robson was carried off injured after what looked very much like a premeditated assault on the mainstay of the Gunners effort. United's midfield at that time comprised the cultured trio, Whiteside, Moses and Robson (the latter, obviously, Man of the Match).

| 1986 | Sheffield Wednesday | A | Division 1 | 0–2 |
| 1994 | Chelsea | H | Premier League | 1–0 |

APRIL 17TH

1892	Henry White was born in Watford, Hertfordshire.			
1897	Leicester Fosse	H	Division 2	2–1
1900	Tottenham Hotspur	A	Southern District Combination	2–4
1907	Notts County	A	Division 1	1–4
1908	Newcastle United	A	Division 1	1–2
1909	Bradford City	H	Division 1	1–0
1911	Liverpool	A	Division 1	1–1
1915	Preston North End	A	Division 2	0–3
1920	Preston North End	A	Division 1	1–1

1922	West Bromwich Albion	A	Division 1	3–0
1926	Huddersfield Town	H	Division 1	3–1
1937	Portsmouth	H	Division 1	4–0
1939	Tottenham Hotspur	A	Friendly	2–1

George Marks made his first senior appearance.

1940	Chelsea	A	League South 'C' Division	2–2
1943	Luton Town	A	Friendly	4–1
1948	Derby County	H	Division 1	1–2
1954	Newcastle United	A	Division 1	2–5
1971	Newcastle United	H	Division 1	1–0

A brilliant Charlie George goal in the 71st minute gave Arsenal a 1–0 victory at home to Newcastle United. The game looked to be heading for a draw when George claimed the ball on the edge of the area and took it past one defender before hitting an explosive drive past McFaul in the Newcastle goal.

1976	Ipswich Town	H	Division 1	1–2
1982	Nottingham Forest	H	Division 1	2–0
1985	Tottenham Hotspur	A	Division 1	2–0
1991	Manchester City	H	Division 1	2–2
1995	Aston Villa	A	Premier League	4–0

APRIL 18TH

1891	Clapton	H	Friendly	3–1
1892	Bootle	H	Friendly	1–1
1894	New Brompton	A	Friendly	4–2
1896	Darwen	H	Division 2	1–3
1903	Millwall	H	London League Premier Division	0–2
1906	West Hartlepool	A	Friendly	4–0
1908	Everton	H	Division 1	2–1
1914	Clapton Orient	H	Division 2	2–2
1919	Crystal Palace	A	London Combination	3–0
1922	West Bromwich Albion	H	Division 1	2–2
1924	Everton	A	Division 1	1–3
1925	Burnley	H	Division 1	5–0
1927	Aston Villa	A	Division 1	3–2

Herbie Roberts made his League debut.

1928	Middlesbrough	A	Division 1	2–2
1930	Leicester City	H	Division 1	1–1
1931	Liverpool	H	Division 1	3–1
1934	Portsmouth	A	Division 1	0–1
1936	Aston Villa	H	Division 1	1–0
1938	Brentford	A	Division 1	0–3
1942	Brighton & Hove Albion	H	London War Cup	5–1
1949	Blackpool	H	Division 1	2–0
1953	Stoke City	H	Division 1	3–1
1955	Sheffield United	A	Division 1	1–1
1956	Racing Club de Paris	A	Friendly	4–3
1959	Blackpool	A	Division 1	2–1
1960	Fulham	A	Division 1	0–3

Last game for Gordon Nutt. He Played 49 (10 goals) League and 2 FA Cup matches.

1964	Liverpool	A	Division 1	0–5
1969	Stefan Schwarz was born in Malmo, Sweden.			
1979	Matthew Upton born in Hartismere.			
1981	Ipswich Town	A	Division 1	2–0
1987	Wimbledon	A	Division 1	2–1
1990	Liverpool	H	Division 1	1–1
1992	Sheffield United	A	Division 1	1–1
1993	Sheffield Wednesday	Wembley	Coca-Cola Cup final	2–1

Goals by Man of the Match Paul Merson and the unlikely hero, Steve Morrow, secured the first part of the first ever domestic Cup Double for the Gunners. It was the second time that Arsenal had won the Football League (Coca-Cola) Cup. The presentation was held up when during the post-match celebrations Tony Adams had dropped Steve Morrow off his back causing the Irishman to break his shoulder. As Morrow was carried from the pitch on a stretcher Adams went up the famous stairs to pick up the trophy.

1998	Wimbledon	H	Premier League	5–0

Wimbledon arrived at Highbury knowing they had not been beaten in their last 5 visits there and with the reputation of the side that took delight in spoiling the party. However, Arsenal were immediately flowing with confidence and a determination and after only 11 minutes Tony Adams rose at the far post to head home the first goal and ease the tension. Overmars scored another of his trademark goals after being released from Anelka after 17 minutes, and a further 2 minutes later the game was dead and buried as Bergkamp finished a superb move that had been set up by Anelka. The Gunners increased their lead to 4–0 when a long clearance by Seaman found Bergkamp who squared to Overmars to pass to Anelka who rolled it into the path of Petit who smashed the ball home. Wimbledon hit the post on the 75th minute with their first real attempt but it was left for Wreh to finish off the proceedings with a fine goal after nipping in between the keeper and 2 defenders to nod home into an empty net which prompted the performance of his cartwheel style celebration. The Gunners were now within 9 points of claiming the title as the winning sequence continued.

APRIL 19TH

1889	Boston Town	A	Friendly	1–4
1890	Chatham	H	Friendly	1–0
1897	Darwen	H	Division 2	1–0
1902	Burton United	A	Division 2	0–2
1904	Bradford City	A	Division 2	3–0
1913	Tottenham Hotspur	A	Division 1	1–1

Final game for Hugh McDonald. His record: 94 League and 9 FA Cup appearances.

1919	Clapton Orient	A	Friendly	3–1
1924	Sunderland	A	Division 1	1–1
1930	Huddersfield Town	A	Division 1	2–2
1935	Middlesbrough	H	Division 1	8–0
1937	Portsmouth	A	Friendly	2–0
1941	Leicester City	H	Football League War Cup	1–0
1946	Derby County	A	Football League – South	1–1
1947	Charlton Athletic	A	Division 1	2–2
1952	Stoke City	H	Division 1	4–1
1954	Portsmouth	A	Division 1	1–1
1957	Blackpool	H	Division 1	1–1
1958	Burnley	H	Division 1	0–0

1965	Blackpool	H	Division 1	3–1
1965	Perry Groves was born in Bow, London.			
1967	Fulham	A	Division 1	0–0
1969	Stoke City	A	Division 1	3–1
1972	Stoke City	Everton	FA Cup semi-final replay	2–1

George and Radford scored the goals that took the Gunners to the Centenary FA Cup final.

| 1975 | Queen's Park Rangers | A | Division 1 | 0–0 |
| 1976 | Queen's Park Rangers | A | Division 1 | 1–2 |

Final appearance of Brian Kidd. He had played 77 (30 goals) League, 9 (3 goals) FA Cup and 4 (1 goal) FL Cup games.

1980	Liverpool	A	Division 1	1–1
1994	Wimbledon	H	Premier League	1–1
1997	Blackburn Rovers	H	Premier League	1–1

APRIL 20TH

1889	Spartan Rovers	H	Friendly	6–0
1895	Burton Wanderers	A	Division 2	1–2
1896	Nathaniel Whittaker's XI	H	Friendly	3–2
1897	Norfolk County	A	Friendly	3–4
1901	Notts County	H	Friendly	3–0
1908	Sheffield Wednesday	H	Division 1	1–1

James Ashcroft made final league appearance, number 273 in his Arsenal career which also included 30 FA Cup matches. James Henry Bigden (75 League and 12 FA Cup games) and James Sharp, who had played 103 (4 goals) League and 13 (1 goal) FA Cup matches, also bowed out after this match.

1912	Glasgow Rangers	A	Friendly	0–0
1918	Millwall Athletic	A	National War Fund	1–0
1925	Luton Town	H	Friendly	4–1
1925	Debut made by Bill Seddon.			
1929	Manchester United	A	Division 1	1–4
1935	Huddersfield Town	H	Division 1	1–0
1940	Notts County	H	Football League War Cup	4–0
1946	Leicester City	H	Football League – South	1–2
1957	Charlton Athletic	H	Division 1	3–1
1962	Ipswich Town	A	Division 1	2–2
1963	Manchester City	H	Division 1	2–3
1964	Dave Bacuzzi was sold to Manchester City for £25,000. He had made 46 League and 2 FA Cup starts for Arsenal.			
1966	Sunderland	A	Division 1	2–0
1968	Sunderland	A	Division 1	0–2
1971	Burnley	H	Division 1	1–0

Arsenal were forced to play Burnley at Highbury without Bob McNab and Peter Storey who were called up for England duty. The Gunners had the incentive of knowing that a victory would put them on top of the table for the first time in the season. On a nervy night Charlie George scored the only goal with a 29th-minute penalty. Arsenal were top of the table by 2 points with a game in hand after their 9th successive League win.

| 1974 | Derby County | H | Division 1 | 2–0 |
| 1981 | Crystal Palace | H | Division 1 | 3–2 |

1983	Norwich City	A	Division 1	1–3

League debut for Colin Hill in a game that marked the end of George Wood's Arsenal career. The goalkeeper's final figures: 60 League, 1 FA Cup, 7 FL Cup and 2 European appearances. Wood's tally of games played was enhanced when he was preferred to Pat Jennings for an extended run when the Irishman was in contractual dispute with Terry Neill over his demand for improved terms. There was never a justification to penalise the team (and its fans) by making Jennings sweat in the stiffs. George Wood was Willie Young with gloves.

1985	Queen's Park Rangers	A	Division 1	0–1
1987	Leicester City	H	Division 1	4–1
1992	Liverpool	H	Division 1	4–0
1995	Sampdoria	A	Cup Winners Cup semi-final 2nd leg	2–3

Stefan Schwarz played what was probably the best game of his brief Arsenal career and scored a goal that took the game to a penalty shoot-out in which David Seaman excelled to help the Gunners reach a second successive European Cup Winners Cup final.

APRIL 21ST

1894	Burnley	H	Friendly	2–0
1900	Burton Swifts	A	Division 2	0–2
1905	New Brompton	H	Friendly	3–1
1906	Middlesbrough	A	Division 1	0–2
1908	Heart of Midlothian	A	Friendly	1–3
1916	Chelsea	A	London Combination	0–9
1917	West Ham United	H	London Combination	2–1
1919	Crystal Palace	H	London Combination	3–2
1923	Preston North End	A	Division 1	2–1
1924	Everton	H	Division 1	0–1
1928	Newcastle United	A	Division 1	1–1
1930	Leicester City	A	Division 1	6–6

Last senior game for goalkeeper Dan Lewis. His record finished: 142 League and 25 FA Cup matches but he will always be remembered for the error that led to the FA Cup final defeat by Cardiff City in 1927. Having seemingly gathered a shot safely he allowed the ball to squirm out of his hands and under his body into the goal. He blamed the sheen of his new jersey claiming that the greasy ball had slipped off it to elude him. Thus folklore dictates that, since this incident, all new Arsenal goalkeepers shirts be washed prior to being worn (though they are no longer knitted).

1934	Sunderland	H	Division 1	2–1
1936	Work began on the demolition of the old East Stand.			
1945	Watford	A	Football League – South	2–3
1948	Portsmouth	A	Division 1	0–0
1951	Bolton Wanderers	H	Division 1	1–1
1952	West Bromwich Albion	A	Division 1	1–3
1956	West Bromwich Albion	A	Division 1	1–2
1958	Nottingham Forest	H	Division 1	1–1
1959	Glasgow Rangers	H	Friendly	0–3
1962	West Ham United	A	Division 1	3–3
1963	Jock Rutherford died in Neasden.			
1964	Don Howe signed from WBA for £42,000, a record fee for a full-back at the time.			
1969	West Ham United	A	Division 1	2–1

| 1970 | Sammy Nelson came on as substitute for Northern Ireland to make his international debut in the 3–1 defeat by England at Wembley. |
| 1971 | Peter Storey made his international debut for England in the 3–0 victory over Greece at Wembley. |

1973	Everton	A	Division 1	0–0
1979	Derby County	A	Division 1	0–2
1984	Tottenham Hotspur	H	Division 1	3–2
1990	Luton Town	A	Division 1	0–2
1993	Nottingham Forest	H	Premier League	1–1
1997	Coventry City	A	Premier League	1–1

APRIL 22ND

1889	2nd Scots Guards	H	Friendly	7–2
1893	Derby County	H	Friendly	0–0
1899	Barnsley	H	Division 2	3–0
1901	Small Heath	H	Division 2	1–0
1903	Bristol City	A	Friendly	2–1
1905	Everton	H	Division 1	2–1

Final game for James Jackson. His record: 183 League and 21 (1 goal) FA Cup matches.

| 1908 | Raith Rovers | A | Friendly | 0–1 |

1908 James Sharp was transferred to Glasgow Rangers for £400.

| 1911 | Preston North End | H | Division 1 | 2–0 |
| 1912 | Blackburn Rovers | H | Division 1 | 5–1 |

Andy Ducat's final game. Played 175 (19 goals) League and 13 (2 goals) FA Cup matches.

1922	Tottenham Hotspur	H	Division 1	1–0
1929	Everton	H	Division 1	2–0
1931	Corinthians	H	Friendly	5–3
1933	Chelsea	A	Division 1	3–1

This victory confirmed Arsenal as League Champions for the second time in three years. The total of 118 goals scored was the club's second highest ever.

1935	Middlesbrough	A	Division 1	1–0
1939	Stoke City	A	Division 1	0–1
1944	Tottenham Hotspur	H	Football League – South	3–3
1946	Derby County	H	Football League – South	0–1

1947 Death of Frederick Coles.

1950	Wolverhampton Wanderers	A	Division 1	0–3
1953	Cardiff City	A	Division 1	0–0
1957	Blackpool	A	Division 1	4–2

1959 Dave Bowen made his 19th and last appearance for Wales in the 4–1 defeat by Ireland in Belfast. He scored 1 goal in his international career.

1961	Wolverhampton Wanderers	H	Division 1	1–5
1964	Dublin Select	A	Friendly	2–0
1967	Nottingham Forest	H	Division 1	1–1
1970	Anderlecht	A	European Fairs Cup final 1st leg	1–3

Substitute Ray Kennedy scored a priceless late away goal to give Arsenal a lifeline and a realistic chance of overhauling the Belgians in the second leg.

| 1972 | West Ham United | H | Division 1 | 2–1 |

| 1978 | Leeds United | A | Division 1 | 3–1 |

John Devine's League debut.

| 1998 | Tony Adams gained his 50th English international cap in his sides 3–0 win over Portugal at Wembley. |

APRIL 23RD

| 1892 | Clapton | H | Friendly | 4–1 |
| 1898 | Small Heath | A | Division 2 | 1–2 |

Final League game for John Caldwell. Record: 93 (2 goals) League and 4 FA Cup appearances.

1900	Barnsley	A	Division 2	2–3
1902	Tottenham Hotspur	H	Southern Professional Charity Cup	0–0
1908	Aberdeen	A	Friendly	1–4
1910	Preston North End	H	Division 1	1–3
1913	Robert Davidson was born in Lochgelly, Fifeshire.
1914	Grimsby Town	H	Division 2	2–0
1917	Laurie Scott was born in Sheffield.
1921	Newcastle United	H	Division 1	1–1
1927	Cardiff City	Wembley FA Cup final	0–1

The Gunners suffered defeat in their first major cup final when Welsh goalkeeper Dan Lewis committed the error that saw Cardiff score the goal that won them the game. Thus the FA Cup left England for the only time in the history of the competition, to reside in Wales.

| 1932 | Newcastle United | Wembley FA Cup final | 1–2 |

Another highly controversial goal changed the course of this final (Arsenal's third appearance) when, after taking the lead with a goal from Bob John, the Gunners were pegged back by an equaliser from Jack Allen just before half-time. Photographic evidence appeared to prove that before the ball was crossed to Allen it had run over the goal line and was out of play. Whilst the Arsenal defenders waited for a goal kick to be given, Allen converted and referee Bill Harper allowed the goal to stand. The Gunners, without the injured Alex James, could not rally and Allen scored again to win the game for the Geordies.

Arsenal finished as runners-up in the League as well.

1938	Preston North End	A	Division 1	3–1
1949	Chelsea	H	Division 1	1–2
1955	Manchester United	H	Division 1	2–3
1960	Manchester United	H	Division 1	5–2
1962	Ipswich Town	H	Division 1	0–3
1966	Sunderland	H	Division 1	1–1
1973	Southampton	A	Division 1	2–2
1975	Newcastle United	A	Division 1	1–3
1977	Coventry City	H	Division 1	2–0
1980	Juventus	A	Cup Winners Cup semi-final 2nd leg	1–0

Arsenal won on a ground where no British club had triumphed before. Paul Vaessen scored the only goal of the game just two minutes before the end of the game.

1983	Manchester City	H	Division 1	3–0
1984	Birmingham City	A	Division 1	1–1
1991	Queen's Park Rangers	H	Division 1	2–0
1994	Aston Villa.	A	Premier League	2–1

APRIL 24TH

1893	London Welsh	H	Friendly	4–2
1897	Millwall Athletic	A	United League	1–3
1899	Notts County	H	Friendly	2–1
1900	Tottenham Hotspur	H	Southern District Combination	2–1
1905	Dundee	H	Friendly	3–0
1915	Nottingham Forest	H	Division 2	7–0

The last League game played by Arsenal outside the top division saw 4 goals scored by King. With Arsenal's elevation to Division 1 immediately upon resumption of the Football League (at the end of the First World War) in 1919, the club embarked on a still unbroken record sequence of football in the top flight.

Also last appearance of goalkeeper Joseph Lievesley (who played 73 League and 2 FA Cup games for the club) and the end of Percy Sands time at Arsenal wherein he achieved 327 (10 goals) League and 23 (2 goals) FA Cup matches.

1916	Chelsea	H	London Combination	1–3
1920	Preston North End	H	Division 1	0–0
1926	West Bromwich Albion	A	Division 1	1–2
1937	Chelsea	A	Division 1	0–2
1940	Tottenham Hotspur	H	League South 'C' Division	2–4
1943	Queen's Park Rangers	Chelsea	Football League Cup – South semi-final	4–1
1948	Manchester City	A	Division 1	0–0
1954	Middlesbrough	H	Division 1	3–1
1957	Hereford Town	A	Friendly	4–0
1963	Everton	A	Division 1	1–1
1965	Everton	A	Division 1	0–1
1971	West Bromwich Albion	A	Division 1	2–2

It was no more than they deserved when West Bromwich Albion went ahead after 37 minutes at the Hawthorns. Harford played a one-two with Astle and slotted the ball past Arsenal keeper Bob Wilson. The lead lasted for 5 minutes when Frank McLintock finally fired a George Armstrong corner home after Charlie George's shot was blocked on the line. Ten minutes into the 2nd half George chipped the ball to the far post to Peter Storey but Albion's Hartford unluckily intercepted the ball and in doing so placed the ball beyond his own goalkeeper, Cumbes. With 5 minutes left Brown equalised and the 2–2 draw set up the most important match of the season against Leeds United at Elland Road 2 days later. A substitute appearance by Jon Sammels brought to an end an increasingly unhappy Highbury career. Although he had managed 215 (39 goals) League, 21 (3 goals) FA Cup, 19 (3 goals) FL Cup and 15 (7 goals) European games, he never captivated the crowd and was often the whipping-boy for their displeasure.

1974	Liverpool	A	Division 1	1–0

Arsenal League debut for Jimmy Rimmer.

1976	Manchester City	A	Division 1	1–3

Final senior appearance of Terry Mancini. He played 52 (1 goal) League, 8 FA Cup and 2 FL Cup matches.

Had spent the majority of his career in the lower divisions with Watford, Port Elizabeth (South Africa) and Orient before joining QPR from whom Bertie Mee bought him to bolster, on a short term basis only, a young and inexperienced defence.

It did rather beg the question though as to why Mee had earlier (prematurely) sold Double-winning captain Frank McLintock, an infinitely superior player, to QPR for only a few thousand pounds more.

1982	Everton	A	Division 1	1–2
1988	Luton Town	Wembley	Littlewoods Cup final	2–3

This was the final in which Arsenal snatched a defeat from the jaws of victory. Trailing 1–0 at the hour, the Gunners brought on Hayes as substitute who scored soon after his introduction. This was followed by a goal from Smith, several near misses and a fluffed penalty by Winterburn (Hayes had been the regular penalty-taker the previous year, scoring 12 times from the spot). Luton, having been let off the hook, then took advantage of a Gus Caesar error (a mistake that Gus had been practising all season) to equalise and Stein netted the winner in the dying minutes.

APRIL 25TH

1891	Sunderland	H	Friendly	1–3
1894	Corinthians	A	Friendly	2–3
1895	Royal Ordnance	A	Friendly	0–1
1896	Luton Town	H	Friendly	5–2
1901	West Ham United	A	Friendly	0–0
1902	Plymouth Argyle	A	Friendly	4–1
1903	Chesterfield	H	Friendly	1–0
1903	Chesterfield Municipal	H	Friendly	1–0
1904	Port Vale	H	Division 2	0–0
1906	Sunderland	A	Division 1	2–2
1908	Dundee	A	Friendly	1–2

First appearance of Matthew Thomson.

1914	Glossop North End	A	Division 2	2–0
1921	Preston North End	H	Division 1	2–1
1925	Leeds United	A	Division 1	0–1
1931	Newcastle United	A	Division 1	3–1
1932	Aston Villa	A	Division 1	1–1

Leslie Compton's League debut.

1936	Sheffield United	Wembley	FA Cup final	1–0

Ted Drake scored in the 74th minute to seal a win against the second division side as Arsenal won the Cup for the second time. Drake had played despite not having fully recovered from a recent cartilage operation and although he remained on the field he effectively made no further contribution.

1938	Wolverhampton Wanderers	A	Friendly	0–1
1942	Millwall	A	Friendly	2–2
1951	Anderlecht	A	Friendly	3–2
1953	Preston North End	A	Division 1	0–2
1956	Nottingham Forest	A	Friendly	1–1
1959	Portsmouth	H	Division 1	5–2
1961	Terry Neill made his international debut for Northern Ireland in the narrow 3–2 defeat by Italy in Bologna.			
1966	Sheffield United	A	Division 1	0–3
1967	Everton	H	Division 1	3–1
1972	Manchester United	H	Division 1	3–0
1977	Aston Villa	H	Division 1	3–0

Last League game for Wilf Rostron. He played 17 (2 goals) League and 1 FA Cup match.

1978	Liverpool	A	Division 1	0–1

1979	Aston Villa	A	Division 1	1–5
1981	Wolverhampton Wanderers	A	Division 1	2–1
1987	Manchester City	A	Division 1	0–3

Ian Allinson came on as substitute during the match to make his final senior appearance for the club.

| 1992 | Chelsea | A | Division 1 | 1–1 |
| 1998 | Barnsley | A | Premier League | 2–0 |

Barnsley, after being beaten by fellow relegation strugglers Spurs the previous week, were desperate for points and needed nothing short of victory to help their almost lost cause against the drop. The Arsenal midfield took control despite of the absence of Ray Parlour and Vieira almost scored with a header after 12 minutes. Ten minutes later Bergkamp picked up the ball on the edge of the box before skipping past 2 defenders and curling a spectacular shot past Watson in the Barnsley goal. Later Overmars uncharacteristically missed when it was easier to score from 10 yards out after good work from Anelka. In what became one-way traffic, Arsenal could have sealed the game before Overmars eventually made up for his glaring earlier miss when he glided through the defence on to a David Platt precision pass to score Arsenal's second and decisive goal. The Arsenal players left the field to a standing ovation from both sets of fans with those from Barnsley paying tribute to the Gunners by chanting 'Champions' along with the Londoners own clan.

APRIL 26TH

1890	Clapton	H	Friendly	6–1
1892	Bolton Wanderers	H	Friendly	3–2
1893	Sevenoaks	A	Friendly	11–0
1897	Sheffield United	H	Friendly	1–1
1898	Thames Ironworks	A	Friendly	2–2
1899	Woolwich League	H	Friendly	3–0

Final senior game for Frederick Davis. His record: 137 (8 goals) League and 13 (2 goals) FA Cup.

1902	West Bromwich Albion	A	Friendly	0–1
1905	Ipswich Town	A	Friendly	3–1
1913	Middlesbrough	H	Division 1	1–1
1917	Brentford	A	London Combination	0–0
1919	Brentford	A	Friendly	3–3
1924	Preston North End	A	Division 1	2–0
1926	Hibernian	H	Friendly	5–0

Last game for John Mackie. He played 108 League and 10 (1 goal) FA Cup matches.

| 1930 | Huddersfield Town | Wembley FA Cup final | 2–0 |

This was the first major trophy to be won by Arsenal and the start of an unprecedented era of success in the English game.

Cliff Bastin, at 18 years 1 month, became the youngest player to appear in the FA Cup final as Arsenal won the game with goals from Lambert and James.

1941	Leicester City	A	Football League War Cup	2–1
1947	Grimsby Town	H	Division 1	5–3
1948	Hendon	A	Friendly	4–1
1952	Manchester United	A	Division 1	1–6

Reg Lewis made his final League appearance. He had played 154 (103 goals) League and 21 (13 goals) FA Cup games.

Had it not been for the war, which severely disrupted the prime of his career, Lewis might well have laid a claim to the tag of Arsenal's greatest ever goalscorer, as evidenced by his prolific post-war strike rate.

He won a League Championship medal in 1947–48 and an FA Cup winners medal in 1950.

1958	Preston North End	A	Division 1	0–3

Final appearance of Mike Tiddy who played 48 (8 goals) League and 4 FA Cup games.

1965	Manchester United	A	Division 1	1–3
1971	Leeds United	A	Division 1	0–1

The most important match of the season took place at Elland Road where Leeds United, one point behind Arsenal and having played a game more, had to win. The match hinged on a controversial goal by Charlton in the 91st minute. There was stalemate for the first 90 minutes, which suited the Gunners, as the draw would have almost certainly meant the Championship was going to Highbury. Charlton appeared to be offside when he collected the ball and strode towards the Arsenal penalty area. Charlton's shot hit the post and rebounded across the goal where both he and Bob McNab bundled the ball over the line. The Arsenal players surrounded referee Norman Burtenshaw after the goal and at the full-time whistle where he had to be escorted to the changing rooms by the police. William Hill bookmakers still made Arsenal 4/5 favourites for the League, with Leeds at evens.

1975	Tottenham Hotspur	H	Division 1	1–0
1980	West Bromwich Albion	H	Division 1	1–1
1986	West Bromwich Albion	H	Division 1	2–2

APRIL 27TH

1889	London Caledonians	H	Friendly	0–1
1895	Millwall Athletic	H	Friendly	3–1
1896	Luton Town	A	Friendly	0–2
1898	Alfred Baker born Ilkeston, Derbyshire.			
1901	New Brighton Tower	A	Division 2	0–1

Final appearance James Tennant who played 51 (8 goals) League and 3 (2 goals) FA Cup games.

1903	Chatham	A	Chatham Charity Cup	0–2
1904	Charlie Satterthwaite was signed from West Ham United.			
1905	Norwich City	A	Friendly	1–2
1907	Derby County	H	Division 1	3–2
1908	Motherwell	A	Friendly	1–1
1909	Manchester United	A	Division 1	4–1

Final game for Thomas Fitchie who played 56 (27 goals) League and 7 (3 goals) FA Cup matches during two spells with the club.

1912	Notts County	H	Division 1	0–3
1918	Brentford	H	National War Fund	3–1
1929	Leeds United	H	Division 1	1–0
1932	Huddersfield Town	A	Division 1	2–1
1935	Leicester City	A	Division 1	5–3
1936	Chelsea	H	Division 1	1–1
1940	Notts County	A	Football League War Cup	5–1
1949	Manchester City	A	Division 1	3–0
1954	Racing Club de Paris	H	Friendly	4–0
1959	Crystal Palace	A	Southern Floodlight Challenge Cup	2–0

1963	Blackpool	A	Division 1	2–3

Debut for Jon Sammels.

1968	Burnley	H	Division 1	2–0
1974	Coventry City	A	Division 1	3–3
1985	Sheffield Wednesday	H	Division 1	1–0
1991	Liverpool	H	Ray Kennedy Benefit Match	1–3
1994	Queen's Park Rangers	A	Premier League	1–1
1996	Blackburn Rovers	A	Premier League	1–1

APRIL 28TH

1897	Manchester City	H	Division 2	1–2

Final League game James Boyle. Played 61 (7 goals) League and 5 (2 goals) FA Cup matches.

1898	Tottenham Hotspur	H	Friendly	5–0
1900	Barnsley	H	Division 2	5–1
1904	Millwall Athletic	A	Southern Professional Charity Cup	1–2
1906	Tottenham Hotspur	H	Southern Professional Charity Cup	5–0
1908	Glasgow Rangers	A	Friendly	1–1
1910	Colchester United	A	Friendly	3–2
1917	Crystal Palace	H	London Combination	4–0
1920	Bradford Park Avenue	A	Division 1	0–0
1923	Sheffield United	H	Division 1	2–0
1924	Burnley	A	Division 1	1–4

Alexander Graham's last senior appearance. Record: 166 (17 goals) League and 13 (3 goals) FA Cup games.

1926	Bolton Wanderers	A	Division 1	1–1
1927	Blackburn Rovers	A	Division 1	2–1
1928	Manchester United	H	Division 1	0–1
1930	Sunderland	H	Division 1	0–1
1934	Chelsea	A	Division 1	2–2

Charlie Jones finished his career with this last game prior to retirement. His record: 176 (8 goals) League and 17 FA Cup match. He won 3 League Championship medals with Arsenal.

1945	Chelsea	H	Football League – South	3–0
1948	Colchester United	H	Friendly	3–0
1956	Cardiff City	A	Division 1	2–1

Last game for Alex Forbes. His record: 217 (20 goals) League and 22 FA Cup appearances including the FA Cup finals of 1950 and 1952.

1962	Sheffield United	H	Division 1	2–0
1970	Anderlecht	H	European Fairs Cup final 2nd leg.	3–0

In front of a packed Highbury, Arsenal won their first major trophy for 17 years. Goals from Kelly, Radford and Sammels gave the Cup to Arsenal by an aggregate score of 4–3.

1973	West Ham United	A	Division 1	2–1
1975	West Ham United	A	Division 1	0–1
1979	Norwich City	H	Division 1	1–1
1980	Liverpool	Aston Villa		
		FA Cup semi-final 2nd replay		1–1

Once again Alan Sunderland scored (this time in 13 seconds) but Kenny Dalglish's equaliser meant a fourth game would be needed to settle the tie.

| 1984 | Leicester City | H | Division 1 | 2–1 |
| 1990 | Millwall | H | Division 1 | 2–0 |

APRIL 29TH

1893	Stoke	H	Friendly	0–1
1895	Grimsby Town	H	Friendly	1–2
1896	Chatham	A	Friendly	1–0
1897	Southampton St Mary's	A	Friendly	5–1
1899	Tottenham Hotspur	A	United League	2–3

Final game for Adam Haywood who played 84 (31 goals) League and 7 (5 goals) FA Cup matches.

1902	Tottenham Hotspur	A	Southern Professional Charity Cup	1–2
1905	Sheffield United	H	Friendly	2–3
1908	Greenock Morton	A	Friendly	0–1
1911	Notts County	A	Division 1	2–0
1912	Tottenham Hotspur	A	Friendly	3–0
1916	Watford	A	London Combination	1–2
1922	Bradford City	A	Division 1	2–0
1929	Cliff Holton was born in Oxford.			
1933	Huddersfield Town	H	Division 1	2–2
1936	Bolton Wanderers	A	Division 1	1–2
1939	Derby County	A	Division 1	2–1
1944	Queen's Park Rangers	A	Football League – South	1–1
1946	Brentford	H	Football League – South	1–1

Final senior appearance of George Marks. He was signed as a professional shortly before the outbreak of the war and made just two League starts in goal for Arsenal, however, he did play 126 times during the hostilities.

| 1950 | Liverpool | | Wembley FA Cup final | 2–0 |

Arsenal wore shirts of old gold (beginning the preference for this colour change strip) in the club's fifth FA Cup final appearance at Wembley. Two goals by Reg Lewis won the game and the Cup for the Gunners.

| 1961 | Everton | A | Division 1 | 1–4 |

David Herd's last game. He appeared in 166 (97 goals) League and 14 (10 goals) FA Cup matches.

1967	Burnley	A	Division 1	4–1
1969	Everton	A	Division 1	0–1
1978	Middlesbrough	H	Division 1	1–0
1986	Chelsea	H	Division 1	2–0
1995	Tottenham Hotspur	H	Premier League	1–1
1998	Derby County	H	Premier League	1–0

With 2 victories needed from the last 4 games this was always going to be a tense match with stiff opposition from Derby who were chasing a European place. Unfortunately Derby's approach to the game was to be aggressive and as a result of a foul on Anelka in the 13th minute inside the penalty area, Bergkamp, normally the most reliable of penalty takers, was required to step forward for the kick and promptly blasted the ball straight at Poom. One of the saddest sights of the season occurred on the 30 minute mark when Bergkamp, undoubtedly the player of the season so far, stretched and limped off with what looked like a hamstring injury. The gloom was lifted 5 minutes later when the outstanding Petit crashed home a shot from 25 yards for his 2nd goal in two weeks.

Overmars was denied just before half-time after a great run, when his shot was saved by Poom. Arsenal survived the second half battering which saw Derby have 5 players booked in all in which they managed only 1 shot during the whole game. The title was now just 3 points away with the visit of Everton in the next game at Highbury. It was reported after that Bergkamp had indeed pulled his hamstring and he would be out for the rest of the season and could even miss the Cup final.

APRIL 30TH

Year	Opponent	H/A	Competition	Score
1891	London Caledonians	H	Friendly	1–1
1892	Glasgow Rangers	H	Friendly	2–3
1896	Tottenham Hotspur	A	Friendly	2–3
1898	Millwall	A	Friendly	0–2

Gavin Crawford's final game. His record: 122 (13 goals) League and 16 (4 goals) FA Cup.

Year	Opponent	H/A	Competition	Score
1904	Fulham	A	London League Premier Division	0–1
1906	Reading	A	Southern Professional Charity Cup	1–0
1908	Kilmarnock	A	Friendly	2–1
1910	Ilford	A	Friendly	2–3

Last game for Archie Cross. Finished with 132 League and 17 FA Cup appearances. Also for John Dick 262 (12 goals) League and 22 (1 goal) FA Cup.

Year	Opponent	H/A	Competition	Score
1914	Norwich City	A	Friendly	3–0
1921	Newcastle United	A	Division 1	0–1
1927	Birmingham	H	Division 1	3–0
1932	Middlesbrough	H	Division 1	5–0
1938	Liverpool	H	Division 1	1–0
1955	Portsmouth	A	Division 1	1–2

1959 Ian McKechnie signed professional forms. He came to Arsenal as an outside-left but converted to goalkeeper after impressing in a practice match. Played 23 League and 2 European games.

Year	Opponent	H/A	Competition	Score
1959	Bath City	A	Coronation Cup	3–4
1960	West Bromwich Albion	A	Division 1	0–1

1964 Ernest Williamson died in Norwich.

Year	Opponent	H/A	Competition	Score
1965	Torino	A	Friendly	2–2

1965 Eddie McGoldrick was born in Islington, London.

Year	Opponent	H/A	Competition	Score
1966	Aston Villa	A	Division 1	0–3
1968	Sheffield Wednesday	H	Division 1	3–2

1969 John Roberts was signed from Northampton Town for £35,000.

Year	Opponent	H/A	Competition	Score
1974	Queen's Park Rangers	H	Division 1	1–1

Final game for Ray Kennedy. He had played 158 (53 goals) League, 27 (6 goals) FA Cup, 11 (4 goals) FL Cup and 16 (8 goals) European. matches. With Arsenal, he won European Fairs Cup, Football League Championship and FA Cup medals.

Also the end of the road for Bob Wilson who chose to retire at the top of his profession to pursue a career in TV. His final record: 234 League, 32 FA Cup, 18 FL Cup and 24 European appearances. Like Kennedy, a Fairs Cup and Double winner.

Year	Opponent	H/A	Competition	Score
1977	Newcastle United	A	Division 1	2–0
1983	Watford	A	Division 1	1–2

1984 James Tullis 'Jimmy' Logie died in London.

Year	Opponent	H/A	Competition	Score
1988	Sheffield Wednesday	A	Division 1	3–3

1993 Tommy Caton died in Bampton, Oxfordshire, at only 30 years of age.

Year	Opponent	H/A	Competition	Score
1994	West Ham United	H	Premier League	0–2

MAY 1ST

1902   The original 'Tim' Coleman joined from Northampton Town and Roderick McEachrane arrived from West Ham United.

1907   Joseph (Joe) Shaw completed a move from Accrington Stanley.

1920	Bradford Park Avenue	H	Division 1	3–0

Last senior appearance David Greenaway who played 161 (13 goals) League and 9 FA Cup games.

1926	Birmingham	H	Division 1	3–0
1937	Bolton Wanderers	H	Division 1	0–0

Alex James played his last League game.

1943	Charlton Athletic	Wembley Football League Cup – South final		7–1
1948	Grimsby Town	H	Division 1	8–0

League debut given to Lionel Smith.

1953	Burnley	H	Division 1	3–2

Arsenal pipped Preston on goal average to win the League Championship title for the seventh time.

1961	DOS Utrecht	A	Friendly	2–2
1962	Everton	H	Division 1	2–3

Jack Kelsey made his final appearance for Arsenal. Record: 327 League and 24 FA Cup games.

Many would argue that Kelsey was the finest goalkeeper ever to play for Arsenal. Brave beyond question and remarkably agile for a big man, he was automatic first choice for club and country (Wales) for the best part of a decade.

While Pat Jennings enjoyed his peak years with Tottenham Hotspur and David Seaman has had one of the most dependable back-fours to protect him, Jack Kelsey had to do it all and did it with aplomb.

1971	Stoke City	H	Division 1	1–0

In their last home match of the season Arsenal played Stoke City who were out for revenge for their FA Cup semi-final defeat. Over 55,000 spectators saw another hard fought match with Peter Storey sustaining an injury 11 minutes into the 2nd half and then leaving the pitch to be replaced by substitute Eddie Kelly. Arsenal were camped in the Stoke penalty area for most of the match and finally broke the deadlock in 65th minute. George Armstrong crossed for John Radford to tussle with Stoke goalkeeper Banks and the ball broke for Kelly to shoot home. Arsenal won 1–0 and were one point behind Leeds United going into the last League match of the season.

1980	Liverpool	Coventry FA Cup semi-final 3rd replay		1–0

A goal from Brian Talbot finally put paid to the Liverpool challenge at the fourth attempt.

1982	West Ham United	H	Division 1	2–0
1989	Norwich City	H	Division 1	5–0
1993	Everton	A	Premier League	0–0
1996	Liverpool	H	Premier League	0–0

MAY 2ND

1891	1st Highland Light Infantry	H	Friendly	5–1
1921	Liverpool	H	Division 1	0–0

Last game for John Peart. His record: 63 League and 3 FA Cup appearances.

1925	Bury	A	Division 1	0–2

TOP: The opening of the East Stand at Highbury
BOTTOM: The Arsenal team of 1930

Cliff Bastin and Ted Drake, two of the stars of the 1930s

TOP LEFT: The programme from Arsenal's first FA Cup final appearance, in 1927 against Cardiff City. City won 1–0 to take the cup out of England for the only time

TOP RIGHT: The programme from the Inter-Cities Fairs Cup match against Staevnet, which Arsenal won 7–1

BOTTOM: The programme and ticket stub from the 1930 FA Cup final between Arsenal and Huddersfield Town. Arsenal won 2–0 to lift their first major trophy

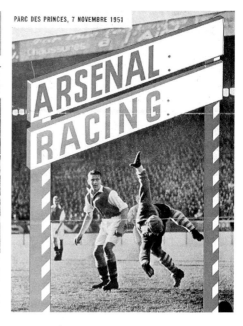

CLOCKWISE FROM TOP LEFT: The programme from the friendly match against Hibernian in 1955 which finished in a 2–2 draw; the programme from the friendly match against Racing Club de Paris which Arsenal won 5–0; and the programme from the 1953 Coronation Cup involving Celtic, Arsenal, Hibernian and Spurs

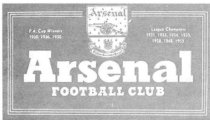

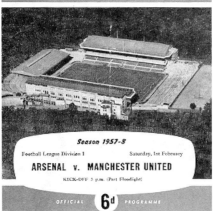

TOP: The programme from the 1950 FA Cup final
BOTTOM: The programme from the 1958 Division One match against
Manchester United

Caricatures of Emmanuel Petit, Patrick Vieira and Ted Drake

Caricatures of Marc Overmars and Joe Mercer, captain of the 1950
FA Cup-winning side

TOP: Tony Adams has just
scored the winning goal in the
1993 FA Cup semi-final
against Spurs at Wembley

LEFT: George Graham, the
manager who guided Arsenal
to two League titles, the FA
Cup, two League Cups and the
European Cup-Winners' Cup

| 1928 | Sheffield Wednesday | H | Division 1 | 1–1 |
| 1931 | Bolton Wanderers | H | Division 1 | 5–0 |

Final game of Arsenal's first League Championship-winning season in which the Gunners established a record points total (66) and scored 127 goals (38 by Jack Lambert).

1936	Leeds United	H	Division 1	2–2
1938	Southampton	A	Friendly	3–2
1942	Brentford	Chelsea	London War Cup Semi final	0–0
1951	Blackpool	A	Division 1	1–0
1958	David O' Leary was born in Stoke Newington, London.			
1965	Lazio	A	Friendly	2–0
1967	David Rocastle was born in Lewisham, London.			
1970	Tottenham Hotspur	A	European Fairs Cup 3rd round 1st leg	0–1
1972	Coventry City	A	Division 1	1–0
1981	Aston Villa	H	Division 1	2–0
1983	Manchester United	H	Division 1	3–0
1987	Aston Villa	H	Division 1	2–1
1988	Coventry City	H	Division 1	1–1
1990	Southampton	H	Division 1	2–1

Brian Marwood's last game in the first team. He played 52 (16 goals) League, 2 FA Cup and 6 (1 goal) FL Cup.

Although he only enjoyed a relatively short career at Highbury, Marwood made an instant impact in the team and in the affections of the supporters. He was a vital component in the League Championship-winning team of 1988–89 as was another who played their final game for Arsenal in this match, Kevin Richardson.

Richardson achieved 96 (5 goals) League, 9 (1 goal) FA Cup and 16 (2 goals) FL Cup appearances for the Gunners who made a neat £500,000 profit on him when he was sold to Real Sociedad.

| 1992 | Southampton | H | Division 1 | 5–1 |

Few who attended this game would have believed they were to witness the final League match of David Rocastle in Arsenal colours but such was the case. Rocastle played 228 (24 goals) League, 20 (4 goals) FA Cup, 33 (6 goals) FL Cup and 4 European games before being given the shock news by George Graham that a deal had been agreed with Leeds United for his transfer.

With the Gunners he picked up medals for the Littlewoods League Cup in 1986–87 and the League Championships of 1988–89 and 1990–91, but when he left his career went rapidly downhill.

MAY 3RD

1890	London Caledonians/Clapton XI	H	Friendly	3–2
1919	West Ham United	A	Friendly	0–1
1924	Preston North End	H	Division 1	1–2
1930	Aston Villa	H	Division 1	2–4
1933	Cliftonville	A	Friendly	4–0
1941	Tottenham Hotspur	A	London War Cup	3–3
1948	Benfica	A	Friendly	4–0
1950	Portsmouth	H	Division 1	2–0

Dennis Compton's final game before retirement. He achieved 54 (15 goals) League and

5 (1 goal) FA Cup appearances in a career shared with cricket duties for Middlesex and England and severely interrupted by the war.

1951	Ellesmere Port	A	Friendly	7–0
1952	Newcastle United	Wembley FA Cup final		0–1

Arsenal had to play most of this game with ten men after an injury to Wally Barnes had forced him to leave the pitch. Even so the Gunners held out until, with two further Arsenal players down injured and calling for assistance from the trainer, Newcastle's Chilean George Robledo hit the winning goal.

1965 John Jensen was born in Copenhagen, Denmark.

1966	Swansea Town	A	Friendly	3–1
1967	Apoel	H	Friendly	1–1

1969 Bob McNab won the last of his 4 international caps for England in the 3–1 victory over Northern Ireland in Belfast.

1971	Tottenham Hotspur	A	Division 1	1–0

The final League match of the season was against North London rivals, Tottenham Hotspur at White Hart Lane. The Gunners needed a win or a 0–0 draw to secure the Championship. Any other draw would mean that Leeds United would win the title on goal average. There were about 100,000 people locked out of the match and the official attendance of 51,992 was clearly incorrect and only counted the paid entrants. Arsenal fans had broken the turnstile doors around the ground and there were between 65,000-70,000 fans on the terraces. The Gunners defence was as solid as ever and they took the game to Tottenham, who were allowed very infrequent efforts on the Arsenal goal. The game seemed to be heading for a 0–0 draw when Ray Kennedy rose to head home a George Armstrong cross 2 minutes from time. At the final whistle Arsenal fans congratulated their heroes and covered the pitch. Within 3 minutes of reaching the dressing-room the Arsenal players received a telegram from Bill Shankly, the manager of Liverpool, who they were due to play in the FA Cup final the following Saturday, congratulating them on becoming champions.

1977	Derby County	H	Division 1	0–0
1980	Coventry City	A	Division 1	1–0

Final League appearance for Paul Barron.

1986	Birmingham City	A	Division 1	1–0
1997	Newcastle United	H	Premier League	0–1
1998	Everton	H	Premier League	4–0

Thousands of fans flocked to the area to be part of a fantastic day and they were not to be let down. Ian Wright was back from his 3-month lay-off to claim a place on the bench, and even though he spent most of his time running up and down the touchline, his story was to have a happy ending. Everton, fighting for survival, came to defend and try for a point whereas the Gunners needed to win to clinch the title and avoid the need to take points from their two remaining (tricky) away games at Liverpool and Aston Villa. Wreh almost opened the scoring on 90 seconds when his shot was well saved. Then with 5 minutes gone Petit floated a great corner which in a tussle between Tony Adams and Slaven Bilic entered the net off the Croatian defender. Arsenal looked for the second goal and Parlour and Anelka both went close before, just on the half-hour mark, Overmars picked up the ball and shot into the bottom corner with the keeper unsighted, Highbury erupted!

On half time Petit was subjected to one of the worst tackles of the season when Don Hutchinson's 2-footed challenge put him out of the game, amazingly though the Evertonian was not even booked for the offence. With the party in full flow, Overmars, who had been in devastating form, sped past the defence to shoot home for Arsenal's 3rd goal. On 73 minutes Ian Wright finally joined in the action to the delight of the crowd. Fittingly the final and best goal of the game came from skipper Tony Adams who, after missing the mid-part of the season with injury and loss of form, returned in the new year to lead by example. Steve Bould who came on as substitute and played in midfield set up Adams with a lovely pass for Adams to run onto the ball and volley home with his left foot. Arsenal were Champions having achieved the feat in fantastic style. It was also their 10th consecutive victory in a run of matches that had seen them overhaul the bookmakers' favourites and make Arsène Wenger the first ever foreign manager to win the English League title.

With this victory, Arsenal clinched their first FA Carling Premiership title since the inception of the FA Premier League in 1992. Overall it marked the Gunners eleventh League Championship and gave them the first part of their double Double.

MAY 4TH

1918	Brentford	A	National War Fund	1–1
1921	Wigan Borough	A	Friendly	1–2
1927	Bury	A	Division 1	2–3
1929	Burnley	A	Division 1	3–3
1931	Northampton Town	A	Friendly	1–0
1932	Plymouth Argyle	A	Friendly	2–1
1935	Derby County	H	Division 1	0–1
1940	Crystal Palace	H	Football League War Cup	3–1
1946	West Ham United	H	Football League – South	2–1
1949	Portsmouth	H	Division 1	3–2
1953	Tottenham Hotspur	H	Friendly	0–2
1959	Birmingham City	H	Division 1	2–1

Dave Bowen's last League game. He amassed 146 (2 goals) League and 16 FA Cup games for the Gunners.

1962	Berlin City Select XI	A	Friendly	5–0

1962 Ian McKechnie transferred to Southend United.

1968	Sheffield Wednesday	A	Division 1	2–1
1969	Reykjavik	A	Friendly	3–1

Marked the start of Charlie George and Eddie Kelly's first-team careers.

1982	Birmingham City	A	Division 1	1–0
1985	Luton Town	A	Division 1	1–3
1987	Queen's Park Rangers	A	Division 1	4–1
1991	Sunderland	A	Division 1	0–0
1993	Queen's Park Rangers	H	Premier League	0–0
1994	Parma	Copenhagen		
			Cup Winners Cup final	1–0

Without the suspended Ian Wright and injured local hero John Jensen (who had been crocked playing for Denmark in the Parken Stadium a fortnight earlier), Arsenal secured their second European trophy in a determined performance against highly rated Italian opposition. Alan 'Smudger' Smith cracked a glorious first-half goal that gave the Gunners a platform to defend, as the team gave one of the most inspiring performances of the Graham era. John Jensen was later seen rather worse for wear as he partied in a Copenhagen night club unsteady on his crutches!

1995	Wimbledon	H	Premier League	0–0

MAY 5TH

1907	Belgian XI	A	Friendly	?–1
1908	William Garbutt transferred to Blackburn Rovers.			
1917	Portsmouth	A	London Combination	0–0
1928	Everton	A	Division 1	3–3

Charles Buchan's final game before retirement. He played 102 (49 goals) League and 18 (7 goals) FA Cup for Arsenal.

On this occasion he was overshadowed by another legend as Dixie Dean scored a hat-trick for Everton.

1930	Northampton Town	A	Friendly	7–0
1934	Sheffield United	H	Division 1	2–0

Final game of the season in which, despite the death of manager Herbert Chapman, Arsenal had enough character and skill to retain the League Championship trophy. It was their third title in four seasons.

Last game, prior to retirement, for David Jack. An Arsenal legend, and integral part of the Chapman dynasty, he played 181 (113 goals) League and 25 (10 goals) FA Cup matches winning 3 League Championship and 1 FA Cup winners medals.

Jack was also the first Arsenal player to captain England.

1945	West Ham United	A	Football League – South	1–1

Ted Drake made his last appearance. His record: 168 (124 goals) League and 14 (12 goals) FA Cup.

After completing his Highbury career, Drake went on to manage at Reading and Chelsea where he supervised their only winning League Championship campaign.

1951	Millwall	A	Friendly	0–2
1954	Grasshoppers	A	Friendly	3–2

Final match in Lionel Smith's Arsenal career. He made 162 League and 18 FA Cup appearances without scoring a goal.

1957	Eintracht Frankfurt	A	Friendly	2–0
1961	Racing Club de Paris	A	Friendly	4–1
1965	Brescia	A	Friendly	1–1
1966	Leeds United	H	Division 1	0–3
1970	Folkestone	A	Armory & Cheesmur Testimonial	4–0
1979	Birmingham City	A	Division 1	0–0
1980	Nottingham Forest	H	Division 1	0–0
1984	West Bromwich Albion	A	Division 1	3–1
1986	Oxford United	A	Division 1	0–3

Last appearance of Tony Woodcock who played 131 (56 goals) League, 14 (7 goals) FA Cup, 22 (5 goals) FL Cup and 2 European games. Class act who, unfortunately, too often played for himself and not for the team. Did not survive the George Graham takeover, rejoining the Cologne club.

1990	Norwich City	A	Division 1	2–2

David O'Leary came on as substitute for Steve Bould in the 66th minute and played the game he needed to beat Geordie Armstrong's League record of 500 appearances.

Also the final outing for Martin 'Whoops-a-Daisy' Hayes who amassed 102 (26 goals) League, 9 (3 goals) FA Cup and 21 (5 goals) FL Cup games. The question remains, why didn't Hayes take the penalty against Luton Town in the 1988 Littlewoods Cup final?

1992	Apoel	A	Friendly	1–1
1996	Bolton Wanderers	H	Premier League	2–1

MAY 6TH

1914 William Blyth joined Arsenal on a free transfer from Manchester City.

1916	Rest of London Combination	H	Friendly	2–2
1922	Bradford City	H	Division 1	1–0
1933	Sheffield United	A	Division 1	1–3
1935	Norwich City	A	Friendly	1–0
1939	Brentford	H	Division 1	2–0

Final first-class appearance for Eddie Hapgood, one of the finest full-backs ever to have played for the Gunners.

He amassed 393 (2 goals) League and 41 FA Cup games before becoming a flying-officer during the war.

He won 5 League Championship and 2 FA Cup winners medals whilst at Highbury and a total of 30 full England caps.

This was the last League game before the Second World War and was used to make the film *The Arsenal Stadium Mystery* wherein Brentford played the fictional part of 'The Trojans'.

1944	Aldershot	H	Football League – South	3–1
1948	Oporto	A	Friendly	2–3
1950	Stoke City	A	Division 1	5–2
1954	Young Boys	A	Friendly	1–3
1963	Manchester United	A	Division 1	3–2
1967	Stoke City	H	Division 1	3–1

1968 Ray Kennedy joined as an apprentice professional.

1972	Leeds United		Wembley FA Cup final	0–1

Geoff Barnett, deputising for the injured Bob Wilson, took no blame for the goal that settled this dour final between bitter rivals. This was the Gunners eighth FA Cup final appearance and they had now won four and lost four of the games.

1974	Kettering Town	A	Opening of Stand	3–0

John Matthews first senior outing.

1978	Ipswich Town		Wembley FA Cup final	0–1

An injury-hit Arsenal side did not do themselves justice against the underdogs, Ipswich Town who had made much of their own injuries in the week before the final. Liam Brady started a game that he was clearly not fit enough to play in and had to be replaced by Graham Rix. Roger Osborne found his moment of fleeting fame by scoring the winner for Ipswich. He went on to become a postman.

1985	Southampton	H	Division 1	1–0
1989	Middlesbrough	A	Division 1	1–0
1991	Manchester United	H	Division 1	3–1

By the time that this game kicked off, Arsenal had already been confirmed as League Champions for the tenth time. Nottingham Forest's victory over Liverpool in an earlier match had left the Gunners with an unassailable lead at the top of the table despite being hindered by the deduction of two points imposed by the FA earlier in the season. It was with some pleasure, therefore, that the crowd at this game were able to advise the FAC in no uncertain terms what they could do with their points.

Arsenal finished seven points clear of their nearest rivals in a season in which they lost just once in the League.

1993	Sheffield Wednesday	A	Premier League	0–1

League debut for Gavin McGowan and Scott Marshall.

1998	Liverpool	A	Premier League	0–4

It was a case of 'After The Lord Mayor's Show' with this performance in which Arsenal played only 3 of the team that had clinched the League title against Everton. With a team made up of Squad players, it was never going to be a fair contest. The Liverpool fans and players gave the Champions a rapturous welcome and that was about all the Gunners enjoyed on the evening. The travelling fans didn't care though and were still in party mood and even cheered a Liverpool goal! The only disturbing point on the night was a rash challenge on Ian Wright by his so-called best friend, Paul Ince, that saw the Arsenal striker carried off on a stretcher and put his World Cup hopes in doubt.

Scott Marshall made his last appearance in an Arsenal shirt as unused substitute. He was released in the summer on a free transfer under the dictates of the Bosman ruling.

MAY 7TH

1883	Joe Shaw was born in Bury, Lancashire.				
1907	The Hague	A	Friendly		6–3
1921	Liverpool	A	Division 1		0–3
1927	Tottenham Hotspur	A	Division 1		4–0
1929	Goalkeeper Charlie Preedy signed from Wigan Borough. He went on to make 39 League and Cup appearances between the sticks in senior competitions for the Gunners.				
1931	Ted Beasley signed from Stourbridge FC for £550.				
1932	Blackburn Rovers	H	Division 1		4–0
1938	Bolton Wanderers	H	Division 1		5–0
	With this victory Arsenal clinched the League Championship title for the fifth time in eight years.				
1949	Charlton Athletic	H	Division 1		2–0
	League debut for Ray Daniel.				
1960	Grasshoppers	A	Friendly		4–2
1966	Leicester City	H	Division 1		1–0
1968	Leeds United	H	Division 1		4–3
1977	Middlesbrough	H	Division 1		1–1
1983	Sunderland	H	Division 1		0–1
1984	West Ham United	H	Division 1		3–3
1988	Everton	A	Division 1		2–1

Kevin Campbell made his first senior appearance as substitute after a prolific scoring record at youth and reserve levels.

In the same game Kenny Sansom made his final senior start for Arsenal. He played 314 (6 goals) League, 26 FA Cup, 48 FL Cup and 6 European matches but ultimately paid the price for a rather public disagreement with manager George Graham who removed the captaincy of the team from him and dropped him to the reserves for a spell before arranging a sale to Newcastle United.

1994	Newcastle United	A	Premier League		0–2

The final senior game of Alan Miller before his transfer to Middlesbrough.

MAY 8TH

1910	George Male was born in West Ham, London.			
1923	Jimmy Brain arrived from Ton Pent.			
1934	Charlie Jones on retirement, joined Notts County as Manager.			
1930	George Male turned professional.			
1938	Feyenoord	A	Friendly	0–1

1942	Terry Neill was born in Belfast, N. Ireland.			
1943	Tottenham Hotspur	A	Friendly	2–1
1957	Grasshoppers	A	Friendly	4–2
1959	Bristol XI	A	Friendly	4–5
1962	Gothenburg Alliance	A	Friendly	5–1

1963   George Eastham made his international debut for England in the 1–1 draw with Brazil at Wembley.

1969	Watford	A	Friendly	2–0

John Roberts made his League debut.

1971   Liverpool   Wembley FA Cup final   2–1

Attempting to become the 2nd team this century to complete the League Championship and FA Cup Double, Arsenal faced Liverpool in the FA Cup final at Wembley. On a very hot and steamy day both teams toiled in the sun but could not find a way through the tight defences. The closest effort came with 12 minutes remaining when George Graham headed against the bar from a John Radford throw-in and an acrobatic scissors kick from Liverpool defender Smith gave Arsenal a corner. George Armstrong took the kick and Graham headed goalwards only for Lindsey to kick the ball off the line. There were no goals at the end of 90 minutes and after only 2 minutes of extra time Liverpool's Heighway picked up the ball on the wing and cut in towards goal. He shot between Arsenal keeper Bob Wilson and the near post to register the first goal. Most teams would have thought it was not going to be their day but the Gunners fought back 9 minutes later when a mix-up in the Liverpool defence allowed Eddie Kelly (but we still think Graham scored!) to scramble the ball in for the equaliser. After 111 minutes Charlie George belted home a pass from John Radford to seal a 2–1 win and make history by becoming the team to have played most games in a season to win the Double. Arsenal played 64 matches, 42 League, 9 FA Cup, 8 Fairs Cup and 5 League Cup.

1972	Liverpool	H	Division 1	0–0
1982	Middlesbrough	A	Division 1	3–1
1985	Tottenham Hotspur	H	Pat Jennings Farewell Match	2–3

Pat Jennings took his final bow. A cut price buy from Tottenham Hotspur who discarded him in favour of Barry Daines, Jennings gave the Gunners magnificent service until his retirement and always seemed to excel against his former club.

His record finished: played 237 League, 38 FA Cup, 32 FL Cup and 19 European games.

1993	Crystal Palace	H	Premier League	3–0

MAY 9TH

1891   Dr James Paterson was born in London.

1907	Preussen	A	Friendly	9–1
1921	Southend United	A	Friendly	4–0

1922   Andrew Kennedy joined from Crystal Palace.

1922	Southend United	H	Friendly	2–1

1931   Dan Lewis transferred to Gillingham.

1935   Reg Lewis joined as an amateur player from Margate.

1936   Bernard Joy created history when he became the last amateur player to represent England in a full international match (against Belgium).

1942	Crystal Palace	A	London League	3–3

1954   Derek Tapscott made his international debut for Wales in the 2–0 defeat by Austria in Vienna.

| 1965 | Latina | A | Friendly | 3–0 |

Peter Storey's first senior game.

| 1973 | Leeds United | A | Division 1 | 1–6 |

League debut for David Price.

| 1978 | Derby County | A | Division 1 | 0–3 |

Alan Hudson's final League appearance for Arsenal. He played a total of 47 League and Cup games without scoring a goal.

It was also the last game for John Matthews who had been severely hampered by injury and, perhaps unfairly, singled out for abuse by certain sections of the crowd. His performance record finished: 45 (2 goals) League, 6 (1 goal) FA Cup and 6 (2 goals).

| 1981 | Eastern Athletic Association | Hong Kong Po Leung Kuk Cup | | 3–0 |

Last game in an Arsenal shirt for Frank Stapleton who bowed out with 225 (75 goals) League, 32 (15 goals) FA Cup, 27 (14 goals) FL Cup and 15 (4 goals) European appearances. In the prime of his career when he decided, primarily for monetary reasons (allegedly), to leave Arsenal to pursue his rewards. His lack of loyalty to the club that had nurtured him from a boy always led to a vociferous response from the crowd on his return visits to Highbury in opposition colours.

| 1987 | Norwich City | H | Division 1 | 1–2 |

Final appearance of Viv Anderson for the Gunners.

| 1990 | South Korea | Singapore | Caltex Cup | 2–1 |

MAY 10TH

1890	Millwall Athletic	A	Friendly	3–3
1899	James Jackson joined from Newcastle United.			
1908	David Geenaway signed. Previous experience in Scottish junior football only.			

Another Scot, Angus McKinnon, also joined from Petershill FC (Glasgow).

| 1919 | West Ham United | H | Friendly | 3–2 |
| 1923 | Frem | A | Friendly | 4–2 |

First appearance Samson Haden.

1924	TSC99	A	Friendly	6–3
1932	Northampton Town	A	Friendly	3–2
1939	Sweden	A	Friendly	4–0
1941	Preston North End	Wembley	Football League War Cup final	1–1
1947	Derby County	A	Division 1	1–0
1957	Fortuna Dusseldorf	A	Friendly	2–2
1962	Skeid Oslo	A	Friendly	3–0

Danny Clapton's last senior game having played 207 (25 goals) League and 18 (2 goals) FA Cup matches.

1966	Torquay/Plymouth XI	A	Friendly	4–5
1966	Charlie George signed apprentice forms for the club he had supported all his life!			
1969	Dennis Bergkamp was born in Amsterdam.			
1970	Omonia	A	European Fairs Cup 4th round 1st leg	4–3
1975	Malaysian Select XI	A	Friendly	0–2
1977	Hajduk Split	H	John Radford's Testimonial	5–0
1980	West Ham United	Wembley	FA Cup final	0–1

Following the four attempts it had taken to dispose of Liverpool in the semi-final and coupled with the two European Cup Winners Cup semi-finals with Juventus that had also been squeezed into the weeks just prior to this game, it was little wonder that the

Arsenal players looked weary and never performed to their capabilities. Brooking scored West Ham's goal.

| 1983 | West Ham United | A | Division 1 | 3–1 |
| 1995 | Real Zaragoza | Paris | Cup Winners Cup final | 1–2 |

An injury and suspension hit Arsenal fell to a goal in the last minute of extra time from former Spurs player, Nayim.

Earlier John Hartson had equalised for the Gunners after they had fallen behind to a goal from Zaragoza's Argentinian forward Esnider. The turning point in the game was an injury to Martin Keown that saw him retire from the field of play.

| 1998 | Aston Villa | A | Premier League | 0–1 |

Despite putting out a near full-strength team Arsenal failed to raise a gallop with priorty obviously on the Cup final the following week. Dwight Yorke scored from the spot after Grimandi was judged to have held Yorke.

MAY 11TH

1912	Hertha BSC	A	Friendly	5–0
1921	Clapton Orient	H	Friendly	2–0
1924	FC Preussen	A	Friendly	6–1

1925 Advertisement for the Arsenal manager's job appeared in *The Athletic News* but Herbert Chapman had already been approached to take the position.

| 1940 | Crystal Palace | A | Football League War Cup | 2–0 |
| 1948 | Liege Selection | A | Friendly | 2–1 |

Final game for George Male. Played 285 League and 29 FA Cup matches.

A fixture at right-back throughout the glorious decade of the thirties, Male won four League Championship winners medals and an FA Cup winners medal. Captain of Arsenal and England, for whom he won 19 full international caps.

| 1953 | Glasgow Celtic | Hampden Park | Coronation Cup 1st round | 0–1 |
| 1955 | Grasshoppers | A | Friendly | 5–5 |

1959 Jimmy Magill signed from Portadown in Northern Ireland for £5,000

1960	Racing Club de Paris	A	Friendly	3–4
1963	Burnley	H	Division 1	2–3
1965	Grasshoppers	A	Friendly	3–0
1968	West Bromwich Albion	H	Division 1	2–1
1972	Tottenham Hotspur	H	Division 1	0–2
1982	Liverpool	H	Division 1	1–1
1985	West Bromwich Albion	A	Division 1	2–2

Brian Talbot's last game after 254 (40 goals) League, 30 (7 goals) FA Cup, 27 (1 goal) FL Cup and 15 (1 goal) European matches.

'Noddy' was one of the most popular recent players to wear the Arsenal shirt. If not the most gifted of individuals he made up for his lack of skill by giving maximum effort. The unique fact oft quoted about Talbot relates to his winning two successive FA Cup finals with different teams (Ipswich Town and Arsenal).

| 1987 | Apoel | A | Cyprus Super Cup | 2–2 |
| 1988 | Millwall | A | Bob Pearson Testimonial | 2–2 |

Last appearance of Graham Rix who had played 351 (41 goals) League, 44 (7 goals) FA Cup, 47 (2 goals) FL Cup and 21 (1 goal) European games in his Arsenal career. Had the misfortune to inherit the creative midfield responsibilities from Liam Brady when he quit to join Juventus and suffered the inevitable comparisons made between their respective efforts. He was unfairly barracked by sections of the Highbury crowd when, in truth, they failed to appreciate that he never gave less than 100 per cent effort in the Gunners cause.

| 1991 | Coventry City | H | Division 1 | 6–1 |
| 1993 | Tottenham Hotspur | H | Premier League | 1–3 |

Pal Lydesen made his final senior appearance before returning to his former club, IK Start, in Norway.

| 1997 | Derby County | A | Premier League | 3–1 |

When Paul Merson limped off after just 8 minutes to be replaced by Nicolas Anelka, few would have imagined that it would turn out to be his last appearance for the club he had joined as a boy. His record finished 327 (78 goals) League, 31 (4 goals) FA Cup, 40 (10 goals) FL Cup and 22 (7 goals) European games.

| 1998 | Arsène Wenger named Carling Manager of the Year, the first Arsenal manager to receive the honour. |

MAY 12TH

1907	SK Slavia Ips	A	Friendly	7–5
1912	Viktoria 89	A	Friendly	2–2
1923	B93 Copenhagen	A	Friendly	1–0
1939	Swedish XI	A	Friendly	8–2
1945	Alan Ball was born in Farnworth, Lancashire.			
1978	Tottenham Hotspur	A	John Pratt Testimonial	5–3
1979	Manchester United	Wembley	FA Cup final	3–2

So called 'Five-minute Cup Final'. Arsenal cruised to an early two-goal lead through Talbot and Stapleton and looked well in control until conceding two late goals. However, from the restart after United's equaliser and before panic could take hold, Brady set up Rix whose cross found Sunderland waiting to tuck the ball under the body of despairing goalkeeper Gary Bailey. The Cup came back to Highbury for the fifth time.

| 1984 | Watford | A | Division 1 | 1–2 |

MAY 13TH

1904	Archibald 'Baldie' Gray joined from Hibernian.			
1923	Danish XI	A	Friendly	2–1
1926	MTK/VM	A	Friendly	2–2
1933	Eddie Hapgood made his international debut in the 1–1 draw with Italy in Rome, Cliff Bastin scored England's goal.			
1940	Millwall	A	League South 'C' Division	2–0
1967	Sheffield Wednesday	A	Division 1	1–1
1970	Appolon	A	European Fairs Cup 4th round 2nd leg	2–0
1989	Derby County	H	Division 1	1–2
1991	Barnet	A	Friendly	4–2

MAY 14TH

1922	IFK Gothenburg	A	Friendly	3–2
1924	Hamburg XI	A	Friendly	2–2
1931	Danish XI	A	Friendly	2–0
1935	Mel Charles was born in Swansea.			
1937	Alf Kirchen scored on his international debut in England's 6–0 victory over Norway in Oslo.			
1952	Anderlecht	A	Friendly	0–1

| 1959 | Juventus | A | Friendly | 1–3 |
| 1960 | Anderlecht | A | Friendly | 4–1 |

Bill Dodgin made last senior appearance. He played 191 League and 16 (1 goal) FA Cup matches.

| 1963 | Fulham | H | Division 1 | 3–0 |
| 1964 | Transvaal–Orange Free State | A | Friendly | 2–0 |

Don Howe's first game.

1971 Arsenal's Cup final record 'Good Old Arsenal' entered the charts where it reached number 16 and stayed in the top 40 for 5 weeks in total.

| 1975 | Malaysian Select XI | A | Friendly | 1–1 |

Christopher Wreh was born in Monrovia, Liberia.

1977	Manchester United	A	Division 1	2–3
1979	Chelsea	A	Division 1	1–1
1980	Valencia	Brussels	Cup Winners Cup final	0–0

Just four days after tasting defeat in the FA Cup final at Wembley, Arsenal put on an altogether improved performance in this game against the Spaniards. David O'Leary was in particularly outstanding form as he snubbed out the threat of Valencia's world-rated Mario Kempes but, despite the addition of extra time, neither side could manage to break the deadlock. It was thus left to a penalty shoot-out to decide the winners. Famously both Brady and Rix failed with their attempts and Valencia won a competition in which Arsenal had gone undefeated in regular play throughout.

| 1983 | Aston Villa | A | Division 1 | 1–2 |

Last appearance of Vladimir Petrovic who had taken part in only 22 competitive senior games after one of the most drawn-out transfer sagas ever. He was released and went to play for Antwerp.

| 1987 | Apoel/Omonia Combined XI | A | Cyprus Super Cup | 3–2 |
| 1995 | Chelsea | A | Premier League | 1–2 |

MAY 15TH

1926	SK Slavia Ips	A	Friendly	5–1
1943	Blackpool	A	Friendly	2–4
1949	Fluminense	A	Friendly	5–1
1952	Grasshoppers	A	Friendly	5–2
1955	Young Boys	A	Friendly	3–0
1962	Staevnet	A	Friendly	1–1
1967	Romford	A	Bill Seddon Testimonial	3–1

1971 John Roberts made his international debut for Wales in the 0–0 draw with Scotland in Cardiff.

| 1979 | Lyngby Boldklub | A | Friendly | 4–2 |

Final appearance Malcolm Macdonald. Played 84 (42 goals) League, 9 (10 goals) FA Cup, 14 (5 goals) FL Cup and 1 European games.

Terry Neill's first and, probably, most charismatic signing scored freely in his limited time at the club before having to retire through injury.

| 1982 | Southampton | H | Division 1 | 4–1 |

1990 David Seaman was purchased from Queen's Park Rangers for a (then) British record fee for a goalkeeper of £1,300,000.

| 1993 | Sheffield Wednesday | Wembley FA Cup final | | 1–1 |

Arsenal's 12th FA Cup final appearance as they tried to complete a first by winning the League and FA Cup double in the same season ironically against the same opposition of a few weeks earlier. Ian Wright scored for the Gunners.

MAY 16TH

1907	SK Slavia Ips	A	Friendly	4–2
1912	Deutscher F.C.	A	Friendly	4–1
1922	Gais	A	Friendly	4–1
1923	Swedish Combined XI	A	Friendly	3–2
1934	Jack Crayston joined from Bradford for £5,250.			
1939	Gothenburg Alliance	A	Friendly	3–0
1942	Brentford	Tottenham		
			London War Cup semi-final replay	1–2
1961	Staevnet	A	Friendly	1–0

1962 Jack Kelsey severely injured his back during his 41st international appearance for Wales in the 3–1 defeat by Brazil in Sao Paulo. The injury was to prove so severe he had to retire from football.

1980	Wolverhampton Wanderers	A	Division 1	2–1
1984	Charlton Athletic	A	Les Berry Testimonial	4–3

1993 Arsenal's Wembley tune 'Shouting For The Gunners' entered the charts at Number 34 where it was to stay for only a couple of weeks.

1997 Matthew Upson, England Under-18 international, was signed from Luton Town in a £1,200,000 deal after making just one senior appearance for the Hatters.

1998	Newcastle United	Wembley FA Cup final	2–0

Arsenal won the FA Cup for the seventh time and in so doing clinched the League Championship and FA Cup Double for the second time in the club's history. This equalled the post-war record established by Manchester United two years earlier.
The Littlewoods 'Man of the Match' was awarded to Ray Parlour and the Gunners won a game they had dominated with goals from Marc Overmars and Nicolas Anelka.

MAY 17TH

1901	Thomas Briercliffe joined from Stalybridge.			
1919	Chelsea	H	Friendly	1–2
1928	Danish FA XI	A	Friendly	3–2
1929	Cliff 'Boy' Bastin signed from Exeter City for £2,000.			
1931	Danish XI	A	Friendly	5–1
1939	Eddie Magill was born in Carrickfergus, N. Ireland.			
1941	West Ham United	H	London War Cup	3–0
1950	Bohemians Select	A	Friendly	5–2
1962	Skane Alliance	A	Friendly	4–0
1964	Natal XI	A	Friendly	8–2
1975	Singapore National XI	A	Friendly	3–2
1977	Rosenborg	A	Friendly	4–0
1983	Gillingham	A	Bill Collins Testimonial	3–1

Final appearance John Devine. Record: 89 League, 6 FA Cup, 8 FL Cup, 8 European games.
Also last game for John Hollins who played 127 (9 goals) League, 12 FA Cup, 20 (3 goals) FL Cup and 13 European matches.

1989	Wimbledon	H	Division 1	2–2
1991	Liverpool	A	Caltex Cup	1–1
1993	Manchester United	H	David O'Leary farewell match	4–4
1995	Guo An	A	Friendly	1–2

MAY 18TH

1899	James Tennant joined from St Bernards.			
1907	Vienna	A	Friendly	4–2
1923	Swedish Combined XI	A	Friendly	2–1
1924	Spiel–Vereinigung Fürth	A	Friendly	1–0
1926	Rapid Vienna	A	Friendly	3–3
1928	Charlie Jones signed from Nottingham Forest for £4,800.			
1930	Dennis Evans was born in Ellesmere Port, Cheshire.			

1939 Eddie Hapgood played his 30th and last game for England in the 2–1 defeat by Yugoslavia in Belgrade.

1940	Birmingham	H	Football League War Cup	1–2
1949	Palmeiras	A	Friendly	1–1
1961	Swedish National XI	A	Friendly	3–2
1963	Sheffield Wednesday	A	Division 1	3–2
1969	Floriana	A	Friendly	4–0
1977	Nessegoten	A	Friendly	3–0
1982	ASL Club	Trinidad	Friendly	2–3
1995	Tianjin Samsung	A	Friendly	2–0

MAY 19TH

1907	Budapest	A	Friendly	9–0
1912	Ferencvarosi Torna	A	Friendly	2–1
1922	Orgryte IS	A	Friendly	2–0
1931	Copenhagen Combination XI	A	Friendly	1–1

1932	Frank Robert 'Tiger' Hill bought from Aberdeen for £3,000.			
1940	Jack McClelland was born in Lurgan, Northern Ireland.			
1945	Tottenham Hotspur	A	Friendly	0–4
1950	Glentoran	A	Friendly	4–2
1955	Munich 1860	A	Friendly	2–1

Joe Wade finished his Arsenal career having achieved 86 League and 7 FA Cup appearances.

| 1960 | Fortuna Geleen | A | Friendly | 5–5 |
| 1980 | Middlesbrough | A | Division 1 | 0–5 |

Just five days after defeat in the European Cup Winners Cup final, the Gunners were called on to play their 70th game of the season. This reverse meant that the club had failed to qualify for European competition the following year and, perhaps even more significantly, it marked the end of Liam Brady's glittering career for Arsenal having played 235 (43 goals) League, 35 (2 goals) FA Cup, 23 (10 goals) FL Cup and 13 (4 goals) European games .

Brady had long since decided that he wanted to test himself in a foreign environment and his immediate success with Juventus showed just what a class act the Gunners had lost, not that it was ever in doubt.

The questions that remain unanswered, however, are why didn't the Board of Directors try harder to tempt him to stay a while longer and, having lost the battle for Brady's services, why was a class replacement not signed?

MAY 20TH

1907	Budapest	A	Friendly	2–2
1926	Amateure FK Austria	A	Friendly	5–3
1928	Danish FA XI	A	Friendly	1–0

Debut for Charlie Jones.

1951	Fluminense	A	Friendly	0–2
1952	Basle	A	Friendly	1–0
1959	Fiorentina	A	Friendly	2–1
1963	Glasgow Rangers	H	Jack Kelsey Testimonial	2–2
1964	Western Province XI	A	Friendly	5–1
1967	Omonia	A	Friendly	4–1
1969	Hibernians (Malta)	A	Friendly	0–0
1975	Thailand National XI	A	Friendly	3–0
1977	Roros	A	Friendly	6–0
1982	Trinidad Representative	A	Friendly	2–0

Danny O'Shea made his first-team debut.

1993   Sheffield Wednesday   Wembley FA Cup final replay   2–1

Andy Linighan's last-minute winner in extra time sealed Arsenal's sixth FA Cup final victory and created history as the second part of the first ever domestic Cup double, the Gunner's having beaten the same opponents in the Coca-Cola League Cup in April.

The game was the last for David O'Leary who, with 558 (11 goals) League, 70 (1 goal) FA Cup, 70 (2 goals) FL Cup and 21 European matches, took over from Geordie Armstrong as the club's record appearance holder. 'Spider' was one of the best ever players to pull on an Arsenal shirt and achieved his ambition to complete 20 years as a player at Highbury, going out at the very top!

1995   Hong Kong Rangers   A   Friendly   4–0

Paul Davis played his last game for the Gunners. His record: 351 (30 goals) League, 27 (3 goals) FA Cup, 51 (4 goals) FL Cup and 16 European appearances. Given a free transfer, he joined Brentford before retiring as a player. Returned to Arsenal in a junior coaching capacity.

1997   England Under-21 international Matthew Rose joined QPR in a £500,000 move.

MAY 21ST

1897   Fergus Hunt joined from Darwen.

1906   Frank Hill was born in Forfar, Scotland.

1922   Helsingborg   A   Friendly   1–0

1923   Ernest Williamson won the first of his 2 England caps in the space of 3 days when he played in England's 4–2 win over Sweden in Stockholm.

1941   Tottenham Hotspur   H   London War Cup   0–3

1956   Ritchie Powling was born in Barking, Essex.

1961   Vejle Boldklub   A   Friendly   3–0

1966   Besiktas   A   Friendly   0–2

1966   Henry Cooper fought Muhammad Ali in arguably the most famous world heavyweight title fight at Highbury, when Cooper almost became the first British boxer to win the title this century.

MAY 22ND

1902	Jack Lambert was born in Greasbrough, Yorkshire.			
1912	Grazer AK	A	Friendly	6–0
1914	Christopher Buckley signed for the Gunners from Aston Villa.			
1924	Stuttgart Kickers	A	Friendly	2–0
1928	Danish International XI	A	Friendly	5–3
1931	Stockholm Combined XI	A	Friendly	3–2

1931 Final senior appearance of Jimmy Brain. He played 204 (125 goals) League and 27 (14 goals) FA Cup games for the Gunners.

1939	Danish XI	A	Friendly	3–0
1940	Fulham	H	League South 'C' Division	2–1
1946	Leslie Jones given a free transfer to Swansea Town.			
1949	Corinthians	A	Friendly	2–0
1952	Lausanne	A	Friendly	2–2
1953	Paul Mariner was born in Bolton.			
1964	Eastern Province XI	A	Friendly	6–0

1971 Frank McLintock played his 9th and last game for Scotland in the 3–1 defeat by England at Wembley.

1986 Danny Clapton died in Hommerton, London.

MAY 23RD

1918 Dennis Compton was born in Hendon, Middlesex.

1923	SK Lyn Oslo	A	Friendly	0–0

Joe Shaw made his final appearance. He had played 309 League and 17 FA Cup games without scoring a single goal!

After this match, Shaw retired and became manager of Arsenal's reserves graduating eventually to General Assistant with a brief spell in between as acting club manager (on Herbert Chapman's death).

1942	RAF	H	Friendly	1–1

1948 Archie Macaulay won his 7th and last cap for Scotland in the 3–0 defeat by France in Paris.

1968	Japan XI	A	Friendly	3–1
1973	Toronto Select	A	Friendly	1–0

Richie Powling was given his first appearance.

1998 At last a top 10 hit for the Gunners Cup final record. After the success of the film *The Full Monty* the boys recorded their own version of 'Hot Stuff' which shot straight into the charts at Number 9, the highest ever placing for one of their releases. It stayed in the top 40 for 3 weeks.

MAY 24TH

1890	Ernest Williamson was born in Murton, County Durham.			
1899	Horace Cope was born in Treeton, nr Sheffield, Yorks.			
1912	Tottenham Hotspur	A	Friendly	4–0
1919	Tottenham Hotspur	H	Friendly	0–0
1935	Bernard Joy joined as an amateur.			
1939	Danish XI	A	Friendly	4–1

1939 George Male and Wilf Copping made their final appearances for England in the 2–0 victory over Romania in Bucharest, which was to be the last full international England played for the next 7 years due to the war. Male won a total of 19 caps and Copping won 20.

1941	Millwall	A	London War Cup	5–2
1947	Liverpool	H	Division 1	1–2
1951	Botafogo	A	Friendly	0–2
1953	Rapid Vienna	A	Friendly	1–6

Last match for Ray Daniel. Appearance record: 87 (5 goals) League and 12 FA Cup.

| 1959 | Lugano | A | Friendly | 4–1 |
| 1967 | Appollon/AEL Select | A | Friendly | 7–0 |

1975 Alan Ball played his 72nd and last game for England in the famous 5–1 victory over Scotland at Wembley. He scored 8 goals in his international career and captained the side on over 30 occasions. 20 of these appearances occurred whilst he was at Arsenal.

MAY 25TH

| 1923 | Norwegian XI | A | Friendly | 9–2 |
| 1928 | IF Helsingborg | A | Friendly | 3–2 |

1929 'Billy' Blyth was transferred to Birmingham City.

1933 Charlie Jones played his 4th and last game for Wales in the 1–1 draw with France in Paris.

1935 Dennis Compton signed professional forms.

| 1937 | Gothenburg | A | Friendly | 1–1 |
| 1940 | Portsmouth | A | League South 'C' Division | 1–1 |

1944 Joe Wade joined as an amateur.

1948 Charles Satterthwaite died.

| 1949 | Vasco de Gama | A | Friendly | 0–1 |
| 1966 | Besiktas | A | Friendly | 0–0 |

MAY 26TH

1912	Rapid Vienna	A	Friendly	8–2
1924	Cologne Sportklub 99	A	Friendly	9–0
1926	Rapid/Amateure All Stars	A	Friendly	0–1

1938 Both Ted Drake (2 goals) and Cliff Bastin with 1 goal scored in what was to be their last appearance for England in the 4–2 victory over France in Paris. Bastin scored a total of 12 goals in 21 games, whilst amazingly Drake despite scoring 6 goals only won 5 caps.

1939	Danish XI	A	Friendly	6–0
1947	Brentford	A	Division 1	1–0
1968	Japan XI	A	Friendly	1–0

1987 Nigel Winterburn signed from Wimbledon for £407,000.

| 1989 | Liverpool | A | Division 1 | 2–0 |

Probably the most dramatic climax to a League Championship race that has ever been staged!

In a game that had been held over to the end of the season because of the tragic events in the FA Cup semi-final at Hillsborough in which Liverpool were involved, Arsenal needed to win by two clear goals to win the League and prevent their opponents from retaining the title. The Gunners duly obliged with a goal from Alan Smith followed, in the closing seconds, by a strike from Mickey Thomas sending the Arsenal contingent at Anfield into spontaneous celebrations.

It was the tenth time that the League Championship trophy had been brought back to Highbury.

MAY 27TH

1912	Wiener Sport Club	A	Friendly	5–0
1926	Innsbruck Select XI	A	Friendly	4–2
1931	Swedish National XI	A	Friendly	6–1

1933 Alex Wilson was purchased from Greenock Morton for £600.

1948 Doug Lishman signed from Walsall for a fee of £10,500.

1951	America	A	Friendly	1–2
1953	Grasshoppers	A	Friendly	2–1

Final game for Freddie Cox who played 79 (9 goals) League and 15 (7 goals) FA Cup matches for the Gunners including the victorious 1950 FA Cup final against Liverpool. First senior game for Dennis Evans.

1967	Apoel	A	Friendly	1–1
1973	Devonshire Colts	A	Friendly	4–0

Final appearance of Peter Marinello. He had played only 38 (3 goals) League, 1 FA Cup, 5 (1 goal) FL Cup and 7 (1 goal) European games. He had arrived in a blaze of publicity but failed to live up to a reputation built in Scottish football. Some claimed Marinello had found the bright lights of London too hard to resist and that his off-field activities got in the way of his life as a footballer.

1998 Ian Wright was substituted after just 20 minutes during England's 1–0 victory over Morocco in Casablanca, with a torn hamstring, which ended his hopes of making the final 22 for the World Cup in France. Martin Keown made his 17th appearance for England in the same game. In the same tournament Emmanuel Petit played for France in their 1–0 victory over Belgium. Remi Garde signed a new 1 year contract to delay his retirement, whilst John Lukic also signed a new 1 year deal to stay at the club. Scott Marshall and Chris Kiwomya were both released on free transfers.

MAY 28TH

1914 Frank Bradshaw was signed from Everton.

1928	IFK Gothenburg	A	Friendly	3–1
1937	Copenhagen	A	Friendly	4–1

Reg Lewis made his first senior appearance.

1956 Johnny Petts signed as a professional. He went on to appear in 32 League games in his customary wing-half position.

1976 Jimmy Rimmer played the first half in his only appearance for England in the 3–2 win against Italy in an exhibition match in New York.

MAY 29TH

1912	Spiel–Vereinigung Fürth	A	Friendly	6–0

1914 Matthew Thomson was transferred to Swindon Town.

1931	AIK	A	Friendly	5–0
1949	Flamengo	A	Friendly	1–3

First team debut for 'Peter' Goring in a game that marked the final appearance of Ronnie Rooke, a key member of the 1947–48 League Championship-winning team. His record finished: 88 (68 goals) League and 5 (1 goal) FA Cup matches.

1949 Brian Kidd was born in Manchester, Lancashire.

1950	Servette	A	Friendly	3–1

1959 Steve Gatting was born in Park Royal, London.

1968	Japan XI	A	Friendly	4–0

Sammy Nelson was given his first-team debut.

1990   Martin Hayes was transferred to Celtic for £625,000.

MAY 30TH

1928   Staevnet Combined XI   A   Friendly   3–1
1950   Swiss Select   A   Friendly   4–2
1951   Sao Paulo   A   Friendly   1–0
1952   Alex Forbes made his 14th and last appearance for Scotland in the 3–1 defeat by Sweden in Stockholm.
1964   South Africa XI   A   Friendly   5–0
1995   Death of Ted Drake in London. His Arsenal record of 42 League goals in a single season (1934–35) in which he made 41 appearances is unlikely to be broken as is his feat of scoring seven goals in one match (vs. Aston Villa Dec.1935). Ted Drake died age 82. He played over 180 first-team games for Arsenal scoring an amazing 139 goals in this time. In the five seasons he was at the club he finished leading goalscorer on each occasion. After the war he managed Hendon, Reading and then Chelsea where he had further success becoming the first player to win a Division 1 championship medal and then manage a team to the title. He later looked after Fulham's reserves and was elected on to the board and then life president.

MAY 31ST

1884   Frank Bradshaw was born in Sheffield, Yorkshire.
1907   Norman Sidey was born in London.
1937   Copenhagen   A   Friendly   5–1
        First appearance of Lawrie Scott.
1941   Preston North End   Blackburn
                            Football League War Cup final replay   1–2
1947   Everton   H   Division 1   2–1
1961   Peter 'Snouty' Storey joined as an apprentice professional.
1967   Nea Salamis   A   Friendly   2–0
        Don Howe's final game. Record: 70 (1 goal) League, 3 FA Cup and 1 FL Cup appearances.
1972   Miami Gatos   A   Friendly   3–2
1980   Alan Sunderland made his one and only appearance for England in the 2–1 win over Australia in Sydney. In the same fixture Brian Talbot won his 6th and last cap for England.

JUNE 1ST

1929   Alexander Wilson James signed from Preston North End in a deal worth £8,500.
1940   Southampton   H   League South C Division   5–0
1949   Botafogo   A   Friendly   2–2
1953   Alex James died in London, aged 51, on the 24th anniversary of his arrival from Preston.

JUNE 2ND

1934   Wilfred Copping 'The Iron Man' signed for £8,000 from Leeds United.
1937   Copenhagen   A   Friendly   3–0
1968   President's All Star XI   A   Friendly   6–2
        Last appearance of Jim Furnell who played 141 League, 13 FA Cup,12 FL Cup and 1 European games.
1980   Raphael Meade given professional status.

1991   Gus Caesar, on a free transfer from Arsenal, joined Cambridge United.

JUNE 3RD

1931   Gothenburg   A   Friendly   3–2
        Combination
1939   Jimmy Logie joined from Lochore Welfare for £75.
1970   Bobby Gould transferred to Wolverhampton Wanderers for £55,000.
1988   Steve Bould arrived from Stoke City for a fee of £390,000 (set by Tribunal). He had
        chosen Arsenal ahead of Everton who were also keen to secure his services.

JUNE 4TH

1939   Diables Rouges   A   Friendly   5–1
1949   Sao Paulo   A   Friendly   0–1
        Final appearance of Bryn Jones. In a career that was severely disrupted by the war, he
        made 71 (7 goals) League and 3 FA Cup starts for the Gunners.
1977   Alex Manninger was born in Salzburg, Austria.

JUNE 5TH

1991   Kwame Ampadu was sold to West Bromwich Albion for a fee of £50,000.

JUNE 6TH

1930   John Butler sold to Torquay United for £1,000.
1937   Feyenoord   A   Friendly   3–0
        Final appearance of the man many would claim to be the greatest ever Arsenal player,
        Alex James.
        At the hub of the side that dominated English football throughout the thirties, his record
        finished: 231 (26 goals) League and 28 (1 goal) FA Cup. He won 4 League Championship
        and 2 FA Cup medals as well as 4 full Scottish caps during his time at Highbury.
1951   Palmeiras   A   Friendly   1–3

JUNE 7TH

1928   Dave Bowen was born in Maesteg, Wales.
1947   Sheffield United   A   Division 1   1–2

JUNE 8TH

1899   Duncan McNichol signed from St Bernards.
1905   James Sharp joined from Fulham.
1954   Lionel Smith was transferred to Watford.
1982   Tony Woodcock joined from 1FC Koln for £500,000.

JUNE 9TH

1936   FR 'Tiger' Hill sold to Blackpool for £2,000.
1983   VSP   A   Friendly   3–0
1984   John Mackie died in Isleworth.
1986   Martin Keown was sold to Aston Villa for £125,000 rising, with appearances, to
        £200,000. He had refused Arsenal's offer of a new contract as he was not satisfied with
        the prospective terms (reported as a £50 per week increase).

JUNE 10TH

1946   Tommy Baldwin was born in Gateshead.
1966   David Platt was born in Chadderton, Lancashire.
1985   Brian Talbot transferred to Watford for £150,000.

JUNE 11TH

1971   Liam Brady joined the club as an apprentice professional.

JUNE 12TH

1945   Pat Jennings was born in Newry
1946   Bobby Gould was born in Coventry, Warwickshire.
1951   Vasco de Gama   A   Friendly   0–4
        Final appearance of Ian McPherson who had played 152 (19 goals) League and 11 (2
        goals) FA Cup games.
        Won a League Championship medal in 1947–48.
1980   Clive Allen was signed from QPR for £1 million.
1983   VSPSSI   A   Friendly   5–0
1998   Emmanuel Petit was chosen for host nation France in their opening Group C game
        against South Africa in the 1998 World Cup finals. France won the game 3–0.

JUNE 13TH

1998   Marc Overmars starred for Holland in their opening group game of the France 98 World
        Cup against their neighbours, Belgium, which finished in a 0–0 draw. Dennis Bergkamp
        was introduced as a late second-half substitute by the Dutch in an attempt to break the
        deadlock but struggled to impose himself on the proceedings.

JUNE 14TH

1973   Peter Storey made his 19th and last appearance for England in the 2–0 defeat by Italy in
        Turin.
1973   David O'Leary signed as an apprentice professional.
1974   Ian Selley was born in Chertsey, Surrey.
1990   John Lukic left Arsenal to return to Leeds United for £1,000,000.

JUNE 15TH

1912   Andy Ducat sold to Aston Villa for £1,000.
1935   John Vance Milne bought from Blackburn Rovers for £5,000.
1974   Trevor Ross signed professional terms.
1998   David Seaman and Tony Adams were part of an England team that beat Tunisia 2–0 in
        the opening Group G game of the World Cup finals in Marseilles.

JUNE 16TH

1982   Graham Rix and Kenny Sansom became the first Arsenal players to play for England in
        the World Cup final stages when they both appeared in the 3–1 victory over France in
        England's opening match of the tournament.
1983   VSNIAC Mitra   A   Friendly   0–2
1994   Goalkeeper Lee Harper was signed from Sittingbourne for £150,000.

JUNE 17TH

1895   William Blyth was born in Dalkeith, Midlothian.

1952 Gerry Ward signed as an amateur.
1953 Ray Daniel sold to Sunderland for a fee of £27,500.

JUNE 18TH

1962 Andy Linighan was born in 1962.
1979 Paul Davis signed professional forms.
1993 Eddie McGoldrick was bought from Crystal Palace for £1,000,000.

JUNE 19TH

1913 HTW 'Wally' Hardinge joined from Sheffield United.
1944 Death of Herbert Roberts from erysipelas.
1998 Eighteen-year-old David Grodin became the latest French import to join the Gunners ranks when he signed in a £500,000 deal from Saint-Etienne who, it was announced, had agreed a five-year partnership with Arsenal. The purpose of the Anglo-French pact was to develop young players by broadening their experience by means of exchange periods.

JUNE 20TH

1949 Ron Rooke was transferred to Crystal Palace to become player-manager.
1987 Ian Allinson was released on a free transfer to join Stoke City.
1989 Andrew Marriott was sold to Nottingham Forest in a deal worth up to £50,000 (appearance related). He had not made the Arsenal first team but subsequently did appear in goal for Wales at full international level.
1998 Marc Overmars scored Holland's 2nd goal in the 5–0 victory over South Korea in the World Cup group game in Marseilles. In doing so he became the first ever Arsenal player to score in the World Cup final stages. Also present in the Dutch team was Dennis Bergkamp who made his first start to a football match for seven weeks, following a hamstring injury that had forced him to miss the final games of the domestic season including the FA Cup final, Dennis scored the 3rd goal for Holland.

JUNE 21ST

1951 Alan Hudson was born in Chelsea, London.

JUNE 22ND

1894 Robert Turnbull was born in Dumbarton, Scotland.
1900 Fredrick Coles joined from Nottingham Forest.
1904 James Henry Bigden joined Arsenal from West Ham United.
1983 Arsenal won the race for the signature of the precocious Scottish talent Charlie Nicholas for £650,000 from Celtic. Rivals Liverpool and Manchester United had also been keen to secure the player's services after a season in Scotland in which Nicholas had scored 52 goals.
1988 Graham Rix was awarded a free transfer to SM Caen, France.
1998 David Seaman and Tony Adams played in the England team beaten 2–1 by Romania in the second round of qualifying games in the group matches in the France 98 World Cup Tournament.

JUNE 23RD

1955 David Price was born in Caterham, Surrey.
1976 Patrick Vieira was born in Dakar, Senegal.

JUNE 24TH

1949 Bryn Jones was transferred to Norwich City for £3,000 where he took up the position of player-coach.

1998 Manu Petit and Patrick Vieira represented France, in the final game of the group qualifying stages of World Cup 1998 against Denmark. Petit scored the winning goal early in the second half to secure a 2–1 victory for France which meant they finished top of their group with maximum points.

JUNE 25TH

1904 Fred Coles was transferred to Grimsby Town.

1975 Steve Gatting signed as an apprentice professional.

JUNE 26TH

1970 Terry Neill was transferred to Hull City as player-manager.

1972 Frank Stapleton joined Arsenal from school as an apprentice professional.

1998 David Seaman and Tony Adams played for England in their final Group G game in the World Cup in France against Colombia which finished 2–0 in favour of England.

JUNE 27TH

1978 Paul Davis joined as an apprentice professional.

JUNE 28TH

1913 Joseph Lievesley was signed from Sheffield United.

1921 Reg Boreham joined Arsenal from Wycombe Wanderers where he had been an amateur.

1923 Harry Woods was acquired from Newcastle United.

1928 John Mackie transferred to Portsmouth for £2,375.

1929 Stan Charlton was born in Exeter, Devon.

1998 Emmanuel Petit started in the French team that created history: in the first knock-out round of the World Cup final tournament, they overcame Paraguay by scoring the competition's first 'golden goal' in extra time.

JUNE 29TH

1923 Goalkeeper Ernie Williamson who had made over 100 League appearances for the Gunners was given a free transfer to Norwich City.

JUNE 30TH

1932 Derek Tapscott was born in Barry, South Wales.

1995 Kevin Campbell transferred to Nottingham Forest for £2,500,000.

JULY 1ST

1911 Leslie Jones was born in Aberdare, Wales.

1953 Alan Sunderland was born in Mexborough, Yorkshire.

1961 John MacLeod joined from Hibernian for £40,000.

1966 'Flint' McCullough was transferred to Millwall.

1973 Richie Powling signed professional forms.

1977 Kevin Stead was acquired by manager Terry Neill on a free transfer from Tottenham Hotspur.

He made two League appearances for Arsenal, one of which was as a substitute, but despite the short nature of his Highbury career he made sufficient impression to stake his claim as the worst footballer ever to play first-team football for the Gunners! Little wonder as even Spurs had not demanded a fee for his services.

1987   Viv Anderson became a Manchester United player for a fee of £250,000 which was set by a Football League Tribunal and was some way short of Arsenal's valuation of what was an appropriate amount for a (then) current English international.

Anderson, the first black footballer to win a full England cap, made 120 League, 12 FA Cup and 18 Football League Cup appearances for the Gunners during which he contributed a total of 15 goals from his full-back position.

1990   Kevin Richardson was transferred to Real Sociedad for £750,000.

JULY 2ND

1970   Steve Morrow was born in Belfast.

JULY 3RD

1925   Charles Buchan resigned for Arsenal (for whom he had previously represented as an amateur) in a deal that saw Sunderland collect a basic fee of £2,000 and another £100 for each goal scored for the Gunners.

1933   Horace Cope was transferred to Bristol Rovers for £1,500.

1966   George Eastham scored for England in his 19th and last appearance in the 2–0 victory over Denmark in Copenhagen.

He scored twice for his country but, despite being a member of the squad, was unfortunate to miss being a part of the triumphant World Cup team.

1995   Dennis Bergkamp became the club's record signing at £7,500,000 from Internazionale, Milan.

JULY 4TH

1990   Andy Linighan was purchased from Norwich City for £1,200,000.

1998   Dennis Bergkamp made history when he scored the winner for Holland in their quarter-final tie of the World Cup game in Marseilles against Argentina. He became the highest scorer for the Dutch with his fantastic 90th-minute goal. It was his 36th goal in just 62 appearances.

JULY 5TH

1978   Paul Barron joined from Plymouth Argyle for a fee of £70,000.

JULY 6TH

1959   Dave Bowen returned to Northampton Town as player-manager in a deal that cost the Cobblers £5,000.

He later became manager of Wales (in 1964).

1995   Jimmy Carter, released on a free transfer by the Gunners, joined Portsmouth.

JULY 7TH

1921   Joe Wade was born in Shoreditch, London.

1997   Paul Merson moved to Middlesbrough for a fee in the region of £5,000,000.

1998   David Platt, after discussions with Arsène Wenger (who agreed to release him from his contract a year early), decided to retire from the playing side of football to concentrate on management. Platt had a distinguished career in which clubs had paid a combined £22 million in transfer fees for his services and the pinnacle of which saw him captain his country, England, for an extended period. In Italy he won a UEFA winners medal with Juventus and an Italian Cup winners medal with Sampdoria. On his return to England and Arsenal, he finished off his career by helping the Gunners to the Double as a valuable member of the squad. His career total of 500 games and 209 goals is a record that underlined his true qualities as a world-class player if perhaps past his prime by the time he joined the Gunners. Among many of his other achievements he is also England's 6th highest goalscorer with an impressive 27 goals in 62 games.

Holland lost on penalties to Brazil in the World Cup semi-final in Marseilles after the game ended 1–1 in normal time. Dennis Bergkamp scored one of the penalties, but failed to become the first Arsenal player ever to appear in a World Cup final. Marc Overmars missed the game with a hamstring injury.

JULY 8TH

1970 David Court sold to Luton Town for £35,000.
1975 David O'Leary was upgraded to full professional.
1977 Wilf Rostron moved to Sunderland for £40,000.
1990 Anders Limpar was signed from Cremonese for £1,000,000.
1997 St Albans City   A   Friendly   4–1

JULY 9TH

1910 Willis Rippon, formerly with junior clubs Hackenthorpe, Rawmarsh Albion, Sandhill Rovers and Kilnhurst Town, joined Arsenal from Bristol City. However, despite making his debut a few weeks later against Manchester United, his career never took off at the highest level and he finished with just 9 League appearances in which he scored twice.

JULY 10TH

1956 Frank Stapleton was born in Dublin.
1975 Bob McNab given a free transfer to Wolverhampton Wanderers.
1988 There was a threat of a split in the Football League when ITV offered £33m over four years to screen League and Littlewoods Cup matches. The amount to be shared between 10 clubs. The top five of these – Liverpool, Everton, Manchester United, Arsenal and Tottenham Hotspur would have been guaranteed £600,000 a year plus £150,000 per game. The second five – Aston Villa, Newcastle United, Nottingham Forest, Sheffield Wednesday and West Ham United were guaranteed £400,000 a year plus £150,000 per game. BBC and BSB were offering between £39m and £47m over 4 years to be divided between the Football League and the FA.
1998 Boreham Wood   A   Friendly   5–2
      The Double winners started their pre-season win over Boreham Wood with a comfortable victory. One noticeable absentee from the line up was Ian Wright, who according to press speculation was about to leave Highbury in a move to West Ham.

JULY 11TH

1866 James Boyle was born in Springburn.
1890 Alex Graham was born in Hurlford, Ayrshire, Scotland.
1922 Angus McKinnon transferred to Charlton Athletic.

JULY 12TH

1958 Steve Williams was born in Hammersmith, London.
1963 Gerry Ward was transferred to Leyton Orient for £8,000.

1974   Ray Kennedy sold to Liverpool for £200,000 in a deal which proved to be Bill Shankly's last for Liverpool.

1974   Brian Kidd arrived from Manchester United for a fee of £110,000.

1977   Red Star Belgrade   A   Friendly   1–3

1995   George Graham found guilty of misconduct following the transfers of John Jensen and Pal Lydersen to Arsenal.

1997   Leyton Orient   A   Friendly   1–0

1998   Emmanuel Petit and Patrick Vieira became the first Arsenal players ever to appear in a World Cup final, and subsequently the first winners, as France beat Brazil 3–0 to win the trophy. To cap a fantastic performance throughout the tournament, 'Manu' scored the 3rd goal for France after running the length of the field to receive a perfect pass from Vieira, before slotting the ball home. It was announced by the BBC that Dennis Bergkamp had yet again won their Goal of the Month competition, only this time it was 'World Cup Goal of the Tournament', for his magnificent goal against Argentina in the quarter-final.

JULY 13TH

1995   George Graham was handed a one-year ban from football by the FA following an investigation into the payment of alleged 'bungs'. Graham was also told to pay a percentage of the costs of the hearing, believed to be in the region of £50,000.

The ban ended on June 30th 1996 and having been precluded from acting in any capacity for any football club, Graham spent his time gardening, playing golf, acting as a pundit for TV and radio and generally licking his wounds. He would no doubt have reflected upon the fact that he had been made a scapegoat by the FA Premier League Inquiry formed to investigate transfer dealings in general, but more specifically the transfer of Teddy Sheringham from Nottingham Forest to Tottenham Hotspur. The Spurs chairman, Alan Sugar, had brought the dubious nature of this transfer to the public's attention but still the panel preferred to focus on Graham and he became their only big scalp.

Given George Graham's track record of success it was of little surprise that his services were keenly sought at the end of his ban nor that he should end up in tandem with David O'Leary in a partnership that has already started to revive the fortunes of Leeds United.

1998   Ian Wright left the club to join West Ham for an undisclosed fee, seven glorious years after his record-breaking transfer, when George Graham signed him from Crystal Palace for £2.5 million. Wright rewrote the record books when he became the highest goalscorer in the club's history when he scored his 2nd goal in the game against Bolton during the 1997/8 season. His final total of 185 goals in only 288 appearances is unlikely ever to be beaten. Whilst he had his run-ins with the football authorities and referees there was never any question of the great man's commitment to the club, his team and the supporters. There are too many instances to write about in his Highbury career but he finished with 2 FA Cup winners medals, 1 League Cup medal, and of course the much cherished Championship medal he desired so badly. He missed Arsenal's glorious night in Copenhagen through suspension but was at the forefront of the celebrations as he was a major factor in the club reaching the final. When people talk about the history of the club and the legends that have played for Arsenal, Ian Wright will be mentioned every time!

JULY 14TH

1947   Archie Macauley arrived from Brentford in a deal that cost the Gunners £10,000.

1992   John Jensen was signed from Brondby in the deal that was to eventually led to the dismissal of George Graham.

The fee was originally reported as £1,200,000 but it transpired that although Brondby had received approximately this amount, Arsenal had paid closer to £1,700,000 and the balance had been taken by the agent brokering the transfer. It also transpired that a similar scenario applied to the Lyderson transaction.

Graham did not dispute receiving money and indeed, repaid a cash sum to the club, but he has always maintained that he accepted the money as an 'unsolicited' gift.

1995   David Platt joined from Sampdoria in a deal that cost Arsenal £4,750,000.

JULY 15TH

1953   Freddie Cox was sold to West Bromwich Albion for £3,500 where he became player / coach.
1979   John Hollins joined from Queen's Park Rangers in a £75,000 deal.
1995   Stephen Hughes signed his initial professional contract.

JULY 16TH

1946   John Hollins was born in Guildford, Surrey.
1954   Jimmy Bloomfield signed from Brentford for £10,000.
1962   Joe Baker, born in England, raised in Scotland, joined from AC Torino of Italy in a £70,000 transaction.
1963   Robert Primrose Wilson, better known as 'Bob', signed as an amateur from Wolverhampton Wanderers for £5,500.
1977   Singapore   A   Friendly   5–1

JULY 17TH

1897   Roger Ord joined from Hebburn Argyle.
1903   Samson Haden was born in Royston near Barnsley, Yorkshire.
1940   Joe Baker was born in Liverpool.
1965   Dan Lewis died in Scarborough.
1991   Team Malarvik   A   Friendly   4–1

JULY 18TH

1984   Bernard Joy died in Kenton.

JULY 19TH

1954   Joe Haverty signed from St Patrick's Athletic for £3,250.
1975   Qatar XI   A   Friendly   0–1

JULY 20TH

1943   Bob McNab was born in Huddersfield, Yorkshire.
1977   Australia   A   Friendly   1–3
1984   John Kay moved to Wimbledon in a deal worth £25,000.
1991   Trollhatten   A   Friendly   1–0
1993   Leyton Orient   A   Friendly   3–3
        First appearance of Eddie McGoldrick.

JULY 21ST

1953   Brian Talbot was born in Ipswich.
1898   Tom Whitaker was born in Aldershot.
1987   Gloucester City   A   Barrie Vassallo Testimonial   6–0

Alan Smith's first appearance for the Gunners.

JULY 22ND

1934	Danny Clapton was born in Stepney, East London.				
1966	Tony Burns transferred to Brighton and Hove Albion.				
1971	Jon Sammels was sold to Leicester City for £100,000.				
1989	Skelleftea	A	Friendly		3–2
	First senior appearance for Alan 'Maxi' Miller.				
1990	Varberg Bois	A	Friendly		2–0
	Andy Linighan's and David Seaman's debuts.				
1991	Eskilstuna	A	Friendly		6–1
1992	David Rocastle was sold to Leeds United for £2,000,000.				

JULY 23RD

1942	Death of Andy Ducat in London.				
1945	Jon Sammels born in Ipswich, Suffolk.				
1973	Liam 'Chippy' Brady signed his first professional contract for Arsenal.				
1984	Viv Anderson was signed from Nottingham Forest for a fee of £250,000.				
1988	Yeovil Town	A	Alan Skirton Testimonial		5–0
	Steve Bould made his first start in Arsenal's colours.				
1996	Kevin Dennis, with whom the club kept faith despite a custodial jail sentence, was given a free transfer and joined Brentford. Dennis did not fulfil his early potential and did not make a senior appearance for Arsenal.				

JULY 24TH

1946	Arthur Milton signed as professional.				
1966	Martin Keown was born in Oxford.				
1971	Bournemouth & BA	A	Friendly		5–0
1977	Glasgow Celtic	A	Friendly		2–3
1989	FK Mjolner	A	Friendly		4–0
1990	Vastra Frolunda IE	A	Friendly		4–0

JULY 25TH

1983	John Lukic was signed (for the first time) from Leeds United for a fee of £75,000.				
1987	Morton	A	Friendly		1–0
	First appearance of Nigel Winterburn.				
1988	Steve Williams departed for Luton Town in a deal that cost the Hatters £300,000.				
1992	Byafossen	A	Friendly		0–1
	Debut of John Jensen and Ian Selley.				
1993	Manchester United	A	Friendly		2–0
1997	Strasbourg	A	Friendly		2–1

JULY 26TH

1919	Henry Albert White joined from Brentford.				
1920	Ian McPherson was born in Glasgow.				
1950	Dave Bowen joined the club from Northampton Town in a £1,000 transaction.				
1961	David Herd sold to Manchester United for £35,000.				
1969	Borussia Dortmund	A	Friendly		2–2
1973	Peter Marinello was sold to Portsmouth for £80,000.				

| 1977 | Red Star Belgrade | A | Friendly | 1–0 |

This game marked the final first-team appearance of George Armstrong who had amassed 500 (53 goals) League, 60 (10 goals) FA Cup, 35 (3 goals) FL Cup and 26 (2 goals) European games for a club record only subsequently surpassed by David O'Leary.

| 1978 | Kaiserslautern | A | Friendly | 0–3 |

1984 Paul Merson signed apprenticeship forms.

1989	Lulea	A	Friendly	2–2
1990	IFK Varnamo	A	Friendly	2–2
1991	Plymouth Argyle	A	Graham Little Testimonial	2–0
1994	Lyn	A	Friendly	0–1

Arsenal debut for Swede Stefan Schwarz.

1996 John Lukic rejoined Arsenal on a free transfer from Leeds United.

JULY 27TH

1913 Albert Beasley was born in Stourbridge, Worcestershire.

1935 Billy McCullough was born in Woddburn, N. Ireland.

| 1968 | Alemmania Aachen | A | Friendly | 2–3 |

1971 John Matthews joined as an apprentice professional.

JULY 28TH

1901 Bill Seddon was born in Clapton, London.

1951 Ray Kennedy was born in Seaton Delaval, Northumberland.

| 1970 | Gothenburg Alliance | A | Friendly | 4–2 |

The pre-season started in Sweden where the Gunners played against a combined team from the local area of Gothenburg in Sweden played in the Ullevi Stadium. The Gothenburg Alliance side consisted of players from IFK, Gais and OIS. Arsenal fielded the same team that started the Fairs Cup final against Anderlecht at Highbury and were leading 2–0 at the break before finishing winners by 4 goals to 2. Charlie George netted twice with Bob McNab and George Graham scoring one goal each.

1972 David Price signed professional forms.

| 1975 | Notts County | H | Friendly | 2–1 |
| 1978 | Borussia Dortmund | A | Friendly | 1–0 |

First game for goalkeeper Paul Barron.

| 1979 | Munich 1860 | A | Friendly | 1–1 |

John Hollins made his Arsenal debut.

| 1987 | Ayr United | A | Friendly | 6–0 |

1989 Sigurdur 'Siggi' Jonnson signed from Sheffield Wednesday for a fee of £475,000 determined by tribunal.

| 1992 | Fram | A | Friendly | 2–0 |
| 1993 | Orlando Pirates | A | Friendly | 1–0 |

JULY 29TH

1912 David Neave was transferred to Merthyr Town.

| 1972 | Lausanne | A | Friendly | 6–0 |

1976 Malcolm MacDonald was bought from Newcastle United for a fee of £333,333, a club record fee (at the time).

| 1989 | Porto | | Wembley Makita International Tournament | 1–0 |

JULY 30TH

Year	Opponent	Venue	Competition	Score
1915	Archie Macauley was born in Falkirk, Scotland.			
1923	Arthur Hutchins given free transfer to Charlton Athletic.			
1934	Sir Henry Norris, the Arsenal chairman between 1910 and 1929, died.			
1962	Jon Sammels signed a professional deal.			
1968	Borussia Monchengladbach	A	Friendly	0–0
1969	Kaiserslautern	A	Friendly	2–2
1975	Heart of Midlothian	A	Friendly	2–0
1976	Notts County	H	Friendly	2–0
1985	Windsor & Eton	A	Friendly	1–0
1989	Liverpool	Wembley	Makita International Tournament	1–0
1991	Glasgow Celtic	H	Paul Davis Testimonial	2–2
1992	Stabaek	A	Friendly	1–0
1997	PSV Eindhoven	A	Friendly	0–1

JULY 31ST

Year	Opponent	Venue	Competition	Score
1951	Ian McPherson transferred to Notts County.			
1961	Joe Haverty was sold to Blackburn Rovers for £17,500.			
1970	Kungsbacka BI	A	Friendly	5–0

Arsenal made the short journey from Gothenburg to Kungsbacka to play BI in another pre-season tour match and ran out comfortable winners 5–0 after a tighter first half which had Arsenal leading by a single goal at the interval. Included in the starting line-up was young Ray Kennedy who scored along with two each from Jon Sammels and Charlie George, one of which being a penalty.

Year	Opponent	Venue	Competition	Score
1971	Benfica	A	Champions Challenge Match	0–2
1974	Cardiff City	A	Fred Keenor Challenge Cup	2–1

Brian Kidd's debut for the Gunners.

Year	Opponent	Venue	Competition	Score
1979	Duisburg	A	Friendly	1–1
1981	Colin Hill signed first professional contract.			
1983	Meppen	A	Friendly	4–1

First appearance of John Lukic and Charlie Nicholas.

Year	Opponent	Venue	Competition	Score
1993	Kaiser Chiefs	A	Friendly	1–0
1994	Raufoss	A	Friendly	9–0

AUGUST 1ST

Year	Opponent	Venue	Competition	Score
1956	Alex Forbes given a free transfer to Leyton Orient.			
1977	Steve Walford was recruited from Tottenham Hotspur for a fee of £25,000.			
1980	Liam Brady completed his move to Juventus, Italy, which under European regulations returned the Gunners just £514,000 for the loss of their most influential player.			
1980	Glasgow Rangers	A	Friendly	0–2
1987	Glasgow Celtic	A	Friendly	5–1

AUGUST 2ND

Year	Opponent	Venue	Competition	Score
1941	Heart of Midlothian	A	Friendly	1–0
1969	Swindon Town	H	Friendly	3–0
1972	Grasshoppers	A	Friendly	2–1
1975	Dundee	A	Friendly	1–2
1985	Brighton & Hove Albion	A	Friendly	2–1

1988	Orebro	A	Friendly	1–1
1992	Brann Bergen	A	Friendly	2–0
1994	Stromsgodset	A	Friendly	5–1

AUGUST 3RD

1965	Trinidad	A	Friendly	3–1
1968	Glasgow Rangers	A	Friendly	2–2
1974	Haarlem	A	Friendly	0–3
1979	Ajax	A	Amsterdam 704 Tournament	0–0
1980	Aberdeen	A	Friendly	1–2
1986	Sporting Lisbon	A	Friendly	0–0
1990	Wolverhampton Wanderers	A	Friendly	1–0
1991	Panathinaikos	H	Makita International Tournament	1–0
1993	Charlton Athletic	A	Friendly	1–2

AUGUST 4TH

1938	George Allison smashed the British transfer record when he signed Bryn Jones from Wolverhampton Wanderers for £14,000.			
1956	VFB Stuttgart	A	Friendly	1–1
1957	AIK Stockholm	A	Friendly	2–1
1965	Jamaica Sugar Estates	A	Friendly	12–0
1970	Copenhagen Football Alliance	A	Friendly	1–1

In the last of their pre-season tour matches the Gunners travelled from Sweden to Denmark to play a combined Copenhagen team. Charlie George scored for the third consecutive match to put Arsenal ahead at half-time but had to be satisfied with a 1–1 draw.

1971	Benfica	H	Friendly	6–2
1972	Hamburg SV	A	Friendly	0–4
1975	Aberdeen	A	Friendly	1–0
1984	Glasgow Celtic	A	Friendly	2–3

Debut made by Viv Anderson.

1985	Tottenham Hotspur	A	Glen Hoddle Testimonial	1–1
1988	Anunsdjo	A	Friendly	3–1
1991	Sampdoria	H	Makita International Tournament	1–1
1997	Norwich City	A	Friendly	6–2

AUGUST 5TH

| 1946 | Ian Buchanan McPherson DFC joined from Notts County in a part exchange deal involving R. Cumner. | | | |
| 1961 | Middlesbrough | A | Friendly | 1–2 |

John MacLeod made his debut.

1967	Glasgow Rangers	H	Friendly	3–0
1974	Dordrecht	A	Friendly	1–1
1978	PSV Eindhoven	A	Friendly	0–2
1979	Hamburg SV	A	Amsterdam 704 Tournament	3–0
1981	AIK Stockholm	A	Friendly	0–0

Final senior game for Sammy Nelson. He made 255 (10 goals) League, 35 (1 goal) FA Cup,

27 (1 goal) FL Cup and 21 European appearances. Won an FA Cup winners medal in 1979.

| 1983 | VFL Bochum | A | Friendly | 1–1 |

Last senior appearance for Peter Nicholas who had played 60 (1 goal) League, 8 FA Cup, 8 (2 goals) FL Cup and 4 European games.

Always out of his depth at Arsenal, his reputation as a 'hard-man' was laughed off after Ray Kennedy (then with Liverpool) bounced him all over the Highbury pitch during the 1981–82 League Cup encounter.

| 1986 | Glasgow Celtic | H | David O'Leary's Testimonial | 0–2 |
| 1987 | Brighton & Hove Albion | A | Friendly | 7–2 |

AUGUST 6TH

1926	Harry Woods was transferred to Luton Town.			
1930	Leslie Compton signed amateur forms.			
1966	Glasgow Rangers	A	Friendly	0–2
1977	Pat Jennings signed from Tottenham Hotspur for £45,000.			
1982	Feyenoord	A	Rotterdam Tournament	0–2
1989	Independiente	Miami	Zenith Data Systems Challenge Trophy	2–1

Arsenal had Gus Caesar sent off as well as physiotherapist Gary Lewin after some bizarre decisions by the referee in this match. Reserve team physio Vic Akers took over from Lewin on the sidelines.

| 1994 | Athletico Madrid | H | Makita International Tournament | 0–0 |

AUGUST 7TH

1898	James Ramsay was born in Clydebank, Scotland.			
1898	John Dick signed from Airdrie (in exchange for J. Devlin).			
1910	Alf Common signed for £250 from Middlesbrough.			
1965	Jamaica	A	Friendly	2–0
1970	Crystal Palace	A	Friendly	2–0

In their last pre-season match Arsenal played against Crystal Palace in aid of the National Sports Development Fund. The venue was the Crystal Palace National Sports Centre and the Reds won 2–0 with John Radford scoring both goals.

1971	Feyenoord	A	Friendly	0–1
1973	Freddie Cox died in Bournemouth.			
1974	AZ67 Alkmaar	A	Friendly	2–0
1982	Tony Adams made his first appearance for the club in a junior friendly (away) against Colchester United.			
1985	Reading	A	Friendly	3–0
1991	Watford	A	Centenary Match	3–1

Final senior game for Siggi Jonnson prior to retirement due to a back injury. Was restricted to only 8 (1 goal) League and 1 FA Cup appearances.

First team debut for Ray Parlour.

1992	Wolverhampton Wanderers	A	Friendly	0–0
1993	Manchester United	Wembley	Charity Shield	1–1
1994	Napoli	H	Makita International Tournament	1–0

AUGUST 8TH

| 1959 | Sparta | A | Friendly | 2–2 |
| 1962 | Bristol Select XI | A | Restoration Appeal Friendly | 2–1 |

First appearance by Joe Baker.

1964	Eintracht Frankfurt	A	Friendly	2–2
1966	Dunfermline Athletic	A	Friendly	0–0
1977	Aldershot	A	Friendly	1–0

Final time between the sticks for Jimmy Rimmer. He played 124 League, 12 FA Cup and 10 FL Cup games in a short but bright Arsenal career which came to a conclusion when Pat Jennings was signed from Tottenham Hotspur.

| 1978 | Glasgow Celtic | A | Friendly | 3–0 |
| 1982 | Austria Vienna | A | Rotterdam Tournament | 0–4 |

AUGUST 9TH

1914 Joe Mercer was born in Ellesmere Port, Cheshire.

1939 Lionel Smith signed as a professional having originally joined as an amateur from Denaby United.

1944 George Armstrong was born in Hebburn, Durham.

1958	Schalke 04	A	Friendly	1–3
1967	Maccabi Select	H	Friendly	1–0
1969	Everton	H	Division 1	0–1
1980	Vasco de Gama	A	Friendly	1–2
1983	Werder Bremen	A	Friendly	0–2
1988	Enkoping	A	Friendly	6–0

1990 Death of Joe Mercer in the Wirral, Cheshire.

| 1997 | Leeds United | A | Premier League | 1–1 |

League debuts given to new boys Overmars, Petit and Grimandi in a game which saw bookings for all four Frenchmen in the Gunners ranks (Garde, Vieira, Petit and Grimandi). In boiling-hot conditions the Gunners toiled hard against the long ball tactics of George Graham's team. Ian Wright edged nearer to Cliff Bastin's record with an angled shot in the 34th minute. After the game George Graham said he was happy with the result and his team's performance because he thought that Arsenal would win the Premiership!

AUGUST 10TH

1965	Curacao	A	Friendly	3–1
1968	Tottenham Hotspur	A	Division 1	2–1
1974	Partizan Belgrade	A	Friendly	0–1
1976	Grasshoppers	A	Friendly	3–0

Malcolm MacDonald's debut.

| 1980 | Partizan Belgrade | A | Friendly | 0–0 |

Last match for Paul Barron.

1984	Iraklis Salonika	A	Bielefeld Tournament	3–1
1985	Portsmouth	A	Friendly	1–0
1986	Shamrock Rovers	A	Friendly	2–0

The final appearance in the first team for Tommy Caton. At Arsenal he played 81 (2 goals) League, 4 FA Cup and 10 (1 goal) FL Cup games.

1987	Tottenham Hotspur	A	Chris Houghton's Testimonial	1–3
1990	Aston Villa	Wembley Makita International Tournament	2–0
1991	Tottenham Hotspur	Wembley Charity Shield	0–0
1992	Peterborough United	A	Friendly	4–2

1994 Vince Bartram signed from AFC Bournemouth in a deal established by a Transfer Tribunal at £350,000.

| 1994 | Gillingham | A | Friendly | 3–1 |

AUGUST 11TH

1947 Don Roper was bought from Southampton for £11,000 plus T. Rudkin.

1953 Danny Clapton, formerly with Leytonstone, joined Arsenal as an amateur but signed as a professional only four days later.

1961	Ipswich Town	H	Friendly	3–3
1962	Austria FK	A	Friendly	0–2
1964	VFB Stuttgart	A	Friendly	1–1
1965	Aruba	A	Friendly	2–2
1973	Brann	A	Friendly	2–0
1975	Hajduk Split	A	Friendly	0–2

1977 Jimmy Rimmer was sold to Aston Villa for a fee of £70,000.

| 1979 | Liverpool | | Wembley Charity Shield | 1–3 |

1982 Lee Chapman joined from Stoke City in a £500,000 deal as determined by tribunal, an amount five times greater than the valuation Arsenal had submitted!

| 1990 | Sampdoria | | Wembley Makita International Tournament | 0–1 |

1993 Colin Pates given a free transfer to Brighton and Hove Albion.

| 1997 | Coventry City | H | Premier League | 2–0 |

The first home game of the season televised live on Sky saw Arsenal pressurise Coventry from the start, in the 29th minute Ian Wright slotted home the rebound after Vieira's shot was blocked by Ogrizovic. In the second half more relentless pressure forced Coventry's Shaw to underhit a backpass for Wrighty to pounce and slot the ball home. He was now just 1 short of equalling the Bastin record.

AUGUST 12TH

1917 Frank Boulton was born in Chipping Sodbury, Gloucs.

1945	Combined Services	A	Friendly	6–1
1959	ADO	A	Friendly	7–0
1967	Hertha Berlin	A	Friendly	1–2
1972	Leicester City	A	Division 1	1–0
1977	Luton Town	A	Friendly	1–1

First appearance in the Arsenal goal for Pat Jennings.

1978	Crystal Palace	H	Friendly	1–1
1984	Arminia Bielefeld	A	Bielefeld Tournament	1–0
1989	Liverpool		Wembley Charity Shield	0–1

1994 Goalkeeper Alan Miller was transferred to Middlesbrough for £500,000.

AUGUST 13TH

| 1958 | Enschede Sports Club | A | Friendly | 2–1 |
| 1966 | Huddersfield Town | A | Friendly | 1–0 |

George Eastham's last match. He made 207 (41 goals) League, 13 FA Cup and 3 European appearances. Later became manager of Stoke City before emigrating to South Africa.

1968	Leicester City	H	Division 1	3–0
1969	Leeds United	A	Division 1	0–0
1976	Rijeka	A	Friendly	2–2

1980 Clive Allen, after making only 3 appearances in friendly matches, was sold as part of the £1.25 million deal which saw Allen and goalkeeper Paul Barron go to Crystal Palace with Kenny Sansom coming in.

1983	Aberdeen	A	Friendly	1–0
1986	Waterford	A	Friendly	1–1
1988	Tottenham Hotspur	Wembley	Makita International Tournament	4–0
1994	Crystal Palace	H	Friendly	1–3

AUGUST 14TH

1894 Jack Butler was born in Colombo, Ceylon.

1963	Enschede	A	Friendly	2–2

Bob Wilson's senior debut.

1971	Chelsea	H	Division 1	3–0
1973	Frigg	A	Friendly	0–1

1980 George Wood signed from Everton for £150,000.

1982	Alexandria Select XI	A	Friendly	0–0

Lee Chapman's first game.

1988	Bayern Munich	Wembley	Makita International Tournament	3–0
1993	Coventry City	H	Premier League	0–3

1996 Remi Garde signed on a free transfer from Strasbourg and Patrick Vieira arrived from AC Milan for a fee of £3,500,000.

AUGUST 15TH

1886 Charles Lewis was born in Plumstead, London.

1894 John Caldwell joined from Hibernians.

1964	Portsmouth	A	Friendly	5–1
1965	Trinidad	A	Friendly	6–2
1970	Everton	A	Division 1	2–2

The League season commenced at Goodison Park where champions Everton played hosts and Arsenal moved Peter Storey from full-back to midfield. Joe Royle gave Everton a first-half lead with a diving header after 29 minutes and had several chances to extend their advantage. In the second half Arsenal attacked more and eventually broke through with a goal from Charlie George after 71 minutes. This was the last we would see of George until December 16th when he would appear as a substitute away in Beveren in the Fairs Cup. At the time Bertie Mee was quoted as saying that he should be alright as he had only suffered a knock on a nerve and bruises but in fact he had broken his leg. Everton regained the lead 6 minutes from time when a shot rebounded from the post to Morrissey who beat Bob Wilson in the Arsenal goal. However, the Gunners managed to force a 2–2 draw when George Graham scored two minutes later.

1972	Wolverhampton Wanderers	H	Division 1	5–2
1976	Zeljeznicar	A	Friendly	1–1

1983 Due to a technical administrative error on the part of Colchester United, Arsenal were able to secure the services of Ian Allinson on a free transfer from the Essex club. In 75 senior appearances for the Gunners, Allinson scored a creditable 23 goals of which the most significant was probably his effort against Tottenham Hotspur in the 1986–87 Littlewoods Cup semi-final replay at White Hart Lane.

1984	Twente Enschede	A	Friendly	0–1
1986	Southend United	A	Friendly	1–0

The first senior outing for Paul Merson.

1987	Liverpool	H	Division 1	1–2
1992	Norwich City	H	Premier League	2–4

AUGUST 16TH

1912	Ted Drake was born in Southampton, Hampshire.			
1958	Young Fellows	A	Friendly	5–0
1969	West Bromwich Albion	A	Division 1	1–0
1975	Burnley	A	Division 1	0–0
	David O'Leary made his League debut.			
1978	John Matthews is sold to Sheffield United for £90,000.			
1980	West Bromwich Albion	A	Division 1	1–0
	Kenny Sansom's Arsenal debut.			
1981	Olympiakos	A	Friendly	3–2

Steve Gatting's last time in the first team. He played 58 (5 goals) League, 10 (1 goal) FA Cup, 4 FL Cup and 4 European games.

1982	Egypt National Team	A	Friendly	1–0
1988	Birmingham City	A	Friendly	4–0
1993	Tottenham Hotspur	A	Premier League	1–0

AUGUST 17TH

1909	Wilf Copping was born in Middlecliffe, Barnsley, Yorks.			
1963	Hamburg SV	A	Friendly	2–2
1968	Liverpool	H	Division 1	1–1
1970	West Ham United	A	Division 1	0–0

A dour 0–0 draw against West Ham United at Upton Park which saw Ray Kennedy start in place of the injured Charlie George in front of a capacity crowd.

1971	Huddersfield Town	A	Division 1	1–0
1974	Leicester City	A	Division 1	1–0
1984	Brighton & Hove Albion	A	Friendly	1–1
1985	Liverpool	A	Division 1	0–2
1990	Brighton & Hove Albion	A	Steve Gatting Testimonial	2–2
1991	Queen's Park Rangers	H	Division 1	1–1
1996	West Ham United	H	Premier League	2–0

AUGUST 18TH

1951	Huddersfield Town	H	Division 1	2–2
1956	Cardiff City	H	Division 1	0–0
1961	Transfer completed of Laurie Brown for £35,000 from Northampton Town.			
1962	Leyton Orient	A	Division 1	2–1
	League debut by Joe Baker.			
1973	Wolverhampton Wanderers	H	FA Cup 3rd round	1–3
1979	Brighton & Hove Albion	A	Division 1	4–0
1983	Michael Lauriston Thomas signed as an apprentice professional.			
1992	Blackburn Rovers	A	Premier League	0–1

The last appearance of 'TinTin'. Perry Groves took his final bow in familiar fashion, as substitute! In the 156 (21 goals) League, 17 (1 goal) FA Cup, 26 (6 goals) FL Cup and 4 European games 'El Pel' had mustered for the Gunners, no fewer than 83 of his appearances came as a sub. The enduring memory of 'the Ginger One' is, therefore, not of him scoring an absolutely breathtaking goal (as in the Littlewoods Cup semi-final against Everton at Goodison in 1988), but of yet another run up the touchline as he prepared to make his entry into an ongoing game. Groves also made 50 appearances in friendlies for the Gunners, 21 of which were as substitute.

AUGUST 19TH

1939	Tottenham Hotspur	A	Friendly	1–0
1946	Ray Daniel signed as an amateur.			
1950	Burnley	A	Division 1	1–0
1953	West Bromwich Albion	A	Division 1	0–2
1956	Joe Wade was transferred to Hereford Town as player-manager.			
1961	Burnley	H	Division 1	2–2

Laurie Brown's first game for Arsenal.

1966	George Eastham transferred to Stoke City for £35,000.			
1967	Stoke City	H	Division 1	2–0
1969	Leeds United	H	Division 1	1–1

Final appearance of Ian Ure after 168 (2 goals) League, 16 FA Cup, 14 FL Cup and 4 European games.

Commanding, tough centre-half who seems to have entered Arsenal mythology as having been completely useless. This is an aberration of the truth which was enhanced by his mix-up with Bob Wilson in League Cup final against Swindon in 1969 and he was certainly good enough to earn full Scottish international recognition.

1972	Stoke City	H	Division 1	2–0
1975	Sheffield United	A	Division 1	3–1
1978	Leeds United	H	Division 1	2–2
1980	Southampton	H	Division 1	1–1
1987	Manchester United	A	Division 1	0–0
1988	Leicester City	A	Friendly	4–1
1989	Manchester United	A	Division 1	1–4
1996	Liverpool	A	Premier League	0–2

AUGUST 20TH

1938	Tottenham Hotspur	H	Friendly	0–2

Arsenal debut of Bryn Jones.

1949	Burnley	H	Division 1	0–1
1955	Blackpool	A	Division 1	1–3
1960	Burnley	A	Division 1	2–3

Alan Skirton made his League debut.

1966	Sunderland	A	Division 1	3–1
1971	Manchester United	A	Division 1	1–3
1973	Glasgow Rangers	A	Centenary Match	2–1
1974	Ipswich Town	H	Division 1	0–1
1977	Ipswich Town	A	Division 1	0–1

Pat Jennings made his League debut for the Gunners.

1981	Juventus	A	Friendly	2–2
1982	Chelsea	A	Friendly	3–1
1983	Portsmouth	A	Friendly	1–2
1985	Southampton	H	Division 1	3–2
1991	Everton	A	Division 1	1–3
1994	Manchester City	H	Premier League	3–0
1995	Middlesbrough	H	Premier League	1–1

AUGUST 21ST

| 1948 | Huddersfield Town | A | Division 1 | 1–1 |

1948 Huddersfield Town A Division 1 1–1
1954 Newcastle United H Division 1 1–3
Last game for Arthur Shaw. His record finished 57 League and 4 FA Cup appearances.
1956 Burnley H Division 1 2–0
1962 Birmingham City H Division 1 2–0
1965 Stoke City H Division 1 2–1
1968 Wolverhampton A Division 1 0–0
Wanderers
1969 Ian Ure was transferred to Manchester United for £80,000.
1976 Bristol City H Division 1 0–1
1979 Ipswich Town H Division 1 0–2
1981 The price of Frank Stapleton's transfer to Manchester United was fixed by a tribunal at £900,000 which was less than half the valuation submitted by Arsenal. Further acrimony was introduced to the proceedings when the (then) manager of the Old Trafford club declared his delight at the outcome insinuating that United had out-manoeuvred the Gunners.
1992 Perry Groves was sold to Southampton for £750,000.
1993 Sheffield Wednesday A Premier League 1–0

AUGUST 22ND

1914 Tottenham Hotspur A Friendly 5–1
1937 Laurie Brown was born in Shildon, Durham.
1951 Chelsea A Division 1 3–1
1953 Huddersfield Town H Division 1 0–0
Gerry Ward, at the age of 16 years, became the youngest ever Arsenal League debutant.
1959 Sheffield Wednesday H Division 1 0–1
1963 John Francombe 'Ian' Ure was signed from Dundee for £62,500.
1964 Liverpool A Division 1 2–3
1967 Liverpool A Division 1 0–2
1970 Manchester United H Division 1 4–0
The first home match of the season was against Manchester United watched by over 54,000 spectators. John Radford gave the Gunners the lead after 14 minutes and 4 minutes later the same player put Arsenal 2 goals ahead. Manchester United were completely outplayed and could have easily been further behind at the break. John Radford completed his hat-trick after 60 minutes at which point Manchester United goalkeeper Stepney left the field following a previous clash with George Armstrong in which the keeper damaged his shoulder. Sadler took over in goal for United but could not prevent George Graham scoring Arsenal's fourth after 69 minutes. The Gunners appeared content to see out time with a 4–0 victory.
1972 Coventry City A Division 1 1–1
1978 Manchester City A Division 1 1–1
League debut made by Paul Barron.
1981 Portsmouth A Friendly 1–0
1987 Queen's Park Rangers A Division 1 0–2
Charlie Nicholas played his final game. Although a crowd favourite, he never fulfilled his early potential and despite scoring twice in the final of the 1987 Littlewoods (League) Cup to seal victory against Liverpool, he tended to score his goals when the pressure was off or against inferior opposition. Definitely not the genuine article! He made 151 (34 goals) League, 13 (10 goals) FA Cup and 20 (10 goals) FL Cup appearances.

| 1989 | Coventry City | H | Division 1 | 2–0 |

AUGUST 23RD

| 1920 | Lionel Smith was born in Mexborough, Yorkshire. | | | |
| 1947 | Sunderland | H | Division 1 | 3–1 |

Archie Macauley's and Don Roper's debuts.

1950	Chelsea	H	Division 1	0–0
1952	Aston Villa	A	Division 1	2–1
1955	Cardiff City	H	Division 1	3–1
1958	Preston North End	A	Division 1	1–2
1958	Tommy Docherty signed for £20,000 from Preston North End.			
1960	Preston North End	H	Division 1	1–0
1961	Leicester City	A	Division 1	1–0
1966	West Ham United	H	Division 1	2–1

Alan Skirton's final game. He had made 145 (53 goals) League, 8 FA Cup and 1 (1 goal) European appearances.

1969	Nottingham Forest	H	Division 1	2–1
1975	Stoke City	H	Division 1	0–1
1977	Everton	H	Division 1	1–0
1980	Coventry City	A	Division 1	1–3
1986	Manchester United	H	Division 1	1–0
1992	Liverpool	A	Premier League	2–0
1994	Leeds United	A	Premier League	0–1
1995	Everton	A	Premier League	2–0
1996	Paul Dickov was sold to Manchester City in a £1,000,000 deal.			
1997	Southampton	A	Premier League	3–1

All the attention was on Ian Wright, widely tipped to break the Bastin record in this game against opposition that he normally ran riot against. It wasn't to be as he only managed a couple of efforts and picked up a booking. However, on a more positive note Overmars scored his first senior goal after cutting in from the left wing and shooting low with his right foot (something that was to become a trademark for the rest of the season). Dennis Bergkamp scored the other two. His first on 59 minutes was runner-up in the BBC's 'Goal of the Month' competition, as he picked the ball up just inside the Southampton half and ran at the defence beating 4 men on the way before curling the ball majestically past Jones in goal. His second goal of the game was not far behind in quality, when he shrugged off Benali and unleashed a stunning shot from 20 yards that hit the back of the net and came out again. Luis Boa Morte (as substitute for Overmars) made his League debut.

AUGUST 24TH

1928	Tommy Docherty was born in Glasgow.			
1949	Chelsea	A	Division 1	2–1
1953	Sheffield United	A	Division 1	0–1
1954	David Herd bought from Stockport County for £10,000.			
1957	Sunderland	A	Division 1	1–0
1961	George Armstrong signed first professional forms.			
1963	Wolverhampton Wanderers	H	Division 1	1–3

Debut for Ian Ure.

1967	Michael Thomas was born in Lambeth, London.			
1968	Ipswich Town	A	Division 1	2–1
1971	Sheffield United	H	Division 1	0–1
1974	Manchester City	H	Division 1	4–0
1985	Manchester United	H	Division 1	1–2
1991	Aston Villa	A	Division 1	1–3
1993	Leeds United	H	Premier League	2–1
1996	Leicester City	A	Premier League	2–0

David Hillier's final game. He made 104 League, 15 FA Cup, 15 FL Cup and 8 European appearances during which he scored just twice. Although he won a Championship medal in 1991, he never found favour with the Highbury crowd who had quickly recognised his limitations which were even apparent after his move to Portsmouth where he failed to command a regular first-team place at a club in lower level football.

AUGUST 25TH

1923	Newcastle United	H	Division 1	1–4
	Debut of Harry Woods.			
1928	Sheffield Wednesday	A	Division 1	2–3

Herbert Chapman introduced shirt numbering for the first time for this game but was told immediately afterwards by the FA to desist.

1934	Portsmouth	A	Division 1	3–3
	Wilf Copping's first game.			
1945	Coventry City	A	Football League – South	0–2
1948	Stoke City	H	Division 1	3–0
1951	Wolverhampton Wanderers	A	Division 1	1–2
1954	Everton	A	Division 1	0–1

Jimmy Bloomfield and Joe Haverty made their League debuts.

1956	Birmingham City	A	Division 1	2–4
1962	Manchester United	H	Division 1	1–3
1964	Sheffield Wednesday	H	Division 1	1–1
1965	Northampton Town	A	Division 1	1–1
1969	West Ham United	A	Division 1	1–1
1970	Huddersfield Town	H	Division 1	1–0

Bob McNab decided to accept the club's new pay offer and signed a new contract in the morning and then faced his old team Huddersfield Town at Highbury in the evening. This was a drab match in which Arsenal found it very difficult to break down a stubborn defence. Eventually Ray Kennedy netted his first goal of the season after 75 minutes to break the deadlock and give the Gunners a 1–0 win.

1973	Manchester United	H	Division 1	3–0
1976	Norwich City	A	Division 1	3–1
1979	Manchester United	H	Division 1	0–0
1984	Chelsea	H	Division 1	1–1
	Arsenal League debut made by Viv Anderson.			
1990	Wimbledon	A	Division 1	3–0

AUGUST 26TH

1904	Joe Hulme was born in Stafford.

1913	Alf Kirchen was born in Shouldham, Norfolk.			
1922	Liverpool	A	Division 1	2–5
1924	Dan Lewis joined from Clapton Orient.			
1933	Birmingham	H	Division 1	1–1
1939	Wolverhampton Wanderers	A	Division 1	2–2
1944	Luton Town	A	Football League – South	2–2
1950	Tottenham Hotspur	H	Division 1	2–2
1958	Burnley	H	Division 1	3–0
	Tommy Docherty debut.			
1959	Nottingham Forest	A	Division 1	3–0
1961	Tottenham Hotspur	A	Division 1	3–4
1967	Nottingham Forest	A	Division 1	0–2
1972	Manchester United	A	Division 1	0–0
1975	Norwich City	H	Division 1	2–1
1978	Everton	A	Division 1	0–1
1980	Swansea City	A	League Cup 2nd round	1–1
1986	Coventry City	A	Division 1	1–2
1987	Kevin Richardson, a Championship winner with previous club Everton, was signed from Watford for £200,000.			
1989	Wimbledon	H	Division 1	0–0
1992	Oldham Athletic	H	Premier League	2–0
1995	Coventry City	A	Premier League	0–0

AUGUST 27TH

1919	Joseph Toner joined from Belfast United for £200.			
1921	Sheffield United	H	Division 1	1–2
1923	West Ham United	A	Division 1	0–1
1927	Bury	A	Division 1	1–5
1932	Birmingham	A	Division 1	1–0
1938	Portsmouth	H	Division 1	2–0
1945	West Ham United	A	Football League – South	1–1
1947	Charlton Athletic	A	Division 1	4–2
1949	Sunderland	A	Division 1	2–4
1952	Manchester United	H	Division 1	2–1
1955	Chelsea	H	Division 1	1–1
1957	West Bromwich Albion	H	Division 1	2–2
1960	Nottingham Forest	H	Division 1	3–0
1963	West Bromwich Albion	H	Division 1	3–2
1966	Aston Villa	H	Division 1	1–0
1968	Manchester City	H	Division 1	4–1
1974	Ipswich Town	A	Division 1	0–3
1977	Wolverhampton Wanderers	A	Division 1	1–1
1983	Luton Town	H	Division 1	2–1
1985	Luton Town	A	Division 1	2–2
1988	Wimbledon	A	Division 1	5–1
	Steve Bould made his League debut for the Gunners.			
1991	Luton Town	H	Division 1	2–0

1997   Leicester City   A   Premier League   3–3

One of the most amazing games of the campaign and the most controversial of the season, but for the travelling Arsenal fans they were to witness one of the greatest hat-tricks by an Arsenal player. In the 10th minute Bergkamp, after being booked a couple of minutes earlier by Graham Barber for an innocuous tackle, picked up the ball from Overmars on the left side of the penalty box and curled an unstoppable shot past Keller. In the second half Arsenal were still coasting when, from their own penalty area, Vieira released Parlour down the right wing who played it to Bergkamp who calmly lifted the ball over the advancing Keller into the empty net. With just 7 minutes to go Arsenal gave away a sloppy goal which was to produce the inevitable aerial onslaught from Leicester from which they were to get the equaliser in the 90th minute. Arsenal still tried to go forward and David Platt sent what looked to be an overhit pass towards the penalty area. Bergkamp in chase let the ball drop over his shoulder, controlled it and sold Matt Elliott a dummy before curling the ball in the far corner for one of the greatest goals ever seen. The drama was not to end there as Graham Barber let play continue and in the 6th minute of injury time Leicester captain Walsh headed home another equaliser which led to mass hysteria on the terraces from the home fans. After the final whistle Arsenal players surrounded the referee to voice their disapproval of his time-keeping and some pushing took place, to the delight of the media that led to Ian Wright facing misconduct charges. Martin O'Neill later said he thought that Bergkamp's 3rd goal was magnificent and that he had to stop himself from applauding!

AUGUST 28TH

1920	Aston Villa	A	Division 1	0–5
1922	Burnley	H	Division 1	1–1
1926	Derby County	H	Division 1	2–1
1937	Everton	A	Division 1	4–1
1943	Charlton Athletic	A	Football League – South	0–1
1948	Manchester United	H	Division 1	0–1
1954	West Bromwich Albion	A	Division 1	1–3
1956	Burnley	A	Division 1	1–3
1965	Burnley	A	Division 1	2–2
1967	Liverpool	H	Division 1	2–0
1971	Stoke City	H	Division 1	0–1
1973	Leeds United	H	Division 1	1–2

1973   John Matthews graduated from apprentice to full professional.

1976	Sunderland	A	Division 1	2–2
1982	Stoke City	A	Division 1	1–2
1993	Everton	H	Premier League	2–0
1994	Liverpool	A	Premier League	0–3

AUGUST 29TH

1921	Preston North End	A	Division 1	2–3
1925	Tottenham Hotspur	H	Division 1	0–1

Charles Buchan played his first game as a professional after rejoining the club from Sunderland.

1928	Derby County	H	Division 1	1–3
1931	West Bromwich Albion	H	Division 1	0–1
1936	Everton	H	Division 1	3–2
1938	Glasgow Rangers	A	Friendly	0–1

| 1942 | Charlton Athletic | A | Football League – South | 6–2 |

1949 Alfred John 'Jack' Kelsey joined from Winch Wen.

| 1951 | Chelsea | H | Division 1 | 2–1 |

Final game for left-back Lawrie Scott who made 115 League and 11 FA Cup appearances. Another player who had his career disrupted by war, but still managed to win a League Championship medal in 1947–48 and an FA Cup winners medal in 1950.

| 1953 | Aston Villa | A | Division 1 | 1–2 |

1956 Viv Anderson was born in Nottingham.

1959	Wolverhampton Wanderers	A	Division 1	3–3
1961	Leicester City	H	Division 1	4–4
1962	Birmingham City	A	Division 1	2–2
1964	Aston Villa	H	Division 1	3–1

Last game for John MacLeod. His record: 101 (23 goals) League, 8 (4 goals) FA Cup and 3 (1 goal) European matches.

| 1966 | West Ham United | A | Division 1 | 2–2 |
| 1970 | Chelsea | A | Division 1 | 1–2 |

Arsenal's first defeat of the season was at Stamford Bridge and was witnessed by nearly 54,000 fans. John Radford was injured in the previous match and surprisingly replaced by full-back Sammy Nelson therefore playing Ray Kennedy alone up front. John Hollins gave Chelsea the lead when he followed up his own shot which had hit the bar 5 minutes before the interval. Eddie Kelly equalised 6 minutes into the second half and the Gunners appeared to be heading for a well-deserved point when Mulligan scored 5 minutes from time to leave Chelsea as the only undefeated London club. Brazilian World Cup-winning manager Mario Zagallo attended the match.

1972	West Ham United	H	Division 1	1–0
1978	Rotherham United	A	League Cup 2nd round	1–3
1979	Leeds United	A	League Cup 2nd round	1–1
1981	Stoke City	H	Division 1	0–1
1983	Wolverhampton Wanderers	A	Division 1	2–1
1984	Nottingham Forest	A	Division 1	0–2
1987	Portsmouth	H	Division 1	6–0

Kevin Richardson made his League debut (as substitute) for the Gunners.

1990	Luton Town	H	Division 1	2–1
1992	Sheffield Wednesday	H	Premier League	2–1
1995	Nottingham Forest	H	Premier League	1–1

AUGUST 30TH

| 1919 | Newcastle United | H | Division 1 | 0–1 |

First appearance of Alfred Baker, Henry White and Ernie Williamson.

1920	Manchester United	H	Division 1	2–0
1924	Nottingham Forest	A	Division 1	2–0
1930	Blackpool	A	Division 1	4–1
1939	Blackburn Rovers	H	Division 1	1–0
1941	Brentford	A	London League	1–4
1947	Sheffield United	A	Division 1	2–1
1948	Stoke City	A	Division 1	0–1
1950	Chelsea	A	Division 1	1–0

1952	Sunderland	H	Division 1	1–2
1958	Leicester City	H	Division 1	5–1
1960	Preston North End	A	Division 1	0–2
1969	Newcastle United	A	Division 1	1–3
1975	Wolverhampton Wanderers	A	Division 1	0–0
1977	Manchester United	H	League Cup 2nd round	3–2
1980	Tottenham Hotspur	H	Division 1	2–0
1986	Liverpool	A	Division 1	1–2
1989	Bohemians	A	Friendly	2–1
1997	Tottenham Hotspur	H	Premier League	0–0

The media pressure was mounting on Ian Wright as the Bastin record still eluded him. In one of the most one-sided contests of the season Arsenal hit the woodwork on no less than 4 occasions in the first half, with Wright hitting the bar from 14 yards out with Walker flapping in no-man's land. Spurs fans disgruntled with their team's pathetic display booed as they cleared the ball into touch whenever they got the opportunity. In injury time of the first half, Justin Edinburgh was sent off for a late tackle on Lee Dixon; this proved to be the turning point of the game as it meant that Spurs could defend with all 10 men in the 2nd half (instead of just the 9 as they had in the first half). More pressure failed to bring a goal in which Arsenal could have achieved a record victory at home against their North London neighbours. After 5 games and still undefeated, Arsenal were in 5th position.

AUGUST 31ST

1906	Percy Sands signed as a professional.			
1925	Leicester City	H	Division 1	2–2

Joseph Toner's last game having notched up 89 (6 goals) League and 11 FA Cup appearances.

1927	Burnley	H	Division 1	4–1
1929	Leeds United	H	Division 1	4–0

Arsenal debut of the great Alex James.

1931	Blackburn Rovers	A	Division 1	1–1

Last first-team game for William Harper. He represented Arsenal in 63 League and 10 FA Cup matches and won a First Division Championship medal in 1930–31.

1932	West Bromwich Albion	H	Division 1	1–2
1935	Sunderland	H	Division 1	3–1

First appearance of John Vance Milne.

1940	Southend United	A	South Regional League	7–1
1946	Wolverhampton Wanderers	A	Division 1	1–6

League debut for Ian McPherson.

1949	Chelsea	H	Division 1	2–3
1954	Everton	H	Division 1	2–0
1955	Manchester City	A	Division 1	2–2
1957	Luton Town	H	Division 1	2–0
1963	Leicester City	A	Division 1	2–7
1968	Queen's Park Rangers	H	Division 1	2–1
1974	Everton	A	Division 1	1–2
1976	Carlisle United	H	League Cup 2nd round	3–2
1982	Norwich City	H	Division 1	1–1

1985	Leicester City	H	Division 1	1–0
1987	Luton Town	A	Division 1	1–1
1988	Queen's Park Rangers	A	MCT	2–0
1991	Manchester City	H	Division 1	2–1
1994	Blackburn Rovers	H	Premier League	0–0

SEPTEMBER 1ST

1892	Highland Light Infantry	H	Friendly	8–0
1894	Lincoln City	A	Division 2	2–5

John Caldwell's debut.

1896	Rossendale	H	Friendly	4–0
1897	Grimsby Town	H	Division 2	4–1

Debut for Fergus Hunt and Roger Ord.

1897	Andy Kennedy was born in Belfast, Ireland.			
1898	Gravesend	H	Friendly	0–1

John Dick debut.

1900	Gainsborough Trinity	H	Division 2	2–1
1902	West Ham United	A	London League Premier Division	3–1

Debut Roddy McEachrane against his former club.

1903	Tottenham Hotspur	A	London League Premier Division	1–0
1904	Bristol City	H	Friendly	3–2

Debut Archibald Gray and Charlie Satterthwaite.

1906	Manchester City	A	Division 1	4–1
1909	Aston Villa	A	Division 1	1–5
1910	Manchester United	H	Division 1	1–2

Debut Alf Common.

1914	Glossop North End	H	Division 2	3–0

Frank Bradshaw and Christopher Buckley made their League debuts.

1917	Queen's Park Rangers	H	London Combination	2–0
1919	Liverpool	A	Division 1	3–2
1923	Newcastle United	A	Division 1	0–1
1924	Manchester City	H	Division 1	1–0
1926	Bolton Wanderers	H	Division 1	2–1
1928	Bolton Wanderers	H	Division 1	2–0
1930	Bolton Wanderers	A	Division 1	4–1
1934	Liverpool	H	Division 1	8–1

Jack Crayston's first-team debut for the Gunners.

1937	Huddersfield Town	H	Division 1	3–1
1945	Coventry City	H	Football League – South	0–0
1951	Sunderland	H	Division 1	3–0
1953	Sheffield United	H	Division 1	1–1
1953	Ted Platt was transferred to Portsmouth.			
1956	West Bromwich Albion	H	Division 1	4–1
1959	Nottingham Forest	H	Division 1	1–1
1962	Burnley	A	Division 1	1–2
1970	Leeds United	H	Division 1	0–0

Eddie Kelly was sent off at Highbury after 22 minutes but Arsenal still managed to
ensure that Leeds United dropped their first point of the season by gaining a 0–0 draw.
Kelly was in a tussle with Bremner of Leeds and appeared to kick him as the players fell

to the ground. Bremner dived at the feet of referee Jones and Kelly was ordered off. This was an extremely brave performance by the Gunners who gained one of their most important results as the season unfolded.

1973	Newcastle United	A	Division 1	1–1
1979	Leeds United	A	Division 1	1–1
1984	Watford	A	Division 1	4–3
1990	Tottenham Hotspur	H	Division 1	0–0
1993	Blackburn Rovers	A	Premier League	1–1

SEPTEMBER 2ND

| 1893 | Newcastle United | H | Division 2 | 2–2 |

This was Woolwich Arsenal's first game in the Football League against opposition who were also newly promoted .

| 1895 | Grimsby Town | H | Division 2 | 3–1 |
| 1899 | Leicester Fosse | H | Division 2 | 0–2 |

Debut for James Jackson and James Tennant.

| 1901 | Barnsley | H | Division 2 | 2–1 |

First appearance Thomas Briercliffe.

| 1905 | Liverpool | H | Division 1 | 3–1 |

James Sharp made his debut.

1907	Notts County	H	Division 1	1–1
1908	Everton	H	Division 1	0–4
1911	Liverpool	H	Division 1	2–2
1912	Manchester United	H	Division 1	0–0
1916	West Ham United	A	London Combination	1–2

Debut of Arthur Hutchins.

1922	Liverpool	H	Division 1	1–0
1933	Sheffield Wednesday	A	Division 1	2–1
1939	Sunderland	H	Division 1	5–2
1944	Tottenham Hotspur	A	Football League – South	0–4
1950	Sheffield Wednesday	H	Division 1	3–0
1958	Burnley	A	Division 1	1–3

Stan Charlton's final first-team game. He played 99 League and 11 (3 goals) FA Cup matches whilst at Highbury.

Also last League game for Cliff Holton. His record: 198 (83 goals) League and 18 (5 goals) FA Cup appearances.

1961	Bolton Wanderers	A	Division 1	1–2
1961	Chris Whyte was born in Islington, London.			
1964	Sheffield Wednesday	A	Division 1	1–2
1964	John MacLeod sold to Aston Villa for £35,000.			
1967	Coventry City	H	Division 1	1–1
1969	Southampton	A	League Cup 2nd round	1–1
1972	Chelsea	H	Division 1	1–1
1976	Eddie Kelly sold to Queen's Park Rangers for £60,000.			
1978	Queen's Park Rangers	H	Division 1	5–1
1980	Swansea City	H	League Cup 2nd round replay	3–1
1981	West Bromwich Albion	A	Division 1	2–0
1986	Sheffield Wednesday	H	Division 1	2–0
1992	Queen's Park Rangers	A	Premier League	0–0

SEPTEMBER 3RD

1892	Gainsborough Trinity	H	Friendly	4–2
1894	Nottingham Forest	H	Friendly	3–2
1898	Luton Town	A	Division 2	1–0
1904	Newcastle United	A	Division 1	0–3

First League match for James Henry Bigden.

1906	Bury	A	Division 1	1–4
1910	Bury	A	Division 1	1–1
1921	Sheffield United	A	Division 1	1–4
1927	Sheffield United	H	Division 1	6–1
1932	Sunderland	H	Division 1	6–1
1935	Grimsby Town	A	Division 1	0–1
1936	Brentford	A	Division 1	0–2

First League game for George Swindin.

1938	Huddersfield Town	A	Division 1	1–1
1945	Wolverhampton Wanderers	A	Football League – South	1–1
1947	Charlton Athletic	H	Division 1	6–0
1949	Liverpool	H	Division 1	1–2
1952	Manchester United	A	Division 1	0–0
1955	Bolton Wanderers	A	Division 1	1–4
1960	Manchester City	A	Division 1	0–0
1966	Tottenham Hotspur	A	Division 1	1–3
1977	Nottingham Forest	H	Division 1	3–0

Richie Powling made his last appearance in the first team before being forced to retire with a serious knee injury.

He had played 55 (3 goals) League, 2 FA Cup and 2 FL Cup games.

1983	Southampton	A	Division 1	0–1
1985	Queen's Park Rangers	A	Division 1	1–0
1988	Aston Villa	H	Division 1	2–3
1991	Leeds United	A	Division 1	2–2

SEPTEMBER 4TH

1891	Fred Pagnam was born in Poulton Le Fylde, Lancs.			
1893	Doncaster Rovers	H	Friendly	4–1

Debut of Frederick William Davis.

1897	Newcastle United	A	Division 2	1–4
1899	Stoke City	H	Friendly	5–3
1909	Sheffield United	H	Division 1	0–0
1911	Chelsea	A		
			London Professional Footballers Assoc Charity Fund	2–2
1915	Tottenham Hotspur	H	London Combination	2–0
1920	Aston Villa	H	Division 1	0–1
1922	Burnley	A	Division 1	1–4
1923	Jock Rutherford joined Arsenal for a second time, this time from Stoke.			
1926	Sheffield United	A	Division 1	0–4
1929	Manchester City	A	Division 1	1–3
1937	Wolverhampton Wanderers	H	Division 1	5–0

1943	Southampton	H	Football League – South	4–1
1946	Blackburn Rovers	H	Division 1	1–3
1948	Sheffield United	A	Division 1	1–1

First senior game for Doug Lisman.

1954	Tottenham Hotspur	H	Division 1	2–0
1956	Preston North End	H	Division 1	1–2

Final match for Don Roper who played 297 (88 goals) League and 22 (7 goals) FA Cup games. He won 2 League Championship medals as a free-scoring forward for the Gunners.

1957	West Bromwich Albion	A	Division 1	2–1
1962	Aston Villa	H	Division 1	1–2
1963	West Bromwich Albion	A	Division 1	0–4
1965	Chelsea	H	Division 1	1–3
1968	Sunderland	H	League Cup 2nd round	1–0

1968 Jim Furnell was sold to Rotherham United for £8,000.

1969	Southampton	H	League Cup 2nd round replay	2–0
1971	West Bromwich Albion	A	Division 1	1–0
1973	Sheffield United	A	Division 1	0–5

1975 Walley Barnes died in London.

1976	Manchester City	H	Division 1	0–0
1979	Leeds United	H	League Cup 2nd round replay	7–0
1982	Liverpool	H	Division 1	0–2
1984	Newcastle United	H	Division 1	2–0

1986 Perry Groves signed from Colchester United for £65,000.

1996	Chelsea	H	Premier League	3–3

SEPTEMBER 5TH

1891	Sheffield United	H	Friendly	0–2

Gavin Crawford's debut.

1896	Manchester City	A	Division 2	1–1
1898	Burslem Port Vale	A	Division 2	0–3
1903	Blackpool	H	Division 2	3–0

First League outing for Percy Sands.

1908	Notts County	A	Division 1	1–2

Debut for David Greenaway.

1914	Wolverhampton Wanderers	A	Division 2	0–1
1921	Preston North End	H	Division 1	1–0
1925	Manchester United	A	Division 1	1–0
1927	Burnley	A	Division 1	2–1
1931	Birmingham	A	Division 1	2–2
1934	Blackburn Rovers	H	Division 1	4–0
1936	Huddersfield Town	A	Division 1	0–0
1942	Southampton	H	Football League – South	6–1
1951	Liverpool	H	Division 1	0–0
1953	Wolverhampton Wanderers	H	Division 1	2–3
1959	Tottenham Hotspur	H	Division 1	1–1
1964	Wolverhampton Wanderers	A	Division 1	1–0

| 1970 | Tottenham Hotspur | H | Division 1 | 2–0 |

In the North London derby at Highbury Tottenham Hotspur were convincingly beaten 2–0 in front of nearly 49,000 spectators. George Armstrong scored both of the goals before half-time. Armstrong's first came after 17 minutes and his second followed 7 minutes later.

1972	Everton	H	League Cup 2nd round	1–0
1981	Liverpool	A	Division 1	0–2
1987	Derry City	A	Friendly	2–0
1992	Wimbledon	A	Premier League	2–3

SEPTEMBER 6TH

1890	93rd Highlanders	H	Friendly	1–1
1897	Burnley	A	Division 2	0–5
1902	Preston North End	A	Division 2	2–2

League debut JG 'Tim' Coleman.

| 1909 | Aston Villa | H | Division 1 | 3–1 |
| 1913 | Leicester Fosse | H | Division 2 | 2–1 |

HTW 'Wally' Hardinge and Joseph Lievesley made their debuts in the first game to be staged at Highbury.

Although the game went ahead, the stadium was far from complete and was finished to the original specifications as the season progressed.

1919	Newcastle United	A	Division 1	1–3
1920	Manchester United	A	Division 1	1–1
1924	Liverpool	H	Division 1	2–0
1926	Bolton Wanderers	A	Division 1	2–2

John Lambert made his first senior start.

1930	Leeds United	H	Division 1	3–1
1933	West Bromwich Albion	H	Division 1	3–1
1941	Crystal Palace	H	London League	7–2
1947	Manchester United	H	Division 1	2–1
1950	Everton	H	Division 1	2–1
1952	Wolverhampton Wanderers	A	Division 1	1–1
1955	Manchester City	H	Division 1	0–0
1958	Everton	A	Division 1	6–1
1960	Birmingham City	H	Division 1	2–0
1961	Stamford	A	Friendly	9–0

George Armstrong's first-team debut.

1966	Sheffield Wednesday	H	Division 1	1–1
1967	West Bromwich Albion	A	Division 1	3–1
1969	Sheffield Wednesday	H	Division 1	0–0
1975	Leicester City	H	Division 1	1–1
1980	Manchester City	A	Division 1	1–1
1983	Manchester United	H	Division 1	2–3
1986	Tottenham Hotspur	H	Division 1	0–0

Final appearance of Stewart Robson who played 151 (16 goals) League, 13 (1 goal) FA Cup, 20 (3 goals) FL Cup and 2 (1 goal) European games. He should have been an all-time Arsenal great and should have progressed to captain England but a combination of injury and attitude curtailed both aspirations in midflight.

SEPTEMBER 7TH

1889	London Caledonians	H	Friendly	2–2
1895	Manchester City	H	Division 2	0–1
1896	Rushden	H	United League	3–2
1901	Leicester Fosse	H	Division 2	2–0
1903	Fulham	H	London League Premier Division	2–0
1907	Bristol City	H	Division 1	0–4
1908	Everton	A	Division 1	3–0
1912	Liverpool	A	Division 1	0–3
1918	Queen's Park Rangers	A	London Combination	3–2
1925	Leicester City	A	Division 1	1–0
1929	Sheffield Wednesday	A	Division 1	2–0
1935	Birmingham	A	Division 1	1–1
1940	Fulham	H	South Regional League	5–0
1945	Peter Storey was born in Farnham, Surrey.			
1946	Sunderland	H	Division 1	2–2
1949	West Bromwich Albion	A	Division 1	2–1
1957	Blackpool	A	Division 1	0–1
1963	Bolton Wanderers	H	Division 1	4–3
1965	Nottingham Forest	A	Division 1	1–0
1968	Southampton	A	Division 1	2–1
1974	Burnley	H	Division 1	0–1
1982	Brighton & Hove Albion	A	Division 1	0–1
1985	Coventry City	A	Division 1	2–0
1991	Coventry City	H	Division 1	1–2
1996	Aston Villa	A	Premier League	2–2

SEPTEMBER 8TH

1892	2nd Scots Guards	H	Friendly	5–1
1894	Fleetwood Rangers	H	Friendly	4–0
1900	Walsall	H	Division 2	1–1
1902	New Brompton	A	Friendly	3–2
1906	Middlesbrough	H	Division 1	2–0
1914	Glossop North End	A	Division 2	4–0
1917	Clapton Orient	A	London Combination	5–0
1919	Liverpool	H	Division 1	1–0
1923	West Bromwich Albion	A	Division 1	0–4
1928	Portsmouth	A	Division 1	0–2
1934	Leeds United	A	Division 1	1–1
1937	Huddersfield Town	A	Division 1	1–2
1938	Brentford	A	Division 1	0–1
1945	Luton Town	H	Football League – South	0–2
1948	Liverpool	H	Division 1	1–1
1951	Aston Villa	A	Division 1	0–1
1953	Chelsea	H	Division 1	1–2
1954	Manchester City	A	Division 1	1–2
1956	Portsmouth	A	Division 1	3–2
1962	Sheffield Wednesday	H	Division 1	1–2
1964	Blackburn Rovers	H	Division 1	1–1

1970	Ipswich Town	A	League Cup 2nd round	0–0

Arsenal offered £125,000 to West Bromwich Albion for Bobby Hope. In the second round of the League Cup Arsenal were drawn to play Ipswich Town at Portman Road. The Gunners produced a rearguard action for most of the match to earn a 0–0 and force a replay.

1971	Barnsley	H	League Cup 2nd round	1–0
1973	Leicester City	H	Division 1	0–2
1979	Derby County	A	Division 1	2–3
1984	Liverpool	H	Division 1	3–1
1990	Everton	A	Division 1	1–1

SEPTEMBER 9TH

1893	Notts County	A	Division 2	2–3
1895	Millwall Athletic	A	Friendly	3–1
1899	Luton Town	A	Division 2	2–1
1905	Sheffield United	A	Division 1	1–3
1907	Bury	A	Division 1	2–3
1911	Aston Villa	A	Division 1	1–4

League debut George Grant.

1916	Tottenham Hotspur	H	London Combination	1–1
1922	Cardiff City	A	Division 1	1–4

Last game for Ernie Williamson who had played 105 League and 8 FA Cup matches.

1931	Portsmouth	H	Division 1	3–3
1933	Manchester City	H	Division 1	1–1
1936	Brentford	H	Division 1	1–1
1944	Aldershot	H	Football League – South	1–0
1950	Middlesbrough	A	Division 1	1–2
1958	Bolton Wanderers	H	Division 1	6–1
1959	Bolton Wanderers	A	Division 1	1–0
1961	Manchester City	H	Division 1	3–0
1967	Sheffield United	A	Division 1	4–2
1969	Glentoran	H	European Fairs Cup 1st round 1st leg	3–0
1972	Newcastle United	A	Division 1	1–2
1975	Everton	A	League Cup 2nd round	2–2
1978	Nottingham Forest	A	Division 1	1–2
1981	Steve Gatting sold to Brighton and Hove Albion for £200,000.			
1989	Sheffield Wednesday	H	Division 1	5–0

SEPTEMBER 10TH

1892	Casuals	H	Friendly	2–4
1894	Grimsby Town	H	Division 2	1–3
1896	Millwall Athletic	A	Friendly	2–1
1898	Leicester Fosse	H	Division 2	4–0
1904	Preston North End	H	Division 1	0–0
1910	Sheffield United	H	Division 1	0–0
1921	Manchester City	A	Division 1	0–2
1923	West Ham United	H	Division 1	4–1
1927	Aston Villa	A	Division 1	2–2
1930	Blackburn Rovers	H	Division 1	3–2
1931	Jimmy Brain sold to Tottenham Hotspur for £2,500.			

1932	Manchester City	A	Division 1	3–2
1938	Everton	H	Division 1	1–2
1947	Bolton Wanderers	H	Division 1	2–0
1949	Huddersfield Town	A	Division 1	2–2
1952	Portsmouth	H	Division 1	3–1
1955	Tottenham Hotspur	A	Division 1	1–3
1956	Preston North End	A	Division 1	0–3
1957	Everton	H	Division 1	2–3

1958 Death of David Jack in London.

1960	Tottenham Hotspur	H	Division 1	2–3
1962	Aston Villa	A	Division 1	1–3

David Court's League debut.

1963	Aston Villa	H	Division 1	3–0
1966	Manchester City	A	Division 1	1–1

1968 Pat Rice made his international debut for Northern Ireland in the 3–2 win over Israel in Jaffa.

1974	Leicester City	H	League Cup 2nd round	1–1
1977	Aston Villa	A	Division 1	0–1

1980 Graham Rix made his international debut in England's 4–0 victory over Norway in the World Cup qualifier at Wembley.

1983	Liverpool	H	Division 1	0–2
1988	Tottenham Hotspur	A	Division 1	3–2
1994	Norwich City	A	Premier League	0–0
1995	Manchester City	A	Premier League	1–0

Last appearance of Eddie McGoldrick who was on the field of play for 38 League, 2 FA Cup, 9 FL Cup and 7 (1 goal) European games. He had complained that he was not appreciated by the Arsenal crowd and (allegedly) stated that he would not cross the road to spit at an Arsenal fan. A second-rate player, who was not worthy of the shirt!

1996	Borussia Monchengladbach	H	UEFA Cup 1st round 1st leg	2–3

SEPTEMBER 11TH

1893	Walsall Town Swifts	H	Division 2	4–0

Woolwich Arsenal's first win in the Football League. John Heath notched a hat-trick.

1897	Lincoln City	H	Division 2	2–2
1899	Millwall Athletic	A	Southern District Combination	0–1

1900 Jimmy Brain was born Bristol, Gloucestershire.

1909	Middlesbrough	A	Division 1	2–5
1913	Queen's Park Rangers	A	Friendly	2–0
1915	Crystal Palace	A	London Combination	1–3
1920	Manchester City	H	Division 1	2–1
1926	Leicester City	H	Division 1	2–2
1929	Manchester City	H	Division 1	3–2
1935	Grimsby Town	H	Division 1	6–0
1937	Leicester City	A	Division 1	1–1
1943	West Ham United	A	Football League – South	2–2

Alf Kirchen's final match. He amassed 92 (38 goals) League and 7 (6 goals) FA Cup appearances.

1946	Everton	A	Division 1	2–3

1946	John Roberts was born in Swansea, Wales.			
1948	Aston Villa	H	Division 1	3–1
1954	Sheffield United	H	Division 1	4–0
1965	Tottenham Hotspur	A	Division 1	2–2
1971	Leeds United	H	Division 1	2–0
1973	Sheffield United	H	Division 1	1–0
1976	West Ham United	A	Division 1	2–0
1979	Fulham	A	Ted Drake Testimonial	2–2

1979 Paul Davis made his first senior appearance.

| 1982 | Coventry City | A | Division 1 | 2–0 |
| 1993 | Ipswich Town | H | Premier League | 4–0 |

SEPTEMBER 12TH

1891	Casuals	H	Friendly	2–1
1892	Sheffield United	A	Friendly	0–1
1896	Walsall	H	Division 2	1–1
1903	Gainsborough Trinity	A	Division 2	2–0
1904	West Ham United	A	Friendly	1–1
1906	Reading	A	Friendly	1–0
1908	Newcastle United	H	Division 1	1–2
1912	Leslie Compton was born in Woodford, Essex.			
1914	Fulham	H	Division 2	3–0
1925	Liverpool	H	Division 1	1–1
1929	Sidney Hoar sold to Clapton Orient for £1,000.			
1931	Sunderland	H	Division 1	2–0
1934	Glasgow Rangers	H	Friendly	1–1
1936	Sunderland	H	Division 1	4–1
1942	Millwall	A	Football League – South	2–1
1951	Liverpool	A	Division 1	0–0
1953	Sunderland	A	Division 1	1–7

1953 Final senior appearance of George Swindin. In a playing career that spanned 18 years at Highbury (including the war years) he amassed 271 League and 23 FA Cup games. Later returned to manage the club.

1958 Billy 'Flint' McCullough signed from Portadown for £5,000.

| 1959 | Manchester City | H | Division 1 | 3–1 |
| 1964 | Sunderland | H | Division 1 | 3–1 |

1966 Alan Skirton was transferred to Blackpool for £65,000.

| 1967 | Coventry City | A | League Cup 2nd round | 2–1 |
| 1970 | Burnley | A | Division 1 | 2–1 |

1970 Burnley attacked in great numbers and with regularity in the first half at Turf Moor only to be foiled by Arsenal goalkeeper Bob Wilson. It was the visitors who took the lead with a Ray Kennedy header after 4 minutes but Burnley forced a deserved equaliser, their first goal for 11 hours of football, when John Roberts headed into his own net. After the interval Burnley began to tire and John Radford took full advantage with 10 minutes remaining to ensure the Gunners left with two points.

1981	Sunderland	H	Division 1	1–1
1987	Nottingham Forest	A	Division 1	1–0
1992	Blackburn Rovers	H	Premier League	0–1

SEPTEMBER 13TH

1890	Casuals	H	Friendly	5–4
1902	Burslem Port Vale	H	Division 2	3–0
1909	Ray Bowden was born in Looe, Cornwall.			
1913	Wolverhampton Wanderers	A	Division 2	2–1
1919	Sunderland	A	Division 1	1–1
1924	Newcastle United	A	Division 1	2–2
1930	Sunderland	A	Division 1	4–1
1933	West Bromwich Albion	A	Division 1	0–1

John Lambert made his last senior appearance. He compiled 143 (98 goals) League and 16 (11 goals) FA Cup matches.
Lambert collected winners medals for the 1930–31 League Championship and 1930 FA Cup final.

1939	Cardiff City	A	Friendly	4–3
1941	Fulham	A	London League	5–2
1947	Preston North End	A	Division 1	0–0
1949	Freddie Cox was signed from Tottenham Hotspur for £12,000.			
1950	Everton	A	Division 1	1–1
1952	Charlton Athletic	H	Division 1	3–4
1955	England Amateur XI	H	Friendly	2–1
1958	Tottenham Hotspur	H	Division 1	3–1
1962	Real Madrid	H	Friendly	0–4
1966	Gillingham	H	League Cup 2nd round	1–1
1969	Burnley	A	Division 1	1–0
1975	Aston Villa	A	Division 1	0–2

1977 George Armstrong was sold to Leicester City for £15,000. After a subsequent move to Stockport County, 'Geordie' retired from playing and embarked on a coaching career which, following various appointments, eventually brought him back to Highbury as reserve team manager.

1978	Lokomotive Leipzig	H	UEFA Cup 1st round 1st leg	3–0
1980	Stoke City	H	Division 1	2–0
1986	Luton Town	A	Division 1	0–0

Perry Groves first senior outing for the Gunners established the pattern that was to follow, he came on as a substitute.

1997	Bolton Wanderers	H	Premier League	4–1

It was inevitable that when Ian Wright finally broke Cliff Bastin's record he was going to do it in style and that was the case on a hot afternoon as the Highbury faithful saw Wrighty equal the record. In the 21st minute when Wright shot across the goalkeeper from just inside the area and peeled away with his shirt above his head revealing a vest with 179 on it (he later admitted he lost count). His moment of greatness was not too far away, however, and he scored his second and record-breaking goal after Vieira's shot was parried and trickled to Wright who gladly smashed it in from one yard from the goal-line. The remainder of the first half was played to a buzz of excitement and Arsenal's 3rd goal from Ray Parlour almost went unnoticed. In the second half Wright was to complete his 10th hat-trick for the Gunners when he volleyed home a David Platt chipped pass. All this and Bolton had scored first.

SEPTEMBER 14TH

1889	Casuals	H	Friendly	6–0
1895	Lincoln City	A	Division 2	1–1
1896	Burton Wanderers	A	Division 2	3–0
1898	Reading	A	United League	1–1
1901	Preston North End	A	Division 2	0–2
1901	Alex James was born in Mossend, Lanarkshire.			
1903	West Ham United	H	London League Premier Division	4–1
1907	Notts County	A	Division 1	0–2
1912	Bolton Wanderers	H	Division 1	1–2
1918	Millwall Athletic	H	London Combination	4–0
1923	Doug Lisham was born in Birmingham.			
1929	Burnley	H	Division 1	6–1
1932	West Bromwich Albion	A	Division 1	1–1
1935	Sheffield Wednesday	H	Division 1	2–2
1938	Derby County	H	Division 1	1–2
1940	Fulham	A	South Regional League	1–0
1946	Aston Villa	A	Division 1	2–0
1949	West Bromwich Albion	H	Division 1	4–1
	Freddie Cox made Arsenal debut.			
1954	Manchester City	H	Division 1	2–3
1957	Leicester City	H	Division 1	3–1
1960	Birmingham City	A	Division 1	0–2
1963	Fulham	A	Division 1	4–1
1965	Nottingham Forest	H	Division 1	1–0
1968	Stoke City	H	Division 1	1–0
1974	Chelsea	A	Division 1	0–0
1982	Spartak Moscow	A	UEFA Cup 1st round 1st leg	2–3
1985	Sheffield Wednesday	H	Division 1	1–0
1991	Crystal Palace	A	Division 1	4–1

SEPTEMBER 15TH

1888	London Caledonians	H	Friendly	3–3
1890	Arthur Hutchins was born in Bishops Waltham.			
1894	Burton Swifts	A	Division 2	0–3
1897	Gravesend	A	Friendly	3–1
1900	Burton Swifts	A	Division 2	0–1
	First team debut of James Ashcroft.			
1902	Queen's Park Rangers	H	London League Premier Division	3–1
1906	Preston North End	A	Division 1	3–0
1913	Notts County	H	Division 2	3–0
1917	Millwall Athletic	H	London Combination	4–0
1923	West Bromwich Albion	H	Division 1	1–0
	Final senior appearance of Reginald Boreham, played 51 (18 goals) League and 2 FA Cup games.			
1926	Manchester United	A	Division 1	2–2
1928	Birmingham	H	Division 1	0–0
1930	Blackburn Rovers	A	Division 1	2–2
1934	West Bromwich Albion	H	Division 1	4–3

1937	Bolton Wanderers	A	Division 1	0–1
1945	Luton Town	A	Football League – South	2–1
1948	Liverpool	A	Division 1	1–0
1951	Derby County	H	Division 1	3–1
1953	Chelsea	A	Division 1	2–0
1956	Newcastle United	H	Division 1	0–1
1959	Bolton Wanderers	H	Division 1	2–1
1962	Fulham	A	Division 1	3–1
1971	Stromgodset Drammen	A	European Cup 1st round 1st leg	3–1
1973	Norwich City	A	Division 1	4–0
1979	Middlesbrough	H	Division 1	2–0
1984	Ipswich Town	A	Division 1	1–2
1990	Chelsea	H	Division 1	4–1
1993	Odense	A	Cup Winners Cup 1st round 1st leg	2–1
1994	Omonia Nicosia	A	Cup Winners Cup 1st round 1st leg	3–1

SEPTEMBER 16TH

1893	Chatham	H	Friendly	5–0
1899	Burslem Port Vale	H	Division 2	1–0
1901	Tottenham Hotspur	H	London League Premier Division	0–2
1905	Notts County	H	Division 1	1–1
1907	Barnsley	H	Friendly	1–0
1911	Newcastle United	H	Division 1	2–0
1912	Aston Villa	H	Division 1	0–3
1916	Crystal Palace	A	London Combination	0–1
1922	Cardiff City	H	Division 1	2–1
1931	Portsmouth	A	Division 1	3–0
1933	Tottenham Hotspur	A	Division 1	1–1

1937 The first match to be shown live on TV anywhere in the world was broadcast from Highbury when the first team played the reserves in a practice game shown on the BBC.

1939	Chelmsford	A	Friendly	4–0
1944	Southampton	A	Football League – South	2–0
1950	Huddersfield Town	H	Division 1	6–2
1961	West Bromwich Albion	A	Division 1	0–4
1964	Blackburn Rovers	A	Division 1	2–1

1966 Colin Addison was signed from Nottingham Forest for £45,000.

1967	Tottenham Hotspur	H	Division 1	4–0
1969	Tottenham Hotspur	H	Division 1	2–3
1970	Lazio	A	European Fairs Cup 1st round 1st leg	2–2

Defending the Fairs Cup Arsenal were drawn against Italian team Lazio with the first leg being staged at the Olympic Stadium in Rome. A 2-day air trip to Rome cost £28 with the match tickets costing extra. Two headed goals by John Radford in the 50 and 55th minutes had the Gunners coasting at 2–0 until 6 minutes from the end when Chinaglia pulled a goal back for Lazio. With 3 minutes left Chinaglia managed to get the ball past goalkeeper Bob Wilson only for Frank McLintock to cover and head the ball away to safety. The West German referee Schulenburg awarded Lazio a penalty, as he believed that McLintock had punched the ball. After a long dispute Chinaglia stepped up to place the ball wide of Wilson. The tie will be remembered for a banquet held after the match where the disagreements of the match spilled over and fighting broke out between the teams.

1972	Liverpool	H	Division 1	0–0
1978	Bolton Wanderers	H	Division 1	1–0
1981	Panathinaikos	A	UEFA Cup 1st round 1st leg	2–0

Raphael Meade was introduced as substitute and scored in his first senior competitive match.

1989	Nottingham Forest	A	Division 1	2–1
1995	West Ham United	H	Premier League	1–0
1996	Sheffield Wednesday	H	Premier League	4–1
1997	PAOK Salonika	A	UEFA cup 1st round 1st leg	0–1

SEPTEMBER 17TH

1892	Darlington	H	Friendly	3–2
1894	West Bromwich Albion	H	Friendly	0–1

1896 Andrew Young was born in Darlington, County Durham.

1898	Darwen	A	Division 2	4–1
1904	Middlesbrough	A	Division 1	0–1
1910	Aston Villa	A	Division 1	0–3
1921	Manchester City	H	Division 1	0–1
1924	Manchester City	A	Division 1	0–2
1927	Sunderland	H	Division 1	2–1
1932	Bolton Wanderers	H	Division 1	3–2
1934	Blackburn Rovers	A	Division 1	0–2
1938	Wolverhampton Wanderers	A	Division 1	1–0

1943 Wally Barnes joined Arsenal having previously been with Portsmouth and Southampton as an amateur.

1946	Blackburn Rovers	A	Division 1	2–1
1949	Bolton Wanderers	A	Division 1	2–2
1952	Portsmouth	A	Division 1	2–2
1955	Portsmouth	H	Division 1	1–3

Wally Barnes final appearance of his distinguished career, he retired days later having amassed 267 (11 goals) League and 25 (1 goal) FA Cup appearances.

1958	Bolton Wanderers	A	Division 1	1–2
1960	Newcastle United	H	Division 1	5–0

League debut given to Geoff Strong.

1966	Blackpool	H	Division 1	1–1

Colin Addison, who had joined the club the previous day, made his Arsenal League debut in this match.

1977	Leicester City	H	Division 1	2–1
1983	Notts County	A	Division 1	4–0
1988	Southampton	H	Division 1	2–2

SEPTEMBER 18TH

1897	Gainsborough Trinity	H	Division 2	4–0
1905	Preston North End	H	Division 1	2–2
1909	Bolton Wanderers	A	Division 1	0–3
1915	Queen's Park Rangers	H	London Combination	2–1
1920	Manchester City	A	Division 1	1–3
1926	Liverpool	H	Division 1	2–0

1930	Goalkeeper William Harper, who had left the club at the end of 1926–27 to play for Fall River in the USA, returned for his second spell with the Gunners.			
1935	Leeds United	A	Division 1	1–1
1937	Sunderland	H	Division 1	4–1
1943	Portsmouth	H	Football League – South	1–2
1948	Sunderland	A	Division 1	1–1
1950	West Ham United	A	Charles W Paynter Testimonial	1–3
1953	Tommy Lawton signed from Brentford for £10,000.			
1954	Preston North End	A	Division 1	1–3
1965	Everton	A	Division 1	1–3
1971	Everton	A	Division 1	1–2
1974	Leicester City	A	League Cup 2nd round replay	1–2
1976	Everton	H	Division 1	3–1
1976	Stephen Hughes was born in Wokingham, Berkshire.			
1982	Notts County	H	Division 1	2–0
1991	Austria Memphis	H	European Cup 1st round 1st leg	6–1
1994	Newcastle United	H	Premier League	2–3

SEPTEMBER 19TH

1891	Gainsborough Trinity	H	Friendly	1–4
1896	Loughborough Town	H	Division 2	2–0
1898	Thames Ironworks	H	Friendly	4–0
1903	Burton United	H	Division 2	8–0
1906	West Norwood	A	Friendly	1–0
1908	Bristol City	A	Division 1	1–2
1914	Stockport County	A	Division 2	1–1
1925	Burnley	A	Division 1	2–2
1929	Nottingham Forest	H	Friendly	4–0
	Cliff Bastin played his first senior game for the Gunners.			
1931	Manchester City	A	Division 1	3–1
1936	Wolverhampton Wanderers	A	Division 1	0–2
1937	Geoff Strong was born in Kirkheaton, Northumberland.			
1942	Luton Town	H	Football League – South	2–0
1951	Hapoel Tel Aviv	H	Friendly	6–1
1953	Manchester City	H	Division 1	2–2
1959	Blackburn Rovers	A	Division 1	1–1
1963	David Seaman was born in Rotherham, Yorkshire.			
1964	Leicester City	A	Division 1	3–2
1970	West Bromwich Albion	H	Division 1	6–2

Arsenal returned from their mid-week exploits in Rome to play West Bromwich Albion at Highbury. Bobby Hope, for whom Arsenal had previously made a bid, was left out of the Albion side through injury. The match remained goalless until the 35 minute when George Graham turned in Ray Kennedy flick. The Gunners then scored another 4 within 35 minutes and the next was scored by Ray Kennedy to make the half-time score 2–0. Armstrong scored the 3rd; an own goal by Cantello accounted for the 4th before Reed scored a consolation goal for Albion. Reed became the first player to score for the away team at Highbury and reduce the arrears but Graham restored the 4-goal margin with his 2nd goal. Brown scored Albion's second but Kennedy scored for Arsenal in the last minute to make the final score 6–2.

1979	Fenerbahce	H	Cup Winners Cup 1st round 1st leg	2–0
1981	Leeds United	A	Division 1	0–0
1987	Wimbledon	H	Division 1	3–0
1989	Plymouth Argyle	H	Littlewoods Cup 2nd round 1st leg	2–0
1992	Sheffield United	A	Premier League	1–1
1993	Manchester United	A	Premier League	0–1
1995	Hartlepool United	A	Coca-Cola Cup 2nd round 1st leg	3–0

SEPTEMBER 20TH

1890	Ilford	H	Friendly	6–0
1902	Barnsley	A	Division 2	1–1
1913	Hull City	H	Division 2	0–0
1919	Sunderland	H	Division 1	3–2
1924	Sheffield United	H	Division 1	2–0
1930	Leicester City	H	Division 1	4–1
1933	Glasgow Rangers	A	Friendly	0–2
1941	Tottenham Hotspur	H	London League	4–0
1947	Stoke City	H	Division 1	3–0
1952	Tottenham Hotspur	A	Division 1	3–1

1952 George Wood was born in Douglas, Lanarkshire, Scotland.

1955	Clyde	H	Friendly	1–2
1958	Manchester City	H	Division 1	4–1
1961	Sheffield Wednesday	A	Division 1	1–1

1962 Danny Clapton was sold to Luton Town for £6,000.

1969	Manchester United	H	Division 1	2–2
1975	Everton	H	Division 1	2–2
1980	Middlesbrough	A	Division 1	1–2

Goalkeeper George Wood made his League debut.

| 1986 | Oxford United | H | Division 1 | 0–0 |
| 1988 | Liverpool | H | MCT | 2–1 |

1996 Eddie McGoldrick was sold to Manchester City for £300,000.

SEPTEMBER 21ST

1889	Tottenham Hotspur	H	Friendly	10–1
1895	Lincoln City	H	Division 2	4–0
1901	Burnley	H	Division 2	4–0
1905	Faversham Rangers	A	Friendly	9–0
1907	Manchester City	H	Division 1	2–1
1912	Sheffield United	A	Division 1	3–1
1918	Fulham	A	London Combination	2–1
1921	Gillingham	A	Friendly	2–3
1925	West Ham United	H	Division 1	3–2
1927	Corinthians	A	Friendly	0–4

Final outing for Samson Haden who played 88 (10 goals) League and 5 (1 goal) FA Cup games.

1929	Sunderland	A	Division 1	1–0
1935	Manchester City	H	Division 1	2–3
1938	Swiss Wanderers	H	Friendly	3–2
1940	Brentford	H	South Regional League	3–1

1946	Derby County	H	Division 1	0–1
1954	Grasshoppers	H	Friendly	4–5

Debut for David Herd.

1957	Manchester United	A	Division 1	2–4
1962	Eddie Clamp sold to Stoke City for £14,000.			
1963	Manchester United	H	Division 1	2–1
1965	Corinthian Casuals	H	Friendly	5–2

Final game for Jimmy Magill. He played 116 League, 11 FA Cup and 4 European matches.

1968	Leeds United	A	Division 1	0–2
1970	Emmannuel Petit was born in Dieppe, France.			
1974	Luton Town	H	Division 1	2–2
1976	Blackpool	A	League Cup 3rd round	1–1
1985	Chelsea	A	Division 1	1–2
1990	Brian Marwood was transferred to Sheffield United for £350,000.			
1991	Sheffield United	H	Division 1	5–2
1993	Huddersfield Town	A	Coca-Cola Cup 2nd round 1st leg	5–0
1994	Hartlepool United	A	Coca-Cola Cup 2nd round 1st leg	5–0
1996	Middlesbrough	A	Premier League	2–0
1997	Chelsea	A	Premier League	3–2

Another fiercely contested London derby on a very hot afternoon. After early pressure Chelsea took the lead through Poyet who was unmarked at the far post and headed home easily. Arsenal were level within 5 minutes thanks to Bergkamp who slotted home a perfectly weighted headed pass from Ian Wright. The second half didn't start too well with one of the worst fouls possible by Dennis Wise on Vieira for which he received only a booking when a red card should have been brandished. Just on the hour Arsenal took the lead when Bergkamp volleyed home a bad clearance from Duberry but Zola scored an equaliser within a minute of the restart. Chelsea had Leboeuf sent off and a draw looked inevitable as Chelsea defended deep. The winner came from the most unlikely of sources. Nigel Winterburn picked up the ball nearly 30 yards out before taking a couple of paces forward and striking one of his rare thunderbolts straight into the top corner.

SEPTEMBER 22ND

1888	Tottenham Hotspur	H	Friendly	0–1
1891	Charles Buchan was born in Plumstead, London.			
1894	Bury	H	Division 2	4–2
1897	Loughborough Town	A	United League	3–1
1900	Barnsley	H	Division 2	1–2
1906	Newcastle United	H	Division 1	2–0
1909	Rest of Kent	A	Friendly	3–2
1917	Tottenham Hotspur	A	London Combination	2–1
1923	Birmingham	A	Division 1	2–0
1928	Manchester City	A	Division 1	1–4
1934	Sheffield United	A	Division 1	0–0
1945	Aston Villa	H	Football League – South	2–4
1951	Manchester City	A	Division 1	2–0
1954	Dave Bowen made his international debut for Wales in the 3–1 defeat by Yugoslavia in Cardiff. Jack Kelsey, Derek Tapscott and Wally Barnes played in the same game.			

1956	Sheffield Wednesday	A	Division 1	4–2
1962	Leicester City	H	Division 1	1–1
1966	Gillingham	A	League Cup 2nd round replay	1–1
1973	Stoke City	H	Division 1	2–1
1978	Chris 'Huggy Bear' Whyte was given a professional contract.			
1979	Aston Villa	A	Division 1	0–0
1980	Stockport County	A	League Cup 3rd round	3–1
1981	Birmingham City	H	Division 1	1–0
1984	Stoke City	H	Division 1	4–0
1990	Nottingham Forest	A	Division 1	2–0
1992	Millwall	H	Coca-Cola Cup 2nd round 1st leg	1–1

SEPTEMBER 23RD

1893	Middlesbrough	H	Friendly	4–1
1895	Sheffield Wednesday	H	Friendly	2–1
1899	Walsall	A	Division 2	0–2
1905	Stoke	A	Division 1	1–2
1907	Reading	H	Southern Professional Charity Cup	0–1
1911	Sheffield United	A	Division 1	1–2
1916	Brentford	H	London Combination	0–0
1922	Tottenham Hotspur	A	Division 1	2–1
1932	Dennis Compton signed as an amateur.			
1933	Everton	A	Division 1	1–3
1936	Glasgow Rangers	H	Friendly	2–1
	Dennis Compton's senior debut.			
1936	George Eastham was born in Blackpool.			
1939	Brentford	A	Friendly	0–3
1944	Queen's Park Rangers	H	Football League – South	2–0
1950	Newcastle United	A	Division 1	1–2
1953	South Africa	H	Friendly	2–2
	Danny Clapton's first XI debut.			
1955	Gordon Nutt and Mike Tiddy joined from Cardiff City for a combined fee of £20,000.			
1959	PSV Eindhoven	A	Friendly	4–1
1961	Birmingham City	H	Division 1	1–1
1967	Manchester City	H	Division 1	1–0
1970	Lazio	H	European Fairs Cup 1st round 2nd leg	2–0

After drawing 2–2 in Rome Lazio were convincingly beaten 2–0 in the return leg at Highbury in front of a crowd of 53,013 and East German referee Glockner booked five Italians in order to stamp out any violence that may have carried over from the first match. John Radford headed Arsenal into the lead after 10 minutes from a Peter Storey cross and the Gunners sealed the victory in the 74th minute with another header from George Armstrong.

1972	Norwich City	A	Division 1	2–3
1975	Everton	H	League Cup 2nd round replay	0–1
1976	Terry Mancini given a free transfer to Aldershot.			
1978	Manchester United	H	Division 1	1–1
1986	Huddersfield Town	H	Littlewoods Cup 2nd round 1st leg	2–0
1987	Doncaster Rovers	A	Littlewoods Cup 2nd round 1st leg	3–0
1989	Charlton Athletic	H	Division 1	1–0

1995	Southampton	H	Premier League	4–2

SEPTEMBER 24TH

1892	Crusaders	H	Friendly	4–0
1894	Renton	H	Friendly	6–1
1898	Gainsborough Trinity	H	Division 2	5–1
1904	Wolverhampton Wanderers	H	Division 1	2–0
1910	Sunderland	H	Division 1	0–0

1921 William 'Billy' Milne DCM was signed from Buckie Thistle.

1921	Everton	A	Division 1	1–1
1927	Derby County	A	Division 1	0–4

Final senior game for Andrew Kennedy. He played 122 League and 7 FA Cup matches.

1932	Everton	H	Division 1	2–1
1934	St Johnstone	A	Friendly	3–0
1938	Aston Villa	H	Division 1	0–0
1949	Birmingham City	H	Division 1	4–2
1955	Sunderland	A	Division 1	1–3

Debut of Gordon Nutt and Mike Tiddy.

1957	Hapoel	H	Friendly	10–2
1960	Cardiff City	A	Division 1	0–1

1965 Anders Limpar was born in Solna, Sweden.

1966	Chelsea	A	Division 1	1–3
1969	Everton	H	League Cup 3rd round	0–0
1977	Norwich City	A	Division 1	0–1

League debut made by Steve Walford.

1981 Sammy Nelson was sold to Brighton and Hove Albion for £35,000.

1983	Norwich City	H	Division 1	3–0
1988	Sheffield Wednesday	A	Division 1	1–2

1991 Ian Wright, destined to become the club's record goalscorer, was signed from Crystal Palace in a £2,500,000 deal.

1997	West Ham United	H	Premier League	4–0

The pre-match presentation to Ian Wright before the game for becoming Arsenal's highest scorer didn't detract from the work ahead as the Gunners produced possibly one of the best first-half performances seen for many a year at Highbury. Dennis Bergkamp opened the scoring after 10 minutes and Overmars scored his 1st goal at Highbury after 38 minutes cutting in from the left and shooting with his right low into the corner. Overmars was to add another 6 minutes later but only after Ian Wright had converted a penalty after a handball by a West Ham defender. The 2nd half was never going to match the 1st half and the only bright moment was when Nicolas Anelka headed just over after a glorious move involving Bergkamp and Parlour. Arsenal went top of the Premiership with 18 points after 8 games played.

SEPTEMBER 25TH

1893	Grimsby Town	H	Division 2	3–1
1897	Manchester City	A	Division 2	1–4
1909	Chelsea	H	Division 1	3–2
1915	Fulham	A	London Combination	3–4
1920	Middlesbrough	H	Division 1	2–2

1926	Leeds United	A	Division 1	1–4
1929	Aston Villa	A	Division 1	2–5
1935	Glasgow Rangers	A	Friendly	2–2

Bernard Joy's first-team debut.

1937	Derby County	A	Division 1	0–2
1943	Brighton & Hove Albion	A	Football League – South	1–1
1948	Wolverhampton Wanderers	H	Division 1	3–1
1954	Burnley	H	Division 1	4–0
1956	Leyton Orient	H	Friendly	4–0
1962	Racing Club de Paris	A	Friendly	3–0
1963	Staevnet	A	Inter-Cities Fairs Cup 1st round 1st leg	7–1
1965	Manchester United	H	Division 1	4–2
1968	Scunthorpe United	A	League Cup 3rd round	6–1
1971	Leicester City	H	Division 1	3–0
1976	Ipswich Town	A	Division 1	1–3
1979	Southampton	H	League Cup 3rd round	2–1
1982	Manchester United	A	Division 1	0–0
1984	Bristol Rovers	H	Milk Cup 2nd round 1st leg	4–0
1985	Hereford United	A	Milk Cup 2nd round 1st leg	0–0
1990	Chester City	A (Macclesfield)		
			Rumbellows Cup 2nd round 1st leg	1–0
1991	Leicester City	A	Rumbellows Cup 2nd round 1st leg	1–1

Ian Wright's debut. He scored, of course.

1993	Southampton	H	Premier League	1–0
1994	West Ham United	A	Premier League	2–0
1996	Borussia Monchengladbach	A	UEFA Cup 1st round 2nd leg	2–3

SEPTEMBER 26TH

1891	West Bromwich Albion	H	Friendly	1–1
1896	Notts County	H	Division 2	2–3
1903	Bristol City	A	Division 2	4–0
1908	Preston North End	H	Division 1	1–0
1910	Fulham	A		
			London Professional Footballers Assoc Charity Fund	3–2
1914	Hull City	H	Division 2	2–1
1925	Leeds United	H	Division 1	4–1
1928	Derby County	A	Division 1	0–0
1931	Everton	H	Division 1	3–2
1932	St Johnstone	A	Friendly	0–0

Debut for FR 'Tiger' Hill.

1936	Derby County	H	Division 1	2–2
1938	Preston North End	H	Charity Shield	2–1
1942	Portsmouth	A	Football League – South	2–2
1953	Cardiff City	A	Division 1	3–0
1958	Kenny Sansom born.			
1959	Blackpool	A	Division 1	2–1
1964	Chelsea	H	Division 1	1–3

| 1970 | Stoke City | A | Division 1 | 0–5 |

An amazing match at the Victoria Ground saw Stoke City hammer the Gunners 5–0 in a match that Frank McLintock should never have played in. He had been suffering from injury for several weeks but had continued to play and had coped fairly well until this match. The man whom he was marking, John Ritchie, scored twice before half-time and after the break Stoke grew in confidence. They added further goals from Conroy, Greenhoff and Bloor to record Arsenal's worst defeat of the season.

1972	Birmingham City	H	Division 1	2–0
1981	Manchester United	H	Division 1	0–0
1987	West Ham United	H	Division 1	1–0
1991	Joe Hulme died in Winchmore Hill.			

SEPTEMBER 27TH

1890	London Caledonians	H	Friendly	3–1
1899	Reading	A	Southern District Combination	3–0
1902	Gainsborough Trinity	H	Division 2	6–1
1908	Eddie Hapgood was born in Bristol, Gloucestershire.			
1913	Barnsley	A	Division 2	0–1
1919	Blackburn Rovers	A	Division 1	2–2
1920	Clapton Orient	A	Friendly	1–2
1924	West Ham United	A	Division 1	0–1
1930	Birmingham	A	Division 1	4–2
1933	Glasgow Rangers	H	Friendly	1–3
1941	Portsmouth	A	London League	5–1
1947	Burnley	A	Division 1	1–0
1952	Derby County	A	Division 1	0–2

Ted Platt played his last senior game for the club. His record: 53 League and 4 FA Cup appearances.

1958	Leeds United	A	Division 1	1–2
1969	Chelsea	A	Division 1	0–3
1975	Tottenham Hotspur	A	Division 1	0–0
1978	Lokomotive Leipzig	A	UEFA Cup 1st round 2nd leg	4–1
1980	Nottingham Forest	H	Division 1	1–0
1986	Nottingham Forest	A	Division 1	0–1
1997	Everton	A	Premier League	2–2

Arsenal visited troubled Everton looking to continue their bright start to the campaign. They dominated early on with Parlour and Overmars both going close. A nice flick by Bergkamp saw Ian Wright run on and shoot past the goalkeeper. A few moments later Arsenal went 2–0 up when Overmars got to an Ian Wright pass to chip over the advancing Gerrard to score. Almost immediately the flying Dutchman nearly made it 3–0 when his shot just missed the post. After the break it was a different story as Everton came out all guns blazing and eventually scored the 2 deserved goals to get them level. Despite throwing a 2-goal lead away the team still looked solid and the news that Manchester United had lost at Leeds made the result even more acceptable.

SEPTEMBER 28TH

1889	Unity	H	Friendly	8–0
1901	Burslem Port Vale	A	Division 2	0–1
1907	Preston North End	A	Division 1	0–3

Joe Shaw's League debut.

1912	Newcastle United	H	Division 1	1–1
1918	Brentford	H	London Combination	1–1
1929	Bolton Wanderers	H	Division 1	1–2
1935	Stoke City	A	Division 1	3–0
1940	Queen's Park Rangers	A	South Regional League	2–3
1946	Manchester United	A	Division 1	2–5

1946 Cliff Bastin made his final senior appearance. One of the all-time football greats, Bastin finished with 350 (150 goals) League, 42 (26 goals) FA Cup and 4 (2 goals) FA Charity Shield appearances. During his Highbury career he won the League Championship 5 times and the FA Cup twice as well as being a member of the narrowly beaten 1932 FA Cup final team.
At international level Bastin won 21 full England caps scoring 12 goals. The outbreak of the Second World War surely prohibited Bastin from establishing records that would have been virtually unassailable.

1946 Laurie Scott made his international debut for England in the 7–2 win over Northern Ireland in Belfast.

1949	Portsmouth	A	Charles Webb Testimonial	1–2
1957	Leeds United	H	Division 1	2–1
1963	Burnley	A	Division 1	3–0
1965	Northampton Town	H	Division 1	1–1
1966	Gillingham	H	League Cup 2nd round 2nd replay	5–0

Tommy Baldwin's final appearance.

1968	Sunderland	H	Division 1	0–0
1970	Ipswich Town	H	League Cup 2nd round replay	4–0

Arsenal restored some pride after losing 5–0 at Stoke on the previous Saturday to progress to the third round of the League Cup. After a 0–0 draw at Portman Road the Gunners won the replay at Highbury 4–0. Arsenal were 3–0 up at half-time with John Roberts scoring the first with a header after 18 minutes and 3 minutes later a John Radford header increased the lead. Ray Kennedy added the third after 35 minutes and also the last goal in the final seconds.

1974	Birmingham City	A	Division 1	1–3
1976	Blackpool	H	League Cup 3rd round replay	0–0
1985	Newcastle United	H	Division 1	0–0

League debut for David Carlyle Rocastle.

1988	Hull City	A	Littlewoods Cup 2nd round 1st leg	2–1
1991	Southampton	A	Division 1	4–0
1992	Manchester City	H	Premier League	1–0
1996	Sunderland	H	Premier League	2–0

SEPTEMBER 29TH

1888	Old St Paul's	H	Friendly	7–3
1894	Manchester City	H	Division 2	4–2
1895	Manchester City	A	Division 2	0–1
1900	Chesterfield Municipal	H	Division 2	1–0

League debut Frederick Coles.

1906	Aston Villa	A	Division 1	2–2
1917	Chelsea	H	London Combination	0–1
1919	Tottenham Hotspur	H	London Professional Footballers Assoc Charity Fund	0–1

First senior appearance of John Butler.

1923	Birmingham	H	Division 1	0–0
1928	Huddersfield Town	H	Division 1	2–0
1934	Birmingham	H	Division 1	5–1
1945	Aston Villa	A	Football League – South	1–5
1947	Royal Military Academy Sandhurst	A	Friendly	5–0
1948	Bexhill Town	A	Friendly	8–1

First game for Arthur Shaw.

1951	Tottenham Hotspur	H	Division 1	1–1
1952	All Stars	A	Friendly	2–4

Leslie Compton's final senior match. His record: 253 (5 goals) League and 17 (1 goal) FA Cup.

1956	Manchester United	H	Division 1	1–2
1962	Bolton Wanderers	A	Division 1	0–3

Gerry Ward bowed out of first-team action after this game. His final record: 81 (10 goals) League and 3 FA Cup appearances.

1969	Glentoran	A	European Fairs Cup 1st round 2nd leg	0–1

Ray Kennedy made his first senior appearance (as substitute).

1971	Stromgodset Drammen	H	European Cup 1st round 2nd leg	4–0
1973	Everton	A	Division 1	0–1
1979	Wolverhampton Wanderers	H	Division 1	2–3
1982	Spartak Moscow	H	UEFA Cup 1st round 2nd leg	2–5
1984	Coventry City	A	Division 1	2–1
1990	Leeds United	A	Division 1	2–2
1993	Odense	H	Cup Winners Cup 1st round 2nd leg	1–1
1994	Omonia Nicosia	H	Cup Winners Cup 1st round 2nd leg	3–0

SEPTEMBER 30TH

1893	Newcastle United	A	Division 2	0–6
1899	Middlesbrough	H	Division 2	3–0
1901	Millwall Athletic	H	London League Premier Division	1–1
1905	Bolton Wanderers	H	Division 1	0–0
1911	Oldham Athletic	H	Division 1	1–1
1912	Chelsea	A	London Professional Footballers Assoc Charity Fund	3–1
1916	Chelsea	A	London Combination	0–3
1922	Tottenham Hotspur	H	Division 1	0–2
1933	Middlesbrough	H	Division 1	6–0
1939	Reading	A	Friendly	3–1
1944	Millwall	A	Football League – South	4–1
1950	West Bromwich Albion	H	Division 1	3–0
1961	Everton	A	Division 1	1–4
1964	Odense Select XI	A	Friendly	6–3

1966 George Graham joined Arsenal from Chelsea in a deal that cost the Gunners £50,000 plus the services of Tommy Baldwin.

1967	Newcastle United	A	Division 1	1–2
1972	Southampton	H	Division 1	1–0

1978	Middlesbrough	A	Division 1	3–2
1981	Panathinaikos	H	UEFA Cup 1st round 2nd leg	1–0
1989	Chelsea	A	Division 1	0–0
1995	Chelsea	A	Premier League	0–1
1997	PAOK Salonika	H	UEFA Cup 1st round 2nd leg	1–1

OCTOBER 1ST

1887	Alexandria United	H	Friendly	5–1
1892	Marlow	H	Friendly	4–0
1898	Manchester City	A	Division 2	1–3
1900	Aston Villa	H	Friendly	3–0
1904	Bury	A	Division 1	1–1
1910	Oldham Athletic	H	Division 1	0–0
1921	Everton	H	Division 1	1–0
1927	West Ham United	H	Division 1	2–2
1932	Blackpool	A	Division 1	2–1
1938	Sunderland	A	Division 1	0–0
1949	Derby County	A	Division 1	2–1
1952	Racing Club de Paris	A	Friendly	0–2
1953	Preston North End	H	Friendly	2–1

1953 Derek Tapscott joined from Barry Town for £ 2,750.

| 1955 | Aston Villa | H | Division 1 | 1–0 |

1957 Ian Allison was born in Stevenage, Hertfordshire.

| 1960 | West Bromwich Albion | H | Division 1 | 1–0 |
| 1966 | Leicester City | H | Division 1 | 2–4 |

George Graham's Arsenal debut.

1966 Bob McNab signed from Huddersfield Town for £50,000.

1969 Geoff Barnett, goalkeeper, joined from Everton in a £35,000 deal to become the understudy to Bob Wilson.

1969	Everton	A	League Cup 3rd round replay	0–1
1977	West Ham United	H	Division 1	3–0
1983	Queen's Park Rangers	A	Division 1	0–2
1988	West Ham United	A	Division 1	4–1
1994	Crystal Palace	H	Premier League	1–2

OCTOBER 2ND

1897	Luton Town	A	Division 2	2–0
1899	Aston Villa	H	Friendly	1–0
1909	Blackburn Rovers	A	Division 1	0–7
1915	Clapton Orient	H	London Combination	2–0
1920	Middlesbrough	A	Division 1	1–2
1922	Sheffield United	A	Division 1	1–2
1926	Newcastle United	H	Division 1	2–2
1937	Manchester City	H	Division 1	2–1
1943	Fulham	A	Football League – South	4–3
1946	Sparta Prague	A	Friendly	2–2
1948	Bolton Wanderers	A	Division 1	0–1
1954	Leicester City	A	Division 1	3–3
1956	Crystal Palace	H	Southern Floodlight Challenge Cup	4–0

1957	Aston Villa	H	Division 1	4–0
1962	Barnet	A	75th Anniversary Match	5–2
1963	Everton	A	Division 1	1–2
1965	Newcastle United	A	Division 1	1–0
1971	Southampton	A	Division 1	1–0
1973	Tranmere Rovers	H	League Cup 2nd round	0–1
1974	Reading	A	Fred May Testimonial	2–0

First senior game for David O'Leary, Trevor Ross and Wilf Rostron.

1976	Queen's Park Rangers	H	Division 1	3–2
1982	West Ham United	H	Division 1	2–3
1984	Saudi Arabia	A	Friendly	1–1
1991	Austria Memphis	A	European Cup 1st round 2nd leg	0–1
1993	Liverpool	A	Premier League	0–0

OCTOBER 3RD

1891	Birmingham St Georges	H	Friendly	1–5
1896	Luton Town	H	United League	2–2
1898	Reading	H	United League	2–0
1903	Manchester United	H	Division 2	4–0
1908	Middlesbrough	A	Division 1	1–1
1914	Leeds City	A	Division 2	2–2
1925	Newcastle United	A	Division 1	0–7
1931	Grimsby Town	A	Division 1	1–3
1936	Manchester United	A	Division 1	0–2

Final senior appearance of Pat Beasley. He had played 79 (19 goals) League and 10 (5 goals) FA Cup games in total.

| 1942 | Fulham | A | Football League – South | 4–3 |
| 1953 | Preston North End | H | Division 1 | 3–2 |

1958 Jackie Henderson signed from Wolverhampton Wanderers for £17,500.
John Snedden joined (as an amateur) from Bonnyvale Star Juniors.

| 1959 | Everton | H | Division 1 | 1–3 |
| 1970 | Nottingham Forest | H | Division 1 | 4–0 |

Arsenal continued their chase for the Championship with a 4–0 victory at home to Nottingham Forest. The Gunners started the day in 4th place, 3 points behind leaders Leeds United. Ray Kennedy scored his first hat-trick for the club and was now the leading Arsenal scorer. Poor defending allowed Kennedy to score in the 16, 46 and 60th minutes and an excellent goal in the last minute by George Armstrong ended the visitors' misery.

| 1972 | Rotherham United | H | League Cup 3rd round | 5–0 |

Last game for John Roberts. Primarily an understudy he managed to make 59 (4 goals) League, 12 (1 goal) FL Cup and 10 European matches.

1979	Fenerbahce	A	Cup Winners Cup 1st round 2nd leg	0–0
1981	Notts County	A	Division 1	1–2
1987	Charlton Athletic	A	Division 1	3–0
1989	Plymouth Argyle	A	Littlewoods Cup 2nd round 2nd leg	6–1
1992	Chelsea	H	Premier League	2–1
1995	Hartlepool United	H	Coca-Cola Cup 2nd round 2nd leg	5–0

OCTOBER 4TH

1890	Chiswick Park	A	Friendly	4–0
1894	Casuals	A	Friendly	8–0
1897	Kettering Town	H	United League	4–0
1902	Bristol City	A	Division 2	0–1
1913	Bury	H	Division 2	0–1
1919	Blackburn Rovers	H	Division 1	0–1
1924	Blackburn Rovers	H	Division 1	1–0
1930	Sheffield United	H	Division 1	1–1
1941	Chelsea	H	London League	3–0

1942 Terry Mancini was born in Camden Town, London.

1947	Portsmouth	H	Division 1	0–0
1952	Blackpool	H	Division 1	3–1
1955	Brentford	A	Friendly	3–2
1958	West Bromwich Albion	H	Division 1	4–3

Debut Jackie Henderson.

1961 Death of Horace Cope in Nottingham.

1969	Coventry City	H	Division 1	0–1

Geoff Barnett debut for Arsenal.

1972 Jeff Blockley was signed from Coventry City for a fee of £200,000.

1973 Wilf Rostron was given a professional contract.

1975	Manchester City	H	Division 1	2–3
1977	Liverpool	H	Division 1	0–0
1980	Leicester City	H	Division 1	1–0
1983	Plymouth Argyle	A	Milk Cup 2nd round 1st leg	1–1
1986	Everton	A	Division 1	1–0
1997	Barnsley	H	Premier League	5–0

Newly promoted Barnsley arrived at Highbury with a reputation of playing nice football but letting in lots of goals, the trend was to continue. Despite going out of the UEFA Cup a few days earlier there seemed no after-effects on the team's morale as they started brightly even though Barnsley should have scored early on. Bergkamp opened the scoring with another 'Goal of the Month' winner, when on 25 minutes he collected the ball from Winterburn before changing back to his right foot and curling another unstoppable shot wide of the keeper. Six minutes later saw another glorious Bergkamp goal as he curled one with the outside of his foot from a Vieira pass. Ray Parlour on the stroke of half-time made it 3–0 after collecting another superb pass from Bergkamp. David Platt after coming as substitute for Overmars made an immediate impression by scoring with a header from a corner. Ian Wright, not to be outdone, scored the 5th goal shortly before being substituted, a nice touch from Arsène Wenger knowing that the striker would be fit for England's World Cup game against Italy in Rome a few days later. With over a quarter of the season gone Arsenal had gained 22 points in 10 games and remained unbeaten.

OCTOBER 5TH

1889	Lyndhurst	H	FA Cup qualifying round 1	11–0
1895	Rotherham Town	H	Division 2	5–0
1896	Rushden	A	United League	3–5
1901	Chesterfield Municipal	H	Division 2	3–2
1907	Bury	H	Division 1	0–0
1912	Oldham Athletic	A	Division 1	0–0

1918	West Ham United	A	London Combination	4–1
1925	West Ham United	A	Division 1	4–0
1927	Samson Haden sold to Notts County for £1,350.			
1929	Everton	A	Division 1	1–1
	Cliff Bastin League debut for Arsenal.			
1935	Blackburn Rovers	H	Division 1	5–1
1936	Gerry Ward was born in Stepney, London.			
1940	Southend United	H	South Regional League	7–0
1946	Blackpool	A	Division 1	1–2
1953	Queen's Park Rangers	A	Friendly (Floodlight Opening)	3–1
	First game for Len Wills.			
1954	Moscow Dynamo	A	Friendly	0–5
1957	Bolton Wanderers	A	Division 1	1–0
1963	Ipswich Town	H	Division 1	6–0
1964	Frank McLintock signed from Leicester City for £80,000.			
1966	West Ham United	H	League Cup 3rd round	1–3
	Debut for Tony Woodcock.			
1968	Manchester United	A	Division 1	0–0
1974	Leeds United	A	Division 1	0–2
	Final first-team outing for Jeff Blockley; Record: 52 (1 goal) League, 7 FA Cup and 3 FL Cup games.			
1976	Blackpool	H	League Cup 3rd round 2nd replay	2–0
1982	Cardiff City	H	Milk Cup 2nd round 1st leg	2–1
1985	Aston Villa	H	Division 1	3–2
1991	Chelsea	H	Division 1	3–2
1993	Huddersfield Town	H	Coca-Cola Cup 2nd round 2nd leg	1–1
1994	Hartlepool United	H	Coca-Cola Cup 2nd round 2nd leg	2–0

OCTOBER 6TH

1888	Grove House	H	Friendly	2–0
1892	2nd Royal West Kent Regiment	H	Friendly	3–0
1894	Lincoln City	H	Division 2	5–2
1900	Blackpool	A	Division 2	1–1
	Archie Cross made his League debut.			
1906	Liverpool	H	Division 1	2–1
1917	Brentford	A	London Combination	2–2
1923	Manchester City	A	Division 1	0–1
1928	Everton	A	Division 1	2–4
1934	Stoke City	A	Division 1	2–2
1945	Swansea Town	H	Football League – South	4–1
1948	Manchester United	H	Charity Shield	4–3
1951	Preston North End	A	Division 1	0–2
1956	Manchester City	H	Division 1	7–3
1962	Tottenham Hotspur	A	Division 1	4–4
1962	Tommy Caton was born in Kirkby, Liverpool.			
1964	Nottingham Forest	H	Division 1	0–3
	Debut for Frank McLintock.			
1966	Niall Quinn was born in Dublin.			

1970	Luton Town	A	League Cup 3rd round	1–0

Arsenal were drawn away to Second Division Luton Town in the third round of the League Cup and the Gunners won 1–0 in front of a capacity crowd at Kenilworth Road. The home side took the initiative in the first half with their centre-forward Malcolm Macdonald going close to opening the scoring. Luton were also inspired by former Gunner David Court but could not break through the solid Arsenal defence after George Graham had scored what proved to be the winning goal after 26 minutes.

1971	Newcastle United	H	League Cup 3rd round	4–0
1973	Birmingham City	H	Division 1	1–0

Liam Brady, arguably one of the finest talents ever to have played for the club, was introduced as substitute and thus began his distinguished League career.

1979	Manchester City	H	Division 1	0–0
1981	Sheffield United	A	League Cup 2nd round	0–1
1984	Everton	H	Division 1	1–0
1987	Doncaster Rovers	H	Littlewoods Cup 2nd round 2nd leg	1–0
1990	Norwich City	H	Division 1	2–0

OCTOBER 7TH

1893	Casuals	H	Friendly	5–1
1899	Chesterfield	A	Division 2	1–3
1905	Wolverhampton Wanderers	A	Division 1	2–0
1908	Rest of Kent	A	Friendly	3–0

Debut of Angus McKinnon.

1909	Notts County	A	Division 1	1–5
1911	Bolton Wanderers	A	Division 1	2–2
1916	Southampton	H	London Combination	3–3
1922	West Bromwich Albion	H	Division 1	3–1
1931	West Bromwich Albion	A	Charity Shield	1–0
1933	Blackburn Rovers	A	Division 1	2–2
1939	Chelsea	A	Friendly	3–0
1944	Brighton & Hove Albion	H	Football League – South	6–3
1950	Charlton Athletic	A	Division 1	3–1
1961	Blackpool	H	Division 1	3–0
1967	Manchester United	A	Division 1	0–1
1969	West Bromwich Albion	H	Division 1	1–1
1972	Sheffield United	A	Division 1	0–1

Debut for Jeff Blockley.

1978	Aston Villa	H	Division 1	1–1
1980	Birmingham City	A	Division 1	1–3
1986	Huddersfield Town	A	Littlewoods Cup 2nd round 2nd leg	1–1
1992	Millwall	A	Coca-Cola Cup 2nd round 2nd leg	1–1

OCTOBER 8TH

1887	Grove House	H	London Senior Cup	3–1
1891	Royal Engineers Training Bttn.	H	Friendly	8–0
1892	Clapton	H	Friendly	4–1
1898	Millwall Athletic	A	United League	1–1

1904	Aston Villa	H	Division 1	1–0
1910	Bradford City	A	Division 1	0–3
1921	Sunderland	A	Division 1	0–1
1927	Portsmouth	A	Division 1	3–2
1930	Sheffield Wednesday	A	Charity Shield	2–1
1932	Derby County	H	Division 1	3–3

Final appearance of Tom Parker. Captain of the 1930 FA Cup-winning team, the club's first major trophy, and also the League Championship side of 1930–31, he played 258 (17 goals) League and 34 FA Cup games for the Gunners.

1936	'Pat' Beasley sold to Huddersfield Town for £750.			
1938	Grimsby Town	H	Division 1	2–0
1949	Everton	H	Division 1	5–2
1955	Everton	A	Division 1	1–1
1960	Leicester City	A	Division 1	1–2

Last senior match for Jimmy Bloomfield. He had played 210 (54 goals) League and 17 (2 goals) FA Cup games.

1966	Newcastle United	H	Division 1	2–0
1977	Manchester City	A	Division 1	1–2
1985	Hereford United	H	Milk Cup 2nd round 2nd leg	2–1
1991	Jimmy Carter, one-time Millwall star, was signed from Liverpool for £500,000.			
1991	Leicester City	H	Rumbellows Cup 2nd round 2nd leg	2–0
1994	Wimbledon	A	Premier League	3–1

OCTOBER 9TH

1893	Sunderland	H	Friendly	1–4
1897	Luton Town	H	Division 2	3–0
1905	West Ham United	H	Southern Professional Charity Cup	3–2
1909	Nottingham Forest	H	Division 1	0–1
1910	Jack Crayston was born in Grange-over-Sands, Lancs.			
1915	Watford	A	London Combination	0–1
1920	Bolton Wanderers	H	Division 1	0–0
1924	Clapton Orient	A	Friendly	2–2
1926	Burnley	A	Division 1	0–2
1937	Chelsea	A	Division 1	2–2
1943	Clapton Orient	A	Football League – South	1–1
1948	Burnley	H	Division 1	3–1
1954	Sheffield Wednesday	A	Division 1	2–1
1963	Stoke City	A	Division 1	2–1
1965	Fulham	H	Division 1	2–1
1968	Manchester City	A	Division 1	1–1
1971	Newcastle United	H	Division 1	4–2
1976	Tottenham Hotspur	H	Peter Simpson's Testimonial	1–2
1976	Steve Gatting's first senior appearance (as substitute).			
1979	Ipswich Town	A	Division 1	2–1
1982	Ipswich Town	A	Division 1	1–0
1984	Bristol Rovers	A	Milk Cup 2nd round 2nd leg	1–1
1988	Manchester United	Aston Villa	MCT	2–1
1990	Chester City	H	Rumbellows Cup 2nd round 2nd leg	5–0

OCTOBER 10TH

1891	Crusaders	H	Friendly	4–1
1896	Millwall Athletic	H	Friendly	1–5
1898	Luton Town	H	United League	3–2
1903	Glossop North End	A	Division 2	3–1
1904	Tottenham Hotspur	H	Southern Professional Charity Cup	1–3
1908	Manchester City	H	Division 1	3–0
1914	Clapton Orient	H	Division 2	2–1
1925	Bolton Wanderers	H	Division 1	2–3
1931	Blackpool	A	Division 1	5–1
1936	Sheffield Wednesday	H	Division 1	1–1
1942	Clapton Orient	A	Football League – South	4–1
1950	Charlie George was born in Islington, London.			
1953	Tottenham Hotspur	A	Division 1	4–1
1956	Racing Club de Paris	A	Friendly	4–3
1959	Manchester United	A	Division 1	2–4
1960	Northampton Town	A	Friendly (Floodlight Opening)	3–2
1964	Tottenham Hotspur	A	Division 1	1–3

1964 Geoff Strong played his last senior game. His record ended 125 (69 goals) League, 8 (5 goals) FA Cup and 4 (3 goals) European matches.

1966 Tony Adams was born in Romford, Essex.

1970	Newcastle United	A	Division 1	1–1

1970 St James' Park was a notoriously bad hunting ground for Arsenal and things looked bleak when Robson stooped low to head Newcastle United into a 53rd-minute lead. However, the Gunners fought back and deservedly earned a point when George Graham equalised 16 minutes later.

1981	Swansea City	A	Division 1	0–2
1987	Oxford United	H	Division 1	2–0

OCTOBER 11TH

1890	93rd Highlanders	H	Friendly	4–1
1897	Wellingborough	A	United League	3–2
1899	Southampton	A	Southern District Combination	0–3
1902	Bristol City	H	Division 2	2–1
1913	Huddersfield Town	A	Division 2	2–1
1913	Frederick Groves signed as a professional.			
1919	Everton	A	Division 1	3–2

1919 League debut for Joseph Toner.

1924	Huddersfield Town	A	Division 1	0–4
1926	Clapton Orient	A	Friendly	4–0
1930	Derby County	A	Division 1	2–4
1941	Charlton Athletic	A	London League	3–1
1947	Aston Villa	H	Division 1	1–0
1952	Sheffield Wednesday	H	Division 1	2–2
1958	Manchester United	A	Division 1	1–1
1967	Reading	H	League Cup 3rd round	1–0
1969	Stoke City	A	Division 1	0–0

1972 Jeff Blockley made his one and only appearance for England in the 1–1 draw with Yugoslavia at Wembley.

1972	Birmingham City paid £150,000 for the services of John Roberts.			
1975	Coventry City	H	Division 1	5–0
1976	John Devine signed as a professional.			
1980	Manchester United	A	Division 1	0–0
1986	Watford	H	Division 1	3–1

OCTOBER 12TH

1884	Jock Rutherford was born in Percy Main, Northumberland.			
1889	5th Northumberland Fusiliers	H	Kent Senior Cup	6–1
1893	London Caledonians	H	Friendly	10–3
1895	Burton Wanderers	H	Division 2	3–0
1896	Burton Wanderers	H	Division 2	3–0
1901	Gainsborough Trinity	A	Division 2	2–2
1903	West Ham United	H	Southern Professional Charity Cup	1–0
1907	Aston Villa	A	Division 1	1–0
1912	Chelsea	H	Division 1	0–1
1918	Tottenham Hotspur	H	London Combination	3–0
1929	Derby County	H	Division 1	1–1
1935	Chelsea	A	Division 1	1–1
1935	Don Howe was born in Wolverhampton.			
1940	Tottenham Hotspur	A	South Regional League	3–2
1946	Brentford	H	Division 1	2–2
1953	Blackpool	H	Charity Shield	3–1
1957	Tottenham Hotspur	A	Division 1	1–3
1965	Israel Select XI	A	Friendly	2–2
1968	Coventry City	H	Division 1	2–1
1974	Queen's Park Rangers	H	Division 1	2–2
1985	West Ham United	A	Division 1	0–0
1988	Hull City	H	Littlewoods Cup 2nd round 2nd leg	3–0
1996	Blackburn Rovers	A	Premier League	2–0

OCTOBER 13TH

1888	London Caledonians	H	Friendly	4–0
1894	Newton Heath	A	Division 2	3–3
1900	Stockport County	H	Division 2	2–0
1906	Bristol City	A	Division 1	3–1
1917	Crystal Palace	A	London Combination	0–2
1923	Manchester City	H	Division 1	1–2
1924	Bury	H	Division 1	0–1
1928	David Bone Nightingale Jack was signed for a (then) record fee of £10,890 from Bolton Wanderers.			
1928	West Ham United	H	Division 1	2–3
1934	Manchester City	H	Division 1	3–0
1945	Swansea Town	A	Football League – South	2–3
1951	Burnley	H	Division 1	1–0
1956	Charlton Athletic	A	Division 1	3–1
1959	Grasshoppers	H	Friendly	8–2
	First outing for John Snedden.			

1960	John McClelland signed from Glenavon for £7,000.			
1962	West Ham United	H	Division 1	1–1
1971	George Graham and Bob Wilson both made their Scottish international debuts in the 2–1 victory over Portugal at Hampden Park.			
1973	Tottenham Hotspur	A	Division 1	0–2
1979	Bolton Wanderers	A	Division 1	0–0
1984	Leicester City	A	Division 1	4–1
1990	Tottenham Hotspur	H	Graham Rix Testimonial	2–5

Final Arsenal appearance of Gus Caesar who came on as a substitute in the above game. Gus amassed 44 League, 1 FA Cup and 5 FL Cup games for the Gunners. He has since passed into Highbury legend but not for the reasons he may have wished. Best remembered for his part in the 1988 Littlewoods Cup final defeat by Luton Town but in truth his error was a carbon copy of those he had performed in previous games. We know that 'George Knows', so why did he pick Gus?

OCTOBER 14TH

1893	Ashford United	H	FA Cup qual round 1	12–0
1895	Everton	H	Friendly	0–2
1899	Gainsborough Trinity	H	Division 2	2–1
1905	Blackburn Rovers	A	Division 1	0–2
1907	Rest of Kent	A	Friendly	3–1
1911	Bradford City	H	Division 1	2–0
1916	Luton Town	H	London Combination	2–1
1922	West Bromwich Albion	A	Division 1	0–7
1925	Lincoln City	A	Friendly	0–3
1933	Newcastle United	H	Division 1	3–0
1939	Swindon Town	A	Friendly	7–0
1944	Fulham	A	Football League – South	4–4
1950	Manchester United	H	Division 1	3–0
1961	Blackburn Rovers	A	Division 1	0–0
1964	Corinthian Casuals	Crystal Palace		
			Sheriff of London Shield	7–0
1967	Sunderland	H	Division 1	2–1
1972	Ipswich Town	H	Division 1	1–0
1978	Wolverhampton Wanderers	A	Division 1	0–1
1984	Bob Wilson XI	St Albans	Friendly	4–4
1989	Manchester City	H	Division 1	4–0
1995	Leeds United	A	Premier League	3–0
1997	Birmingham City	H	Coca-Cola Cup 3rd round	4–1

Playing a side comprising almost wholly Squad players rather than first-team regulars, the Gunners went through to the next round with a victory achieved in extra time. The game saw senior competitive debuts given to Alex Manninger, Matthew Upson, Paolo Vernazza, Alberto Mendez, Jason Crowe (who was shown the red card just 33 seconds after coming on as a substitute) and Jehad Muntasser who entered the fray on 118 minutes.

Muntasser left the club mid-season to join Bristol City without making a further first-team appearance. He thus assumed Steve Brignall's long-standing mantle as the man with the shortest first-team playing career in Arsenal's history.

OCTOBER 15TH

1887	Clapham Pilgrims	H	Friendly	2–2
1892	Highland Light Infantry	H	FA Cup qualifying round 1	3–0
1894	Sunderland	H	Friendly	2–1
1898	Walsall	A	Division 2	1–4
1904	Blackburn Rovers	A	Division 1	1–1
1910	Blackburn Rovers	H	Division 1	4–1
1921	Sunderland	H	Division 1	1–2
1927	Leicester City	H	Division 1	2–2
1932	Blackburn Rovers	A	Division 1	3–2
1938	Chelsea	A	Division 1	2–4
1949	Middlesbrough	A	Division 1	1–1
1955	Newcastle United	H	Division 1	1–0
1958	Aldershot	A	Southern Floodlight Challenge Cup	3–2
1960	Aston Villa	H	Division 1	2–1
1963	Tottenham Hotspur	H	Division 1	4–4
1966	Leeds United	A	Division 1	1–3

Bob McNab's debut.

1968	Liverpool	H	League Cup 4th round	2–1

1971 Andy Cole was born in Nottingham.

1977	Queen's Park Rangers	H	Division 1	1–0
1983	Coventry City	H	Division 1	0–1
1994	Chelsea	H	Premier League	3–1

OCTOBER 16TH

1889	Crusaders	H	FA Cup qualifying round 2	5–2
1897	Newcastle United	H	Division 2	0–0
1909	Sunderland	A	Division 1	2–6
1912	Crystal Palace	A	Kent Senior Shield	0–1
1915	Millwall Athletic	H	London Combination	1–1

1919 Frederick Pagnam signed from Liverpool for £1,500.

1920	Bolton Wanderers	A	Division 1	1–1
1926	West Ham United	H	Division 1	2–2
1937	Portsmouth	H	Division 1	1–1
1943	Brentford	H	Football League – South	3–3
1948	Preston North End	A	Division 1	1–1
1954	Portsmouth	H	Division 1	0–1

1954 Wally Barnes won his 22nd and last cap for Wales in the 1–0 defeat by Scotland in Cardiff.

1956	CCA Bucharest	H	Friendly	1–1
1957	Everton	A	Division 1	2–2
1965	Blackpool	A	Division 1	3–5
1971	Chelsea	A	Division 1	2–1
1973	Barcelona	A	Friendly	0–1
1974	Manchester City	A	Division 1	1–2
1976	Stoke City	H	Division 1	2–0

The final game in John Radford's Arsenal career that had seen him make 379 (111 goals) League, 44 (15 goals) FA Cup, 34 (12 goals) FL Cup and 24 (11 goals) European appearances. He led the forward line magnificently for more than a decade during which time he picked up a European Fairs Cup medal in 1970 and was a Double winner the following season.

| 1982 | West Bromwich Albion | H | Division 1 | 2–0 |
| 1993 | Manchester City | H | Premier League | 0–0 |

OCTOBER 17TH

1891	Bootle	A	Friendly	2–2
1896	Walsall	A	Division 2	3–5
1898	Rushden	H	United League	2–0
1902	Fergus Hunt rejoined Arsenal from West Ham United.			
1903	Luton Town	H	Friendly	2–2
1908	Liverpool	A	Division 1	2–2
1914	Blackpool	H	Division 2	2–0
1925	Cardiff City	H	Division 1	5–0
1931	Bolton Wanderers	H	Division 1	1–1
1936	Charlton Athletic	A	Division 1	2–0
1936	Robert John played his 15th and last game for Wales in the 2–1 victory over England in Cardiff. He had made his debut some 13 years earlier.			
1942	Brentford	H	Football League – South	0–2
1948	Bohemians	A	Friendly	6–0
1951	Glasgow Rangers	H	Friendly	3–2
1953	Burnley	H	Division 1	2–5
1959	Preston North End	H	Division 1	0–3
1964	Burnley	H	Division 1	3–2
1970	Everton	H	Division 1	4–0

The reversed opening-day fixtures saw the Gunners entertain current Champions Everton at Highbury and a crowd of over 50,000 saw the match. Arsenal, who were in 4th place still 3 points behind Leeds United, scored in the 13th minute through Ray Kennedy and then continued to attack until the final whistle. The same player added a second goal 7 minutes later when he headed in a Pat Rice cross. Eddie Kelly slammed home the third in the 64th minute and a Peter Storey penalty completed a 4–0 win.

1972	Plymouth Argyle	A	Bill Harper Testimonial	1–1
1981	Manchester City	H	Division 1	1–0
1992	Nottingham Forest	A	Premier League	1–0

OCTOBER 18TH

1890	Old St Marks Oval	A	Friendly	4–0
1902	Glossop North End	A	Division 2	2–1
1905	Corinthians	A	Friendly	1–2
1913	Lincoln City	H	Division 2	3–0
1919	Everton	H	Division 1	1–1
1924	Aston Villa	H	Division 1	1–1
	Final senior appearance of Robert Turnbull. His record: 59 (26 goals) League and 7 (2 goals) FA Cup games.			
1930	Manchester United	A	Division 1	2–1
1933	Everton	A	Charity Shield	3–0
1941	West Ham United	H	London League	4–1
1941	Joe Lievesley died.			

| 1947 | Wolverhampton Wanderers | A | Division 1 | 1–1 |

1948 Wally Barnes made his international debut for Wales in the 1–0 defeat by England at Villa Park.

1951 Lawrie Scott transferred to Crystal Palace as player-manager.

| 1958 | Wolverhampton Wanderers | H | Division 1 | 1–1 |

1958 David Herd made his international debut in Scotland's 3–0 victory over Wales in Cardiff.

1968 Jimmy Robertson was signed from Tottenham Hotspur (in exchange for David Jenkins).

1969	Sunderland	A	Division 1	1–1
1975	Manchester United	A	Division 1	1–3
1980	Sunderland	H	Division 1	2–2
1983	Aldershot	A	Glen Johnson Testimonial	3–3

1983 Peter Nicholas returned to Crystal Palace for £150,000.

1985 Bryn Jones died in North London.

1986	Newcastle United	A	Division 1	2–1
1987	Tottenham Hotspur	A	Division 1	2–1
1989	Tottenham Hotspur	A	Division 1	1–2
1997	Crystal Palace	A	Premier League	0–0

A game that produced little in the way of chances as Palace defended and hustled at every opportunity. Bergkamp had his name taken by the totally incompetent Steve Dunn after a challenge on Hreidarsson (who had kicked and obstructed him by fair means and foul all afternoon and not been penalised). This meant Bergkamp faced a 3-match suspension which would include the important clash with Manchester United. Alberto Mendez (as substitute for Ray Parlour) made his League debut.

OCTOBER 19TH

1889	St Marks College (W. Brompton)	A	Friendly	2–1
1891	Sheffield Wednesday	H	Friendly	1–8
1895	Burton Swifts	H	Division 2	5–0
1896	Wellingborough	H	United League	2–1
1901	Middlesbrough	H	Division 2	0–3
1907	Liverpool	H	Division 1	2–1
1912	Sunderland	H	Division 1	1–3
1918	Chelsea	A	London Combination	1–4
1929	Grimsby Town	H	Division 1	4–1
1935	Portsmouth	A	Division 1	1–2
1940	Northampton Town	H	South Regional League	5–4
1946	Stoke City	H	Division 1	1–0
1957	Birmingham City	H	Division 1	1–3
1960	Norwich City	A	Friendly	2–3
1963	Aston Villa	A	Division 1	1–2
1968	West Bromwich Albion	A	Division 1	0–1
1974	Tottenham Hotspur	A	Division 1	0–2
1978	Hajduk Split	A	UEFA Cup 2nd round 1st leg	1–2
1985	Ipswich Town	H	Division 1	1–0
1991	Manchester United	A	Division 1	1–1
1996	Coventry City	H	Premier League	0–0

OCTOBER 20TH

1888	2nd Rifle Brigade	H	Friendly	1–2
1892	Sheffield United	H	Friendly	1–0
1894	Rotherham Town	A	Division 2	2–1
1900	Small Heath	A	Division 2	1–2
1906	Notts County	H	Division 1	1–0
1917	West Ham United	H	London Combination	2–2
1923	Bolton Wanderers	A	Division 1	2–1
1927	Edris Albert 'Eddie' Hapgood signed from Kettering Town for £1,000.			
1928	Newcastle United	A	Division 1	3–0
	David Jack's debut.			
1934	Tottenham Hotspur	H	Division 1	5–1

Ted Drake became the first Arsenal player to score a hat-trick against Spurs. His second-half goals were in front of over 70,500, a new record attendance for Highbury.

1945	Charlton Athletic	H	Football League – South	1–2
1951	Charlton Athletic	A	Division 1	3–1
1954	Racing Club de Paris	A	Friendly	3–1
1956	Tottenham Hotspur	H	Division 1	3–1
1958	Cliff Holton transferred to Watford for £10,000.			
1969	Sporting Lisbon	A	European Fairs Cup 2nd round 1st leg	0–0
1971	Grasshoppers	A	European Cup 2nd round 1st leg	2–0
1973	Ipswich Town	H	Division 1	1–1
1976	Aston Villa	A	Division 1	1–5
1979	Stoke City	H	Division 1	0–0
1981	Winterslag	A	UEFA Cup 2nd round 1st leg	0–1
1984	Sunderland	H	Division 1	3–2
1987	Barnet	A	Floodlight Opening	2–2
	Steve Morrow's first senior game.			
1990	Manchester United	A	Division 1	1–0

As a result of a mass brawl that took place on the field during this game, Arsenal were deducted two League points as a punishment handed out by the FA (Manchester United were deducted a single point for their part in the affair) who justified the severity of their action against the Gunners by reference to a previous incident between Arsenal and Norwich City. They did not explain, however, why action had not been taken in many other previous similar incidents.

1993	Standard Liege	H	Cup Winners Cup 2nd round 1st leg	3–0
1994	Brondby	A	Cup Winners Cup 2nd round 1st leg	2–1

OCTOBER 21ST

1893	Small Heath	A	Division 2	1–4
1899	Bolton Wanderers	A	Division 2	0–1
1901	West Ham United	H	London League Premier Division	0–1
1905	Sunderland	H	Division 1	2–0
1911	Preston North End	A	Division 1	1–0
1916	Portsmouth	A	London Combination	0–1
1922	Newcastle United	A	Division 1	1–1
1933	Leicester City	H	Division 1	2–0
1939	Charlton Athletic	H	League South 'A' Division	8–4
1944	West Ham United	H	Football League – South	0–3

1950	Aston Villa	A	Division 1	1–1
1953	Anderlecht	H	Friendly	2–3
1961	Manchester United	H	Division 1	5–1

1967 Ian Ure won his 11th and last cap for Scotland in the 1–0 defeat by Northern Ireland in Belfast.

1970	Sturm Graz	A	European Fairs Cup 2nd round 1st leg	0–1

Arsenal travelled to Austria for their second round Fairs Cup match against part-timers Sturm Graz. The Gunners had expected a comfortable passage through to the next stage but, on a bitterly cold night, were beaten 1–0 by a 49th minute goal by winger Zamut.

1972	Crystal Palace	A	Division 1	3–2
1978	Southampton	H	Division 1	1–0
1980	Norwich City	H	Division 1	3–1
1989	Everton	A	Division 1	0–3
1995	Aston Villa	H	Premier League	2–0

OCTOBER 22ND

1887	St Luke's	H	Friendly	
1892	Staffordshire Regiment	H	Friendly	1–0
1898	Burton Swifts	H	Division 2	2–1
1904	Nottingham Forest	H	Division 1	0–3
1908	Ryde	A	Friendly	2–0
1910	Nottingham Forest	A	Division 1	3–2

1920 James Paterson joined as an amateur.

1921	Huddersfield Town	A	Division 1	0–2
1927	Sheffield Wednesday	A	Division 1	1–1
1932	Liverpool	A	Division 1	3–2
1938	Preston North End	H	Division 1	1–0

1938 Reg Connor made his international debut for Wales in the 4–2 victory over England in Cardiff. Hapgood and Copping played for England.

1947 Cliff Holton joined as an amateur.

1949	Blackpool	H	Division 1	1–0

Arsène Wenger was born in Strasbourg, France.

1952	Hibernian	H	Friendly	7–1
1955	Luton Town	A	Division 1	0–0
1958	Aston Villa	A	Division 1	2–1
1960	Blackburn Rovers	A	Division 1	4–2
1963	Staevnet	H	Inter-Cities Fairs Cup 1st round 2nd leg	2–3
1966	West Bromwich Albion	H	Division 1	2–3
1975	Tottenham Hotspur	A	Cyril Knowles Testimonial	2–2
1977	Bristol City	A	Division 1	2–0
1983	Nottingham Forest	H	Division 1	4–1
1988	Queen's Park Rangers	H	Division 1	2–1

OCTOBER 23RD

1893	Roston Bourke's XI	H	Friendly	4–3
1897	Leicester Fosse	H	Division 2	0–3
1899	Portsmouth	H	Southern District Combination	0–2
1909	Everton	H	Division 1	1–0
1915	Croydon Common	A	London Combination	4–1

1920	Derby County	A	Division 1	1–1
1922	Southend United	A	Friendly	0–1
1926	Sheffield Wednesday	H	Division 1	6–2
1935	Sheffield Wednesday	H	Charity Shield	0–1
1937	Stoke City	A	Division 1	1–1
1943	Watford	H	Football League – South	4–2
1948	Everton	H	Division 1	5–0

1948 Bryn Jones scored in his 17th and last appearance for Wales in the game against Scotland in Cardiff.

1954	Aston Villa	A	Division 1	1–2

1957 Graham Rix was born in Mexborough, Yorkshire.

1965	Blackburn Rovers	H	Division 1	2–2
1967	Wolverhampton Wanderers	A	Division 1	2–3
1971	Derby County	A	Division 1	1–2
1976	Leicester City	A	Division 1	1–4
1982	Nottingham Forest	A	Division 1	0–3
1991	Benfica	A	European Cup 2nd round 1st leg	1–1
1993	Oldham Athletic	A	Premier League	0–0
1994	Coventry City	H	Premier League	2–1
1996	Stoke City	A	Coca-Cola Cup 2nd round 1st leg	1–1

OCTOBER 24TH

1891	Long Eaton Rangers	H	Friendly	3–1
1896	Gainsborough Town	A	Division 2	6–1
1898	Kettering Town	A	United League	1–2
1903	Burslem Port Vale	A	Division 2	3–2
1908	Bury	H	Division 1	4–0
1914	Derby County	A	Division 2	0–4
1925	Sheffield United	A	Division 1	0–4
1928	Corinthians	A	Friendly	4–1
1931	Leicester City	A	Division 1	2–1
1936	Grimsby Town	H	Division 1	0–0

The inauguration of the East Stand which was quite unlike any other in the country and remains a magnificent (listed) structure still today.

1942	Reading	H	Football League – South	4–1

1949 Len Wills signed as a professional.

1953	Charlton Athletic	A	Division 1	5–1

1956 Tom Whittaker died of a heart attack in a London hospital.

1959	Leicester City	A	Division 1	2–2
1964	Sheffield United	A	Division 1	0–4
1970	Coventry City	A	Division 1	3–1

The Gunners returned from their mid-week trip to Austria in the Fairs Cup to play Coventry City at Highfield Road where they ran out convincing winners by three goals to one. Ray Kennedy gave Arsenal a first-half lead and John Radford increased the lead 3 minutes after the interval. Until the 79th minute it appeared that the Gunners were heading for a comfortable victory and then Martin halved the arrears and it was left to George Graham who restored Arsenal's 2-goal advantage late in the game.

1974	Terry Mancini bought from Queen's Park Rangers for £20,000.			
1979	Magdeburg	H	Cup Winners Cup 2nd round 1st leg	2–1
1981	Ipswich Town	A	Division 1	1–2
1987	Derby County	H	Division 1	2–1
1992	Everton	H	Premier League	2–0
1995	Barnsley	A	Coca-Cola Cup 3rd round	3–0

OCTOBER 25TH

1890	St Bartholomew's Hospital	H	Friendly	1–0
1902	Manchester United	H	Division 2	0–1
1913	Blackpool	A	Division 2	1–1
1919	Bradford City	H	Division 1	1–2
	League debut Frederick Pagnam.			
1920	Tottenham Hotspur	A	London Professional Footballers Assoc Charity Fund	0–2
1924	Tottenham Hotspur	H	Division 1	1–0
	First team debut for Jimmy Brain.			
1930	West Ham United	H	Division 1	1–1
1941	Watford	A	London League	1–3
1947	Everton	H	Division 1	1–1
1952	Newcastle United	H	Division 1	3–0
1958	Blackburn Rovers	A	Division 1	2–4
1958	Mike Tiddy was transferred to Brighton and Hove Albion .			
1969	Ipswich Town	H	Division 1	0–0
1975	Middlesbrough	H	Division 1	2–1
1977	Southampton	H	League Cup 3rd round	2–0
1980	Liverpool	A	Division 1	1–1

The game marked the end of Pat Rice's playing career for Arsenal having achieved 397 (12 goals) League, 67 (1 goal) FA Cup, 36 FL Cup and 27 European appearances He was an integral part of the team that won the League and FA Cup Double in 1970–71 and captain of the side that won the 1979 FA Cup. As first-team coach in 1997–98, played another key role in achieving the double-Double, he surely emerged as one of the most influential figures in the history of the club.

1983	Plymouth Argyle	H	Milk Cup 2nd round 2nd leg	1–0
1986	Chelsea	H	Division 1	3–1
1988	Luton Town	A	Division 1	1–1
1989	Liverpool	H	Littlewoods Cup 3rd round	1–0

OCTOBER 26TH

1889	Thorpe	A	FA Cup qualifying round 3	2–2
1895	Rotherham Town	A	Division 2	0–3
1896	Luton Town	A	Friendly	1–3
1901	Bristol City	A	Division 2	3–0
1903	Leicester Fosse	H	Division 2	8–0
1907	Middlesbrough	A	Division 1	0–0
1912	Bradford City	A	Division 1	1–3
1918	Crystal Palace	A	London Combination	1–2
1929	Manchester United	A	Division 1	0–1

Last game for Harold Peel who played 47 (5 goals) League and 5 (1 goal) FA Cup matches.

1932	Corinthians	H	Friendly	9–2

1932 Alex James played his 8th and last game for Scotland in the 3–2 win over Wales in Edinburgh. He scored 3 goals in his brief international career.

1935	Preston North End	H	Division 1	2–1
1940	Brentford	A	South Regional League	3–3
1946	Chelsea	A	Division 1	1–2
1954	Maccabi Tel–Aviv	H	Friendly	4–1
1957	Chelsea	A	Division 1	0–0
1963	Nottingham Forest	H	Division 1	4–2
1965	Bournemouth & Boscombe	A	Dai Woodward Testimonial	6–2
1968	West Ham United	H	Division 1	0–0

Jimmy Robertson made his Gunners debut.

1971	Sheffield United	H	League Cup 4th round	0–0
1974	West Ham United	H	Division 1	3–0

Terry Mancini made his debut.

1976	Chelsea	H	League Cup 4th round	2–1
1982	Cardiff City	A	Milk Cup 2nd round 2nd leg	3–1
1985	Nottingham Forest	A	Division 1	2–3
1991	Notts County	H	Division 1	2–0
1993	Norwich City	H	Coca-Cola Cup 3rd round	1–1
1994	Oldham Athletic	A	Coca-Cola Cup 3rd round	0–0
1996	Leeds United	H	Premier League	3–0
1997	Aston Villa	H	Premier League	0–0

Another stalemate as Arsenal struggled to get going against a well-organised defence. Vieira had the ball in the net in the 15th minute but it was disallowed for handball for which he received a yellow card. He nearly made up for it a few minutes later when he had a shot that crashed against the post. Seaman made a stunning save to deny Joachim giving Aston Villa the lead on the half-hour as the stalemate continued. The game rambled on with both teams going close until once again the referee took centre stage when Paul Durkin sent off Petit for touching him with his fingertips as the referee ran towards him after booking Steve Bould. Arsenal slipped to 2nd place after their 3rd draw in 4 games.

OCTOBER 27TH

1888	Brixton Rangers	A	Friendly	1–3
1892	Oxford University	H	Friendly	0–4
1894	Notts County	A	Division 2	2–2
1900	Grimsby Town	H	Division 2	1–1
1902	Queen's Park Rangers	A	London League Premier Division	2–0
1906	Sheffield United	A	Division 1	2–4
1913	West Ham United	A	London Professional Footballers Assoc Charity Fund	2–3

1913 Jock Rutherford signed from Newcastle United for £800.

1917	Queen's Park Rangers	A	London Combination	0–2

1919 Tom Whittaker began his long association with the Gunners when he joined the club from the Army.

1923	Bolton Wanderers	H	Division 1	0–0
1928	Liverpool	H	Division 1	4–4
1934	Sunderland	A	Division 1	1–2
1945	Charlton Athletic	A	Football League – South	2–6
1951	Fulham	H	Division 1	4–3
1956	Everton	A	Division 1	0–4
1959	Portsmouth	H	Southern Floodlight Challenge Cup	2–1
1962	Wolverhampton Wanderers	H	Division 1	5–4
1964	Kettering Town	A	Friendly	6–2

1967 Don Howe, who had retired from the playing staff just three months earlier, was appointed as chief coach. He held this position until July 1971 when he resigned to manage West Bromwich Albion.

1973	Queen's Park Rangers	A	Division 1	0–2
1979	Bristol City	A	Division 1	1–0
1981	Sheffield United	H	League Cup 2nd round replay	2–0

Final appearance of Willie Young, the folk hero. He played 170 (11 goals) League, 28 (3 goals) FA Cup, 20 (1 goal) FL Cup and 18 (4 goals) European matches. From the worst possible start (joining from Spurs) he completely won his critics over by never giving less than 100 per cent effort and the odd flash of skill such as his goal against Wrexham in the 1977–78 FA Cup.

1984	West Ham United	A	Division 1	1–3
1987	AFC Bournemouth	H	Littlewoods Cup 3rd round	3–0
1990	Sunderland	H	Division 1	1–0

OCTOBER 28TH

1893	Liverpool	H	Division 2	0–5
1899	New Brompton	H	FA Cup qualifying round 3	1–1
1905	Birmingham	A	Division 1	1–2
1909	Barnsley	A	Friendly	2–3
1911	Manchester City	A	Division 1	3–3
1916	Millwall Athletic	H	London Combination	1–0
1922	Newcastle United	H	Division 1	1–2

Bob John's League debut.

1933	Aston Villa	A	Division 1	3–2
1936	Sunderland	A	Charity Shield	1–2
1939	Clapton Orient	A	League South 'A' Division	6–1
1944	Crystal Palace	A	Football League – South	3–4
1950	Derby County	H	Division 1	3–1
1953	Racing Club de Paris	A	Friendly	4–2
1961	Cardiff City	A	Division 1	1–1
1967	Fulham	H	Division 1	5–3
1970	Crystal Palace	A	League Cup 4th round	0–0

Selhurst Park was the venue for the Fourth round of the League Cup where Arsenal fought out a 0–0 draw with Crystal Palace to earn a replay at Highbury. England manager, Alf Ramsey, was among the 40,000 spectators who witnessed an exciting match without producing any goals.

1972	Manchester City	H	Division 1	0–0
1975	Charlton Athletic	A	Les Gore Testimonial	4–1

Graham Rix made his debut.

1978	Bristol City	A	Division 1	3–1
1986	Manchester City	H	Littlewoods Cup 3rd round	3–1
1989	Derby County	H	Division 1	1–1
1992	Derby County	A	Coca-Cola Cup 3rd round	1–1

OCTOBER 29TH

1887	Barnes	H	London Senior Cup	0–4
1891	Royal Artillery (Shoeburyness)	H	Friendly	10–0
1892	City Ramblers	H	FA Cup qualifying round 2	10–1
1894	Luton Town	H	Friendly	5–0
1898	Southampton	A	United League	1–5
1904	Sheffield Wednesday	A	Division 1	3–0
1908	Alex Wilson was born in Wishaw, Lanarkshire.			
1910	Manchester City	H	Division 1	0–1
1911	Bernard Joy was born in Fulham, London.			
1921	Huddersfield Town	H	Division 1	1–3
1927	Bolton Wanderers	H	Division 1	1–2
1932	Leicester City	H	Division 1	8–2
1938	Bolton Wanderers	A	Division 1	1–1
1949	Newcastle United	A	Division 1	3–0
1955	Charlton Athletic	H	Division 1	2–4
1960	Manchester United	H	Division 1	2–1
1965	Jimmy Magill transferred to Brighton and Hove Albion for £6,000.			
1966	Manchester United	A	Division 1	0–1
1968	Blackpool	H	League Cup 5th round	5–1
1977	Birmingham City	H	Division 1	1–1

Final game for Trevor Ross having played 58 (5 goals) League, 3 (1 goal) FA Cup and 6 (3 goals) FL Cup.

| 1983 | Aston Villa | A | Division 1 | 6–2 |

Tony Woodcock scored 5 goals in the match, all by the 48th minute, to evoke memories of Ted Drake's 7-goal performance at the same venue in 1935.

| 1988 | Coventry City | H | Division 1 | 2–0 |
| 1994 | Everton | A | Premier League | 1–1 |

OCTOBER 30TH

1893	Wolverhampton Wanderers	H	Friendly	1–0
1897	St Albans	H	FA Cup qualifying round 3	9–0
1899	Bristol City	H	Southern District Combination	3–0
1905	Oxford University	H	Friendly	3–1
1909	Manchester United	A	Division 1	0–1
1911	Chelsea	H	London Professional Footballers Assoc Charity Fund	1–0
1915	Chelsea	A	London Combination	1–3
1920	Derby County	H	Division 1	2–0

Debut of Dr James Paterson.

| 1926 | Everton | A | Division 1 | 1–3 |

1937	Middlesbrough	H	Division 1	1–2

Ray Bowden's final appearance having played 123 (42 goals) League and 13 (5 goals) FA Cup matches.

Also last match for Robert Davidson. His record: 57 (13 goals) League and 4 (2 goals) FA Cup.

Most significantly though this game marked the end of Herbie Roberts Arsenal career. He played 297 (4 goals) League and 36 (1 goal) FA Cup matches for the Gunners. Nicknamed 'the Policeman', he had been the symbol of Herbert Chapman's revolutionary brand of football in which he was employed as a stopper-centre-half.

1941	Bob 'Primrose' Wilson was born in Chesterfield, Derbyshire.			
1943	Crystal Palace	A	Football League – South	1–1
1948	Chelsea	A	Division 1	1–0
1954	Sunderland	H	Division 1	1–3
1957	Brentford	A	Southern Floodlight Challenge Cup	1–4
1965	Leicester City	A	Division 1	1–3
1971	Ipswich Town	H	Division 1	2–1
1976	Leeds United	A	Division 1	1–2
1979	Brighton & Hove Albion	A	League Cup 4th round	0–0
1982	Birmingham City	H	Division 1	0–0
1985	Manchester City	A	Milk Cup 3rd round	2–1
1990	Manchester City	A	Rumbellows Cup 3rd round	2–1
1991	Coventry City	A	Rumbellows Cup 3rd round	0–1
1993	Norwich City	H	Premier League	0–0
1995	Bolton Wanderers	A	Premier League	0–1

OCTOBER 31ST

1891	Clapton	A	Friendly	7–0
1896	Clyde	H	Friendly	2–3
1898	Brighton United	H	United League	5–2
1903	Barnsley	A	Division 2	1–2
1904	Cambridge University	H	Friendly	3–0
1908	Sheffield United	A	Division 1	1–1
1914	Lincoln City	H	Division 2	1–1
1925	Everton	H	Division 1	4–1
1931	Aston Villa	H	Division 1	1–1
1932	Racing Club de Paris	A	Friendly	5–2
1936	Liverpool	A	Division 1	1–2
1942	Crystal Palace	A	Football League – South	7–1
1953	Sheffield Wednesday	H	Division 1	4–1
1959	Birmingham City	H	Division 1	3–0
1964	Everton	H	Division 1	3–1
1970	Derby County	H	Division 1	2–0

Derby County visited 2nd place Arsenal and were defeated by two goals to nil. The match was played in blustery conditions and 9 minutes before half-time Eddie Kelly intercepted a poor back-pass by Derby's McFarland and rounded goalkeeper Green before scoring. A 64th-minute John Radford header sealed the victory for the Gunners to take them within two points of Leeds United.

1972	Sheffield United	A	League Cup 4th round	2–1
1981	Coventry City	H	Division 1	1–0

| 1984 | Oxford United | A | Milk Cup 3rd round | 2–3 |
| 1987 | Newcastle United | A | Division 1 | 1–0 |

NOVEMBER 1ST

1890	South Shore	H	Friendly	2–2
1897	Reading	H	Friendly	3–1
1899	New Brompton	A	FA Cup qual round 3, replay	0–0
1902	Manchester City	H	Division 2	1–0
1909	Tottenham Hotspur	A		
			London Professional Footballers Assoc Charity Fund	0–3
1913	Nottingham Forest	H	Division 2	3–2

League debut for Jock Rutherford.

1919	Bradford City	A	Division 1	1–1
1924	Bolton Wanderers	A	Division 1	1–4
1930	Huddersfield Town	A	Division 1	1–1
1936	Racing Club de Paris	A	Friendly	5–0
1941	Aldershot	H	London League	3–2
1947	Chelsea	A	Division 1	0–0
1948	Racing Club de Paris	A	Friendly	3–3
1949	Racing Club de Paris	A	Friendly	2–1
1952	West Bromwich Albion	A	Division 1	0–2
1955	John Matthews was born in Islington, London.			
1958	Newcastle United	H	Division 1	3–2
1960	Royal Antwerp	A	Friendly	2–2
1967	Blackburn Rovers	H	League Cup 4th round	2–1
1969	Crystal Palace	A	Division 1	5–1
1975	Newcastle United	A	Division 1	0–2
1978	Hajduk Split	H	UEFA Cup 2nd round 2nd leg	1–0
1980	Brighton & Hove Albion	H	Division 1	2–0
1982	Barnet	A	Richie Powling Testimonial	4–2
1983	Chelsea	A	Micky Droy Testimonial	1–2

Tony Adams made his first-team debut in the above friendly with his League debut coming just days later.

| 1986 | Charlton Athletic | A | Division 1 | 2–0 |
| 1997 | Derby County | A | Premier League | 0–3 |

The first defeat of the season for the Gunners but it could have been so different if Ian Wright had slotted home a 30th-minute penalty awarded after Vieira was tripped in the area. The normally dependable Wright smashed the penalty against the bar and Anelka missed the rebound with a wayward header. To add to the misery Steve Bould picked up his 5th booking of the season which meant he had to face a 3-game suspension. In the second half it was all Derby and they scored 3 goals and it could have been more. Arsenal slipped to 2nd position in the Premiership race.

NOVEMBER 2ND

1889	Unity	H	London Senior Cup	4–1
1895	Notts County	A	Division 2	4–3
1896	Kettering Town	H	United League	1–1
1901	Reading	H	Friendly	1–0
1907	Sheffield United	H	Division 1	5–1

1912	Manchester City	H	Division 1	0–4
1914	West Ham United	H		
			London Professional Footballers Assoc Charity Fund	1–0
1918	Queen's Park Rangers	H	London Combination	1–0
1928	Ray Daniel was born in Swansea.			
1929	West Ham United	H	Division 1	0–1
1935	Brentford	A	Division 1	1–2
1940	Charlton Athletic	H	South Regional League	2–2
1946	Sheffield United	H	Division 1	2–3

1946 Bernard Joy made his final League appearance. He played 86 League and 6 FA Cup games.

1957	Manchester City	H	Division 1	2–1
1963	Sheffield United	A	Division 1	2–2
1964	Dundee	A	Friendly	7–2
1974	Wolverhampton Wanderers	H	Division 1	0–0

1977 Trevor Ross was transferred to Everton for £170,000 on the same day that Alan Sunderland arrived from Wolverhampton Wanderers for a fee of £220,000.

1983 Martin Hayes upgraded to professional ranks.

1984	Manchester United	A	Division 1	2–4
1985	Manchester City	H	Division 1	1–0
1988	Liverpool	A	Littlewoods Cup 3rd round	1–1
1991	West Ham United	H	Division 1	0–1

1991 Farewell performance of Michael Thomas. He played 163 (24 goals) League, 17 (1 goal) FA Cup, 24 (5 goals) FL Cup and 2 European games. Despite his early successes (2 League Championships and a League Cup final victory) Thomas had clearly lost interest in playing for Arsenal and had been touted for a move abroad before his transfer to the Scouse. His attitude was a remarkable contrast to that of his close friend, David Rocastle, although ultimately they both peaked with Arsenal.

Whatever the circumstances of his departure, Thomas will be forgiven and held in our hearts because at Anfield in '89 . . . MICKEY DID IT!!

1992	Crystal Palace	A	Premier League	2–1

1996 David Hillier moved to Portsmouth for a fee of £250,000. There may possibly have been worse players than Hillier who have represented Arsenal but were there any with inferior qualities who also played in excess of one hundred games?

As a man in a crowd once remarked on witnessing Hillier perform in a League Cup match against Millwall at the (old) Den, 'He can't pass, can't tackle, can't head a ball. What can he do?'

1996	Wimbledon	A	Premier League	2–2

NOVEMBER 3RD

1888	Phoenix	H	London Senior Cup	3–0

1888 Arsenal's first ever game in this competition.

1894	Notts County	H	Division 2	2–1
1900	Leicester Fosse	H	Division 2	2–1
1906	Bolton Wanderers	H	Division 1	2–2
1917	Clapton Orient	H	London Combination	3–1
1923	Middlesbrough	H	Division 1	2–1
1928	Cardiff City	A	Division 1	1–1

1934	Everton	H	Division 1	2–0
1945	Fulham	A	Football League – South	2–5
1951	Middlesbrough	A	Division 1	3–0
1956	Aston Villa	H	Division 1	2–1
1962	Blackburn Rovers	A	Division 1	5–5
1963	Ian Wright was born in Woolwich.			
1971	Grasshoppers	H	European Cup 2nd round 2nd leg	3–0
1973	Liverpool	H	Division 1	0–2
1979	Brighton & Hove Albion	H	Division 1	3–0
1981	Winterslag	H	UEFA Cup 2nd round 2nd leg	2–1
1987	Chelsea	H	Division 1	3–1
1990	Coventry City	A	Division 1	2–0
1993	Standard Liege	A	Cup Winners Cup 2nd round 2nd leg	7–0

Arsenal's record victory in Europe. Even Eddie McGoldrick managed to score.

| 1994 | Brondby | H | Cup Winners Cup 2nd round 2nd leg | 2–2 |

NOVEMBER 4TH

1893	Clapton Orient	H	FA Cup qualifying round 2	6–2
1895	Royal Ordnance	H	Friendly	3–1
1899	Newton Heath	A	Division 2	0–2
1901	Tottenham Hotspur	A	London League Premier Division	0–5
1905	Everton	H	Division 1	1–2
1911	Everton	H	Division 1	0–1
1916	Watford	A	London Combination	4–2
1921	John Hardy Robson (goalkeeper) was acquired from Innerleithen.			
1922	Everton	A	Division 1	0–1

Henry White's final game. His record: 101 (40 goals) League and 8 (5 goals) FA Cup matches.

1931	Bill Dodgin was born in Wardley, Co Durham.			
1933	Portsmouth	H	Division 1	1–1
1937	Leslie Jones joined from Coventry City in exchange for R. Davidson.			
1939	Crystal Palace	H	League South 'A' Division	5–0
1944	Reading	A	Football League – South	1–3
1949	Jim Fotheringham joined as an amateur.			
1950	Wolverhampton Wanderers	A	Division 1	1–0
1959	Aberdeen	A	Friendly	2–1
1955	Stan Charlton and Vic Groves signed for a joint fee of £30,000 from Leyton Orient.			
1961	Chelsea	H	Division 1	0–3
1967	Leeds United	A	Division 1	1–3
1970	Sturm Graz	H	European Fairs Cup 2nd round 2nd leg	2–0

In the return leg of the Fairs Cup Arsenal were expected to easily overcome a 1–0 first-leg deficit against Austrian part-timers Sturm Graz. However, the match proved to be a frustrating night for the Gunners who cancelled out their visitors' first-leg advantage with a Ray Kennedy goal after only 8 minutes. Arsenal spent the rest of the match attacking in vain until they were finally awarded a penalty for handball 4 minutes into second-half injury time. Thankfully Peter Storey converted the kick to send the Gunners through to the next round 2–1 on aggregate.

| 1972 | Coventry City | H | Division 1 | 0–2 |

Last appearance of George Graham as a player. His record stood at 227 (59 goals) League, 27 (2 goals) FA Cup, 29 (9 goals) FL Cup and 25 (7 goals) European games. During his time at Highbury, George had been part of the 1971 Double winning team and picked up a European Fairs Cup Winners' medal in1970. He also appeared in the 1968 and 1969 League Cup finals and the 1972 FA Cup final.

1975	Fenerbahce	A	Friendly	2–0
1978	Ipswich Town	H	Division 1	4–1
1980	Tottenham Hotspur	A	League Cup 4th round	0–1
1989	Norwich City	H	Division 1	4–3

In a game that received notoriety for a mass brawl, David O'Leary beat George Armstrong's all-time Arsenal appearance record, when he played his 622nd game for the Gunners. He also scored a rare goal.

| 1995 | Manchester United | H | Premier League | 1–0 |

NOVEMBER 5TH

1887	Grange Institute	H	Friendly	4–0
1891	Notts County	A	Friendly	3–4
1892	Lincoln City	H	Friendly	4–0
1898	Small Heath	H	Division 2	2–0
1904	Sunderland	H	Division 1	0–0
1906	Oxford University	H	Friendly	7–1

1909 Frank Moss was born in Leyland, Lancashire.

1910	Everton	A	Division 1	0–2
1921	Birmingham	A	Division 1	1–0
1927	Blackburn Rovers	A	Division 1	1–4
1932	Wolverhampton Wanderers	A	Division 1	7–1

1932 Herbert Chapman persuaded London Electric Railway to change the name of the station Gillespie Road to Arsenal, to date the only London Underground station to be named after a football club.

1932 Vic Groves was born in Stepney, London.

1937 Ray Bowden was transferred to Newcastle United for £5,000.

| 1938 | Leeds United | H | Division 1 | 2–3 |
| 1949 | Fulham | H | Division 1 | 2–1 |

1952 Jimmy Logie made his only international appearance for Scotland in the 1–1 draw with Northern Ireland at Hampden Park.

1955	Manchester United	A	Division 1	1–1
1956	British Olympic XI	H	Friendly	3–2
1960	West Ham United	A	Division 1	0–6
1963	Birmingham City	H	Division 1	4–1
1966	Leeds United	H	Division 1	0–1
1973	Portsmouth	A	75th Anniversary Match	1–2
1977	Manchester United	A	Division 1	2–1

Alan Sunderland's Arsenal debut.

| 1983 | Sunderland | H | Division 1 | 1–2 |

Tony Adams was given his League debut in the match against Sunderland and promptly was at fault for one of the opposition's goals. Fortunately it proved to be only a temporary setback!

1987 Tom Parker died in Southampton.

NOVEMBER 6TH

1897	Walsall	A	Division 2	2–3
1899	New Brompton	Millwall	FA Cup qual round 3 2nd replay	2–2
1909	Bradford City	H	Division 1	0–1
1915	Brentford	H	London Combination	3–1
1920	Blackburn Rovers	A	Division 1	2–2
1926	Blackburn Rovers	H	Division 1	2–2
1937	Grimsby Town	A	Division 1	1–2

Debut for Leslie Jones.

1943	Chelsea	H	Football League – South	6–0
1948	Birmingham City	H	Division 1	2–0
1954	Bolton Wanderers	A	Division 1	2–2

Jim Fotheringham's first senior appearance.

1964 Stewart Robson was born in Billericay.

1965	Sheffield United	H	Division 1	6–2

1968 Bob McNab made his international debut for England in the 0–0 draw with Romania in Bucharest.

1971	Liverpool	A	Division 1	2–3
1974	Chelsea	A	John Hollins Testimonial	1–1
1976	Birmingham City	H	Division 1	4–0
1982	Luton Town	A	Division 1	2–2
1988	Nottingham Forest	A	Division 1	4–1
1991	Benfica	H	European Cup 2nd round 2nd leg	1–3
1993	Aston Villa	H	Premier League	1–2
1994	Sheffield Wednesday	H	Premier League	0–0

NOVEMBER 7TH

1891	London Caledonians	A	Friendly	4–3
1892	Fleetwood Rangers	H	Friendly	1–2
1896	Notts County	A	Division 2	4–7

1901 William Henry Gooing signed from Chesterfield.

1903	Lincoln City	H	Division 2	4–0
1908	Aston Villa	H	Division 1	0–1

1913 Hugh McDonald transferred to Fulham.

1914	Birmingham	A	Division 2	0–3
1925	Manchester City	A	Division 1	5–2

Final senior appearance John Robson. His record: 97 League and 4 FA Cup games.

1931	Newcastle United	A	Division 1	2–3
1936	Leeds United	H	Division 1	4–1
1942	Tottenham Hotspur	A	Football League – South	0–1
1951	Racing Club de Paris	A	Friendly	5–0
1953	Manchester United	A	Division 1	2–5
1955	Leeds United	A	Friendly	3–0
1959	Leeds United	A	Division 1	2–3
1964	Birmingham City	A	Division 1	3–2

1964 Geoff Strong departed for Liverpool in a £40,000 move.

1970	Blackpool	A	Division 1	1–0

Arsenal travelled to Bloomfield Road to play lowly Blackpool who were second from bottom of the League table only two points above Burnley. In a rather drab affair John

Radford scored the only goal of the game in the 71st minute by heading in a George Armstrong cross.

1979	Magdeburg	A	Cup Winners Cup 2nd round 2nd leg	2–2
1981	Aston Villa	A	Division 1	2–0
1992	Coventry City	H	Premier League	3–0

NOVEMBER 8TH

1890	Ilford	A	Friendly	3–0
1897	Blackburn Rovers	H	Friendly	3–0
1899	New Brompton	Tottenham		
			FA Cup qual round 3 3rd replay	1–1
1902	Blackpool	H	Division 2	2–1
1913	Fulham	A	Division 2	1–6

Final appearance of Matthew Thomson who played 89 (1 goal) League and 5 FA Cup games.

1919	Bolton Wanderers	H	Division 1	2–2
1924	Notts County	H	Division 1	0–1

1924 Robert Turnbull transferred to Charlton Athletic.

1927 Len Wills was born in Hackney, London.

1930	Aston Villa	H	Division 1	5–2

1932 Gordon Nutt was born in Birmingham.

1941	Millwall	A	London League	2–2
1947	Blackpool	H	Division 1	2–1
1952	Middlesbrough	H	Division 1	2–1
1958	West Ham United	A	Division 1	0–0
1969	Derby County	H	Division 1	4–0
1971	Sheffield United	A	League Cup 4th round replay	0–2
1975	Derby County	H	Division 1	0–1
1980	Leeds United	A	Division 1	5–0

1980 Lionel Smith died in Stoke Newington.

1986	West Ham United	H	Division 1	0–0

NOVEMBER 9TH

1888 Chris Buckley was born in Urmston, Manchester, Lancs.

1889	West Kent	H	Kent Senior Cup	10–1
1895	Newton Heath	H	Division 2	2–1
1896	Tottenham Hotspur	H	United League	2–1
1898	Bristol City	A	United League	2–1
1901	Stockport County	A	Division 2	0–0
1907	Chelsea	A	Division 1	1–2
1912	West Bromwich Albion	A	Division 1	1–2
1918	Millwall Athletic	A	London Combination	3–3

1925 William Harper joined from Hibernian for £4,000.

1929	Birmingham	A	Division 1	3–2
1935	Derby County	H	Division 1	1–1

1938 Les Jones scored his only international goal in his 11th and last appearance for Wales in the 3–2 defeat by Scotland in Edinburgh.

1946	Preston North End	A	Division 1	0–2

First team debut for Wally Barnes.

1954	Moscow Spartak	H	Friendly	1–2
1957	Nottingham Forest	A	Division 1	0–4
1963	West Ham United	H	Division 1	3–3
1968	Newcastle United	H	Division 1	0–0
1970	Crystal Palace	H	League Cup 4th round replay	0–2

In the 4th-round replay of the League Cup Arsenal were put out of the competition by Crystal Palace. This was the only defeat the Gunners would suffer at Highbury all season and writing was on the wall when Queen gave the visitors the lead after 16 minutes. In the second half George Graham had a shot blocked on the line by his own teammate Eddie Kelly before a bizarre incident which saw referee Norman Burtenshaw award Palace a penalty. Queen made an illegal challenge on Arsenal goalkeeper Bob Wilson and defender John Roberts took it upon himself to deal with the matter by striking the Palace forward. Bobby Tambling stepped up to score and complete a 2–0 victory.

1974	Liverpool	A	Division 1	3–1
1981	Stewart Robson signed professional terms.			
1982	Everton	A	Milk Cup 3rd round	1–1
1983	Tottenham Hotspur	A	Milk Cup 3rd round	2–1
1985	Everton	A	Division 1	1–6
1988	Liverpool	H	Littlewoods Cup 3rd round replay	0–0
1994	Oldham Athletic	H	Coca-Cola Cup 3rd round replay	2–0
1997	Manchester United	H	Premier League	3–2

The prospect of facing Manchester United without Bergkamp and only 1 win in 5 games did not phase Arsenal as they got at their opponents right from the kick-off. Nicolas Anelka scored his first goal for the club with a powerful drive from just outside the area leaving Schmeichel helpless after 10 minutes. Arsenal continued to press and it was no surprise when Vieira picked up a loose ball and hit a screamer of a shot from 20 yards from an acute angle to give the Gunners a deserved 2–0 lead. Manchester United bounced back straightaway as Sheringham headed home seemingly unmarked in the area on 34 minutes. A speculative shot 5 minutes later by the United No 10 brought an unearthly silence to Highbury. In the second half Arsenal replaced Vieira who in his wild celebrations at scoring had damaged his knee, which was to put him out for a few games, and Steve Bould came on. With a rearranged back 5 Arsenal pushed forward and David Platt having one of his best games for the club started to control midfield. Chris Wreh came on in the 80th minute for the impressive Anelka and with his first touch mis-kicked the ball from no more than 3 yards after a great run from Ian Wright. In the 83rd minute David Platt outjumped the United defence to head home from a corner setting off wild celebrations around the ground. After 14 games Arsenal had gained 27 points and were in 2nd position.

NOVEMBER 10TH

1888	Horton Kirby (South Darenth)	A	Kent Senior Cup	6–2
1894	Walsall Town Swifts	A	Division 2	1–4
1900	Newton Heath	H	Division 2	2–1
1902	Brentford	H	London League Premier Division	3–0
1906	Manchester United	A	Division 1	0–1
1917	Millwall Athletic	A	London Combination	2–2
1923	Middlesbrough	A	Division 1	0–0
1928	Sheffield United	H	Division 1	2–0
1934	Grimsby Town	A	Division 1	2–2

1945	Fulham	H	Football League – South	2–0

1948 Laurie Scott made his 17th and last appearance for England in the 1–0 victory over Wales at Villa Park.

1951	West Bromwich Albion	H	Division 1	6–3
1956	Wolverhampton Wanderers	A	Division 1	2–5
1958	Southampton	A	Friendly	1–1

Billy McCullough made his senior debut.

1959 Peter Nicholas was born in Newport, Wales.

1962	Sheffield United	H	Division 1	1–0
1973	Manchester City	A	Division 1	2–1
1979	Crystal Palace	A	Division 1	0–1
1981	Norwich City	H	League Cup 3rd round	1–0
1984	Aston Villa	H	Division 1	1–1
1990	Crystal Palace	A	Division 1	0–0
1993	Norwich City	A	Coca-Cola Cup 3rd round replay	3–0

NOVEMBER 11TH

1893	Ardwick	H	Division 2	1–0
1899	Sheffield Wednesday	H	Division 2	1–2
1905	Derby County	A	Division 1	1–5
1911	West Bromwich Albion	A	Division 1	1–1
1916	Clapton Orient	H	London Combination	4–0
1922	Everton	H	Division 1	1–2
1930	Racing Club de Paris	A	Friendly	7–2
1931	Racing Club de Paris	A	Friendly	3–2
1933	Wolverhampton Wanderers	A	Division 1	1–0
1935	Racing Club de Paris	A	Friendly	2–2
1939	Norwich City	A	League South 'A' Division	1–1
1944	Charlton Athletic	H	Football League – South	4–3
1946	Racing Club de Paris	A	Friendly	1–2
1947	Racing Club de Paris	A	Friendly	3–4
1950	Sunderland	H	Division 1	5–1
1957	Racing Club de Paris	A	Friendly	1–1

1958 John Devine was born in Dublin.

1961	Aston Villa	A	Division 1	1–3
1964	Leeds United	A	Division 1	1–3
1967	Everton	H	Division 1	2–2

1970 Gilles Grimandi was born in Gap, France.

1972	Wolverhampton Wanderers	A	Division 1	3–1
1978	Leeds United	A	Division 1	1–0
1980	Southampton	A	Division 1	1–3
1989	Millwall	A	Division 1	2–1

NOVEMBER 12TH

1887	Iona Deptford	H	Friendly	1–1
1891	Erith	H	Friendly	7–0

1892	Cambridge University	H	Friendly	6–6
1894	Roston Bourke's XI	H	Friendly	6–2
1898	Loughborough Town	A	Division 2	0–0
1904	Stoke	H	Division 1	2–1
1910	Sheffield Wednesday	H	Division 1	1–0
1921	Birmingham	H	Division 1	5–2
1927	Middlesbrough	H	Division 1	3–1
1932	Newcastle United	H	Division 1	1–0
1938	Liverpool	A	Division 1	2–2
1949	Manchester City	A	Division 1	2–0
1955	Sheffield United	H	Division 1	2–1

Debut for Vic Groves.

1956	West Ham United	A	Southern Floodlight Challenge Cup	1–1
1960	Chelsea	H	Division 1	1–4
1966	Everton	A	Division 1	0–0
1976	Al'Naser, Egypt	A	Friendly	3–1
1977	Coventry City	H	Division 1	1–1
1983	Ipswich Town	A	Division 1	0–1
1988	Newcastle United	A	Division 1	1–0

NOVEMBER 13TH

1893	Rotherham Town	H	Division 2	3–0
1897	Walsall	H	Division 2	4–0
1909	Sheffield Wednesday	A	Division 1	1–1
1915	Tottenham Hotspur	A	London Combination	3–3
1920	Blackburn Rovers	H	Division 1	2–0

Final appearance Christopher Buckley. Record: 56 (3 goals) League and 3 FA Cup games.

1926	Huddersfield Town	A	Division 1	3–3
1937	West Bromwich Albion	H	Division 1	1–1
1943	Queen's Park Rangers	H	Football League – South	5–0
1948	Middlesbrough	A	Division 1	1–0
1950	Racing Club de Paris	A	Friendly	5–1
1954	Huddersfield Town	H	Division 1	3–5
1963	Standard Liege	H	Inter-Cities Fairs Cup 2nd round 1st leg	1–1
1965	Leeds United	A	Division 1	0–2
1971	Manchester City	H	Division 1	1–2
1979	Brighton & Hove Albion	H	League Cup 4th round replay	4–0
1982	Everton	H	Division 1	1–1
1996	Stoke City	H	Coca-Cola Cup 2nd round 2nd leg	5–2

NOVEMBER 14TH

1891	Cambridge University	H	Friendly	5–1
1892	Sunderland	H	Friendly	0–4
1896	Small Heath	A	Division 2	2–5
1898	Wellingborough	A	United League	0–3
1899	New Brompton	Gravesend		
			FA Cup qual round 3 4th replay	0–1
1903	Tottenham Hotspur	H	London League Premier Division	1–1
1908	Nottingham Forest	A	Division 1	1–0

1914	Grimsby Town	H	Division 2	6–0
1925	Bury	H	Division 1	6–1

Debut for William Harper.

1928	Nottingham Forest	H	Friendly	0–1
1931	West Ham United	H	Division 1	4–1

1934 One of the most famous internationals in history took place at Highbury when England beat Italy 3–2. Seven Arsenal players, a record that still stands today, appeared for England with Copping, Male and Drake all making their debuts. Ted Drake scored one of England's goals. To complete the Arsenal connection, George Allison did the radio commentary on the game.

1936	Birmingham	A	Division 1	3–1
1942	Queen's Park Rangers	H	Football League – South	3–0
1953	Bolton Wanderers	H	Division 1	5–1
1959	West Ham United	H	Division 1	1–3
1961	Sheffield Wednesday	H	Division 1	1–0
1962	Liverpool	A	Division 1	1–2
1964	West Ham United	H	Division 1	0–3
1967	Feyenoord	A	Friendly	2–3
1970	Crystal Palace	H	Division 1	1–1

Following their mid-week League Cup exit at the hands of Crystal Palace the Gunners were given a chance for revenge in the League encounter at Highbury. Arsenal took the lead after 16 minutes through John Radford but within a minute Birchenall equalised for the visitors. Arsenal had over 75 per cent of the possession but could not turn their superiority into goals and therefore the Reds dropped a valuable point.

1972	Paris XI	A	Friendly	1–0
1987	Norwich City	A	Division 1	4–2

NOVEMBER 15TH

1890	Clapton	A	Friendly	1–2
1897	Bristol City	A	Friendly	2–4
1902	Burnley	A	Division 2	3–0
1913	Grimsby Town	A	Division 2	1–1
1919	Bolton Wanderers	A	Division 1	2–2
1924	Everton	A	Division 1	3–2

First team debut for Dan Lewis.

1930	Sheffield Wednesday	A	Division 1	2–1
1941	Clapton Orient	H	London League	5–2
1947	Blackburn Rovers	A	Division 1	1–0

1950 Leslie Compton won the first of his two caps for England in the 4–2 win over Wales at Roker Park. At the age of 38 years he was the oldest debutant to play for England, a record that is unlikely to be broken. In the same game Ray Daniel made his international debut for Wales.

1951 Lionel Smith made his international debut for England in the 4–2 win over Wales in Cardiff.

1952	Liverpool	A	Division 1	5–1
1958	Nottingham Forest	H	Division 1	3–1
1966	Cardiff City	H	Aberfan Disaster Fund	4–2
1969	Wolverhampton Wanderers	A	Division 1	0–2

1975	Birmingham City	A	Division 1	1–3
1976	Dubai National	A	Friendly	3–0
	Civil Service			
1980	West Bromwich Albion	H	Division 1	2–2
1986	Southampton	A	Division 1	4–0

NOVEMBER 16TH

1895	Liverpool	H	Division 2	0–2
1901	Newton Heath	H	Division 2	2–0
	Debut William Gooing.			
1907	Nottingham Forest	H	Division 1	3–1
1912	Everton	H	Division 1	0–0
1918	Fulham	H	London Combination	1–3
1929	Middlesbrough	H	Division 1	1–0
1935	Everton	A	Division 1	2–0
1940	Tottenham Hotspur	H	South Regional League	1–1
1946	Leeds United	H	Division 1	4–2
1948	Royal Military	A	Friendly	5–0
	Academy Sandhurst			
1952	Death of Roderick McEachrane.			
1957	Portsmouth	H	Division 1	3–2
1962	Steve Bould was born in Stoke on Trent, Staffordshire.			
1963	Chelsea	A	Division 1	1–3
1965	Brazil	H	Friendly	2–0
1968	Nottingham Forest	A	Division 1	2–0
1974	Derby County	H	Division 1	3–1
1985	Oxford United	H	Division 1	2–1
1991	Oldham Athletic	A	Division 1	1–1
1994	Steve Morrow captained Northern Ireland against Eire in the European Championship qualifier in Belfast.			
1996	Manchester United	A	Premier League	0–1

NOVEMBER 17TH

1888	St Luke's	A	Friendly	1–1
1894	Casuals	H	Friendly	4–1
1900	Glossop	A	Division 2	1–0
1902	Tottenham Hotspur	H	London League Premier Division	2–1
1906	Stoke	H	Division 1	2–1
1917	Tottenham Hotspur	H	London Combination	0–1
1923	Tottenham Hotspur	H	Division 1	1–1
1928	Bury	A	Division 1	0–1
1934	Aston Villa	H	Division 1	1–2
1945	Plymouth Argyle	H	Football League – South	3–0
1951	Newcastle United	A	Division 1	0–2
1956	Bolton Wanderers	H	Division 1	3–0
1961	Eddie Clamp signed from Wolverhampton Wanderers for £34,500.			
1962	Nottingham Forest	A	Division 1	0–3
1969	Bobby Gould scored both goals in the 2–0 victory at Wimbledon to win the London Challenge Cup, the last time the club won the trophy.			

1973	Chelsea	H	Division 1	0–0
1979	Everton	H	Division 1	2–0
1980	Pat Rice was transferred to Watford for £8,000.			
1984	Queen's Park Rangers	H	Division 1	1–0
1987	Stoke City	H	Littlewoods Cup 4th round	3–0
1990	Southampton	H	Division 1	4–0

1993 Ian Wright scored 4 goals for England in the 7–1 victory in the World Cup qualifier in Bologna, after San Marino took the lead in the first minute of the match.

NOVEMBER 18TH

1893	Burton Swifts	A	Division 2	2–6
1895	Andrew Neil was born in Kilmarnock, Scotland.			
1901	Southampton	H	Friendly	0–1
1905	Sheffield Wednesday	H	Division 1	0–2
1911	Sunderland	H	Division 1	3–0
1913	The ill-fated Robert Benson joined from Sheffield United.			
1914	Nottingham Forest	A	Division 2	1–1
1916	Fulham	A	London Combination	0–2
1920	Freddie Cox was born in Reading.			
1922	Sunderland	A	Division 1	3–3
1931	Cliff Bastin made his England debut in the 3–1 victory over Wales at Anfield.			
1933	Stoke City	H	Division 1	3–0
1934	Racing Club de Paris	A	Friendly	3–0
1939	Tottenham Hotspur	H	League South 'A' Division	2–1
1944	Watford	H	Football League – South	4–0
1949	Death of James Sharp.			
1950	Liverpool	A	Division 1	3–1

1960 George Eastham was signed for £47,500 from Newcastle in one of the most prolonged transfers in history after nearly 4 months of negotiations and legal obstacles.

| 1961 | Nottingham Forest | H | Division 1 | 2–1 |

Last League game for Jackie Henderson. His record: 103 (29 goals) League and 8 FA Cup matches.

1967	Leicester City	A	Division 1	2–2
1972	Everton	H	Division 1	1–0
1978	Everton	H	Division 1	2–2
1986	Charlton Athletic	H	Littlewoods Cup 4th round	2–0
1989	Queen's Park Rangers	H	Division 1	3–0
1995	Tottenham Hotspur	A	Premier League	1–2
1997	Coventry City	H	Coca-Cola Cup 4th round	1–0

NOVEMBER 19TH

| 1887 | Tottenham Hotspur | A | Friendly | 1–2 |

The first game against Spurs played at Tottenham Marshes. The game was curtailed after 75 minutes due to Arsenal's late arrival at the venue.

1891	Woolwich District League	H	Friendly	6–1
1892	Millwall Athletic	H	FA Cup qualifying round 3	3–2
1897	Tom Parker was born in Woolsten, Hampshire.			
1898	Southampton	H	United League	2–1

1904	Derby County	A	Division 1	0–0
1906	Leyton	A	Friendly	3–1
1910	Bristol City	A	Division 1	1–0
1921	Bolton Wanderers	A	Division 1	0–1
1927	Birmingham	A	Division 1	1–1

Debut for Eddie Hapgood.

1929 Jack Kelsey was born in Llansamlet, Wales.

1932	Aston Villa	A	Division 1	3–5
1933	Racing Club de Paris	A	Friendly	1–0
1938	Leicester City	H	Division 1	0–0
1949	Charlton Athletic	H	Division 1	2–3
1955	Preston North End	A	Division 1	1–0
1958	Racing Club de Paris	A	Friendly	1–0
1960	Blackpool	A	Division 1	1–1

1960 Jimmy Bloomfield was sold to Birmingham City for £30,000. He later played for West Ham and Plymouth before managing at Orient and Leicester City.

1966	Fulham	H	Division 1	1–0
1977	Newcastle United	A	Division 1	2–1
1983	Everton	H	Division 1	2–1
1985	Southampton	H	Milk Cup 4th round	0–0
1988	Middlesbrough	H	Division 1	3–0
1994	Southampton	A	Premier League	0–1

NOVEMBER 20TH

1897	Sheppey United	H	FA Cup Qual round 4	3–0
1909	Bristol City	H	Division 1	2–2
1915	Crystal Palace	H	London Combination	2–2
1920	Huddersfield Town	A	Division 1	4–0
1926	Sunderland	H	Division 1	2–3

1931 Frank Moss was signed from Oldham Athletic for £3,000.

1937	Charlton Athletic	A	Division 1	3–0

1940 Death of John George 'Tim' Coleman.

1943	Aldershot	A	Football League – South	2–3
1948	Newcastle United	H	Division 1	0–1
1954	Manchester United	A	Division 1	1–2

Final senior outing for Jimmy Logie who had made 296 (68 goals) League and 30 (8 goals) FA Cup appearances.

Although the start of his career was delayed by hostilities, Logie nevertheless achieved remarkable success in the time that remained. He won 2 League Championship medals and appeared in the victorious 1950 FA Cup final team.

1961	Dynamo Kiev	H	Friendly	1–1
1965	West Ham United	H	Division 1	3–2
1968	Tottenham Hotspur	H	League Cup semi-final 1st leg	1–0
1971	Wolverhampton Wanderers	A	Division 1	1–5
1973	Mechelen	A	Friendly	2–2
1976	Liverpool	H	Division 1	1–1
1982	Swansea City	A	Division 1	2–1
1993	Chelsea	A	Premier League	2–0

NOVEMBER 21ST

1891	St Bartholomews Hospital	H	Friendly	9–0
1894	Marlow	A	Friendly	4–2
1895	Casuals	A	Friendly	3–0
1896	Millwall Athletic	A	Friendly	2–2
1898	Rushden	A	United League	6–0
1900	Southampton	A	Friendly	1–4
1903	Chesterfield Municipal	H	Division 2	6–0
1908	Sunderland	H	Division 1	0–4
1914	Huddersfield Town	A	Division 2	0–3

League debut for William 'Billy' Blyth.

1925	Blackburn Rovers	A	Division 1	3–2
1931	Chelsea	A	Division 1	1–2

Frank Moss made his League debut.

1936	Middlesbrough	H	Division 1	5–3
1942	Aldershot	A	Football League – South	7–4
1945	Dynamo Moscow	H	Friendly	3–4
1953	Liverpool	A	Division 1	4–1
1955	Glasgow Rangers	A	Friendly	0–2

Stan Charlton's first senior appearance (as substitute).

1959	Chelsea	A	Division 1	3–1
1962	Alan Smith was born in Birmingham.			
1964	West Bromwich Albion	A	Division 1	0–0
1967	Portsmouth	A	Gordon & Wilson joint Testimonial	0–2
1970	Ipswich Town	A	Division 1	1–0

Ipswich Town played hosts to the Gunners who dropped George Graham from the starting line-up and replaced him with Jon Sammels. In the 2nd minute of injury time George Armstrong shot weakly but Ipswich goalkeeper Sivell got both hands to the ball but dropped it over the line. The linesman signalled the goal and Arsenal achieved a valuable if rather soft victory to leapfrog Tottenham Hotspur back into second place.

1972	Norwich City	H	League Cup 5th round	0–3
1981	Nottingham Forest	A	Division 1	2–1
1987	Southampton	H	Division 1	0–1
1992	Leeds United	A	Premier League	0–3
1995	Sheffield Wednesday	H	Premier League	4–2

NOVEMBER 22ND

1890	Gainsborough Trinity	H	Friendly	2–1
1899	Alexander Main signed from Hibernian.			
1902	Doncaster Rovers	A	Division 2	1–0
1904	Cambridge University	A	Friendly	4–2
1913	Birmingham	H	Division 2	1–0

Last senior game for Roddy McEachrane. His record: 313 League and 33 FA Cup games.

1919	Notts County	H	Division 1	3–1
1924	Sunderland	H	Division 1	0–0
1924	Sidney Walter Hoar bought from Luton Town for £3,000.			
1930	Middlesbrough	H	Division 1	5–3

1941	Queen's Park Rangers	H	London League	4–1
1947	Huddersfield Town	H	Division 1	2–0
1952	Manchester City	H	Division 1	3–1
1958	Chelsea	A	Division 1	3–0

1962 Raphael Meade was born in Islington, London.
1963 James 'Fingers' Furnell signed from Liverpool for £18,000.

1969	Manchester City	H	Division 1	1–1
1975	Manchester United	H	Division 1	3–1
1977	Tottenham Hotspur	H	Pat Rice Testimonial	1–3
1978	Red Star Belgrade	A	UEFA Cup 3rd round 1st leg	0–1
1980	Everton	H	Division 1	2–1
1986	Manchester City	H	Division 1	3–0

League debut of Paul Merson.

1989	Oldham Athletic	A	Littlewoods Cup 4th round	1–3
1997	Sheffield Wednesday	A	Premier League	0–2

Ron Atkinson took charge of Wednesday for the first time and had fit again Andy Booth to call on, and he duly obliged by scoring in the 41st minute after Grimandi failed to clear the ball. The second half saw Arsenal attacking without really threatening except for a couple of shots by full-backs Dixon and Winterburn. Whittingham scored a late 2nd goal to kill off the game.

NOVEMBER 23RD

1889	Foxes	H	London Senior Cup	4–1
1891	2nd Scots Guards	H	Friendly	6–0
1892	Ipswich Town	A	Friendly	5–0
1895	Barnsley St Peters	H	Friendly	4–1
1896	Kettering Town	A	United League	1–0

The tragic final game for Joseph Powell. He had played 86 (1 goal) League and 6 (1 goal) FA Cup matches before his death six days later.

1898	Corinthians	A	Friendly	1–4
1901	Glossop North End	A	Division 2	1–0
1903	Brentford	A	London League Premier Division	1–1
1907	Manchester United	A	Division 1	2–4
1912	Sheffield Wednesday	A	Division 1	0–2
1918	Brentford	A	London Combination	1–4

1919 Jimmy Logie was born in Edinburgh.
1929 George Male joined Arsenal as an amateur.

1929	Blackburn Rovers	A	Division 1	1–1
1935	Wolverhampton Wanderers	H	Division 1	4–0

1937 Jim Furnell was born in Clitheroe, Lancashire.
1938 Johnny Macleod was born in Edinburgh, Scotland.

1940	Northampton Town	A	South Regional League	8–1
1946	Liverpool	A	Division 1	2–4
1957	Sheffield Wednesday	A	Division 1	0–2
1959	Leicester City	H	Southern Floodlight Challenge Cup	4–2
1963	Blackpool	H	Division 1	5–3

Jim Furnell's debut.

1968	Chelsea	H	Division 1	0–1

1974	Coventry City	A	Division 1	0–3
1976	Tottenham Hotspur	A	Pat Jennings Testimonial	2–3
1982	Everton	H	Milk Cup 3rd round replay	3–0
1985	West Bromwich Albion	A	Division 1	0–0

Last game for Chris Whyte who had completed 90 (8 goals) League, 5 FA Cup, 14 FL Cup and 4 European appearances.

Joined Crystal Palace on loan with a view to a permanent move for £80,000. The purpose of the temporary deal was to enable the buyers to find a way to come up with the finance for the transfer. However, whilst on loan, Whyte was accused along with his girlfriend of committing a financial offence and Palace pulled out of the deal.

He was later given a free transfer and went to play in the USA.

1988	Liverpool	Aston Villa		
			Littlewoods Cup 3rd round 2nd replay	1–2
1991	Sheffield Wednesday	A	Division 1	1–1
1994	Leicester City	A	Premier League	1–2

NOVEMBER 24TH

1888	Dulwich	H	London Senior Cup	4–2
1892	Norfolk County	A	Friendly	4–1
1894	Newcastle United	A	Division 2	4–2
1895	Billy Milne was born in Buckie, Banffshire, Scotland.			
1900	Middlesbrough	H	Division 2	1–0
1906	Blackburn Rovers	A	Division 1	3–2
1917	Chelsea	A	London Combination	3–4
1923	Tottenham Hotspur	A	Division 1	0–3
1928	Aston Villa	H	Division 1	2–5
1934	Chelsea	A	Division 1	5–2
1945	Plymouth Argyle	A	Football League – South	4–0
1951	Bolton Wanderers	H	Division 1	4–2
1956	Leeds United	A	Division 1	3–3
1962	Ipswich Town	H	Division 1	3–1
1971	Tottenham Hotspur	A	Division 1	1–1
1973	West Ham United	A	Division 1	3–1
1979	Liverpool	H	Division 1	0–0
1990	Queen's Park Rangers	A	Division 1	3–1
1993	West Ham United	A	Premier League	0–0
1996	Tottenham Hotspur	H	Premier League	3–1

NOVEMBER 25TH

1893	Millwall Athletic	H	FA Cup qualifying round 3	2–0
1899	Small Heath	H	Division 2	3–0
1905	Nottingham Forest	A	Division 1	1–3
1909	Shorncliffe Garrison & District	A	Friendly	5–2
1911	Blackburn Rovers	A	Division 1	0–4
1916	West Ham United	H	London Combination	0–2
1922	Sunderland	H	Division 1	2–3

Final senior game for Arthur Hutchins who played 104 (1 goal) League and 4 FA Cup matches.

1933	Huddersfield Town	A	Division 1	1–0
1939	Millwall	A	League South 'A' Division	3–3
1944	Chelsea	A	Football League – South	1–2
1950	Fulham	H	Division 1	5–1
1951	Willie Young was born in Edinburgh, Scotland.			
1961	Wolverhampton Wanderers	A	Division 1	3–2
1967	West Ham United	H	Division 1	0–0
1972	Derby County	A	Division 1	0–5
1978	Coventry City	A	Division 1	1–1
1980	Glasgow Celtic	H	Sammy Nelson's Testimonial	0–0
	Raphael Meade and Chris Whyte made their first-team debuts.			
1984	Sheffield Wednesday	A	Division 1	1–2

NOVEMBER 26TH

1887	Millwall Rovers	A	Friendly	0–3
1892	Clapton	A	Friendly	5–0
1898	Grimsby Town	A	Division 2	0–1
1910	Newcastle United	H	Division 1	1–2
1921	Bolton Wanderers	H	Division 1	0–0
1932	Middlesbrough	H	Division 1	4–2
1938	Middlesbrough	A	Division 1	1–1
1949	Aston Villa	A	Division 1	1–1
1955	Burnley	H	Division 1	0–1

Doug Lishman made his last senior appearance. He played 226 (125 goals) League and 17 (10 goals) FA Cup matches.
He collected a League Championship winners medal for the 1952–53 season.

1958	Juventus	H	Friendly	3–1

1958 Danny Clapton made his only international appearance for England in the 2–2 draw with Wales at Villa Park.

1960	Everton	H	Division 1	3–2
1966	Nottingham Forest	A	Division 1	1–2
1969	Sporting Lisbon	H	European Fairs Cup 2nd round 2nd leg	3–0
1977	Derby County	H	Division 1	1–3
1983	Leicester City	A	Division 1	0–3

The end of the Chapman era. Lee, not Herbert.
Lee Chapman played 28 senior games for Arsenal in all competitions and scored 6 goals.

1985	Southampton	A	Milk Cup 4th round replay	3–1
1988	Derby County	A	Division 1	1–2
1989	Liverpool	A	Division 1	1–2
1994	Manchester United	H	Premier League	0–0

Jimmy Carter's last first-team outing. He was released on a free transfer at the end of the season and joined Portsmouth.

1995	Blackburn Rovers	H	Premier League	0–0

NOVEMBER 27TH

1897	Blackpool	H	Division 2	2–1
1909	Bury	A	Division 1	2–1
1915	Queen's Park Rangers	A	London Combination	1–1

1920	Huddersfield Town	H	Division 1	2–0
1926	West Bromwich Albion	A	Division 1	3–1
1929	Middlesbrough	H	Division 1	1–2
1937	Leeds United	H	Division 1	4–1
1938	Racing Club de Paris	A	Friendly	1–1
1943	Charlton Athletic	H	Football League – South	6–2
1948	Portsmouth	A	Division 1	1–4
1954	Wolverhampton Wanderers	H	Division 1	1–1
1962	Hitchin Town	A	Friendly (Floodlight Opening)	2–1
1971	Crystal Palace	H	Division 1	2–1

1972 Henry Albert White died in Barrow Gurney, Somerset.

1976	Coventry City	A	Division 1	2–1
1982	Watford	H	Division 1	2–4
1984	Australia	H	Friendly	3–2

Martin Hayes made his first-team debut.

1993	Newcastle United	H	Premier League	2–1
1996	Liverpool	A	Coca-Cola Cup 3rd round	2–4

NOVEMBER 28TH

1891	Canadians	H	Friendly	1–1

1895 Sidney Hoar was born in Leagrave, near Luton, Beds.

1896	Grimsby Town	H	Division 2	4–2
1898	Chatham	A	Friendly	1–3
1903	Bolton Wanderers	A	Division 2	1–2
1908	Chelsea	A	Division 1	2–1
1914	Bristol City	H	Division 2	3–0
1925	Sunderland	H	Division 1	2–0

1927 Alf Baker made his only international appearance for England in the 2–1 defeat by Wales at Turf Moor, Burnley.

1931	Liverpool	H	Division 1	6–0
1934	Manchester City	H	Charity Shield	4–0
1936	West Bromwich Albion	A	Division 1	4–2
1937	Racing Club de Paris	A	Friendly	2–0
1942	Charlton Athletic	H	Football League – South	3–0

1951 Arthur Milton made his only appearance for England in the 2–2 draw with Austria at Wembley.

1953	Newcastle United	H	Division 1	2–2

1956 John Barnwell, previously on amateur forms, became a professional.

1959	West Bromwich Albion	H	Division 1	2–4

1962 The Gunners beat Ford United 12–0 in the FA Youth Cup, the highest score Arsenal have recorded in the competition.

1964	Manchester United	H	Division 1	2–3

Last outing for John Snedden who finished with a record of 83 League, 10 FA Cup and 1 European appearances.

1970	Liverpool	H	Division 1	2–0

Arsenal continued to attack at home against Liverpool but it was substitute George Graham, coming on for Eddie Kelly in 65th minute, who changed the game. Five minutes after entering the fray Graham played a one-two with Jon Sammels to hammer an unstoppable volley past Ray Clemence. John Radford sealed a 2–0 victory 10 minutes later when he finished off a move that was started by Graham.

1981	Everton	H	Division 1	1–0
1987	Watford	A	Division 1	0–2
1990	Manchester United	H	Rumbellows Cup 4th round	2–6
1992	Manchester United	H	Premier League	0–1

NOVEMBER 29TH

1893 James Boyle arrived from Celtic.

1896 Joseph Powell died in Plumstead just six days after his final game for the Gunners in which he broke his arm (which was later amputated) and caught a fatal dose of tetanus and blood poisoning.

| 1899 | Eastbourne | A | Friendly | 2–1 |

Debut of Alexander Main.

| 1902 | Lincoln City | H | Division 2 | 2–1 |
| 1913 | Bristol City | A | Division 2 | 1–1 |

First senior appearance of Robert Benson.

| 1919 | Notts County | A | Division 1 | 2–2 |
| 1924 | Cardiff City | A | Division 1 | 1–1 |

Debut for Sidney Hoar.

| 1930 | Chelsea | A | Division 1 | 5–1 |
| 1941 | Reading | H | London League | 3–1 |

1946 Joe Mercer joined from Everton for £7,000.

1947	Derby County	A	Division 1	0–1
1952	Stoke City	A	Division 1	1–1
1958	Blackpool	H	Division 1	1–4

1967 Colin Addison was sold to Sheffield United for £40,000.

1967	Burnley	A	League Cup 5th round	3–3
1969	Liverpool	A	Division 1	1–0
1975	West Ham United	A	Division 1	0–1
1977	Hull City	H	League Cup 4th round	5–1
1980	Aston Villa	A	Division 1	1–1
1983	Walsall	H	Milk Cup 4th round	1–2

Ian Allinson made his first-team debut in the game that sealed the fate of manager Terry Neill and saw the end of Alan Sunderland's Highbury career. Later released on a free transfer to Ipswich Town, it emerged that following a training-ground altercation with skipper Kenny Sansom the pair had spent the following year neither talking to nor passing to each other!

For allowing this ludicrous situation to develop and then fester, let alone his awful track record in the transfer market, Terry Neill thoroughly deserved to be sacked.

Sunderland's high point was scoring the winning goal against Manchester United in the 1979 FA Cup final. His record finished: 206 (55 goals) League, 34 (16 goals) FA Cup, 26 (13 goals) FL Cup and 14 (7 goals) European appearances.

| 1986 | Aston Villa | A | Division 1 | 4–0 |
| 1995 | Sheffield Wednesday | H | Coca-Cola Cup 4th round | 2–1 |

NOVEMBER 30TH

| 1889 | Great Marlow | A | Friendly | 0–2 |
| 1891 | Sheffield Wednesday | A | Friendly | 1–5 |

1893	London Caledonians	A	Friendly	1–1

James Boyle made his debut.

1895	Newton Heath	A	Division 2	1–5
1896	Wellingborough	A	United League	1–4
1901	Doncaster Rovers	H	Division 2	1–0
1903	The Army	H	Friendly	4–0
1907	Blackburn Rovers	H	Division 1	2–0

1910 Thomas Winship joined from Wallsend Park Villa.

1912	Blackburn Rovers	H	Division 1	0–1

Final match for Alf Common. Played 77 (23 goals) League and 3 FA Cup games.

1918	West Ham United	H	London Combination	0–2
1929	Newcastle United	H	Division 1	0–1
1932	Racing Club de Paris	H	Friendly	3–0
1935	Huddersfield Town	A	Division 1	0–0
1940	Crystal Palace	H	South Regional League	2–2

1944 George Graham was born in Bargeddie, Scotland.

1946	Bolton Wanderers	H	Division 1	2–2

Arsenal debut for Joe Mercer.

1957	Newcastle United	H	Division 1	2–3
1963	Blackburn Rovers	A	Division 1	1–4
1965	Moscow Dynamo	H	Friendly	3–0
1968	Burnley	A	Division 1	1–0
1974	Middlesbrough	H	Division 1	2–0
1982	Huddersfield Town	H	Milk Cup 4th round	1–0

1983 Tommy Caton bought from Manchester City for £500,000.
Niall Quinn joined straight from school.

1985	Birmingham City	H	Division 1	0–0
1993	Aston Villa	H	Coca-Cola Cup 4th round	0–1
1994	Sheffield Wednesday	H	Coca-Cola Cup 4th round	2–0

Vince Bartram was introduced as substitute goalkeeper and kept a clean sheet in his first senior appearance.

1996	Newcastle United	A	Premier League	2–1
1997	Liverpool	H	Premier League	0–1

Despite the return of Bergkamp Arsenal once again failed to produce a winning display despite a promising start which saw good efforts from Hughes and Adams. Michael Owen showed his great pace on a couple of occasions and went very close producing an excellent save from Seaman. In the 54th minute Steve McManaman volleyed an unstoppable shot into the far corner giving Seaman no chance and the visitors had the lead which they were to hang on to. Arsenal slipped to 5th position and Arsène Wenger said in his post match interview he thought it unlikely that Manchester United could be stopped in the title race!

DECEMBER 1ST

1888	Phoenix (Leyton)	A	Friendly	0–0
1890	Cambridge University	H	Friendly	5–1
1894	Stoke	H	Friendly	3–1
1900	Burnley	A	Division 2	0–3
1902	Tottenham Hotspur	A	London League Premier Division	0–1
1906	Sunderland	H	Division 1	0–1

1917	Brentford	H	London Combination	4–1
1923	Blackburn Rovers	H	Division 1	2–2
1928	Leicester City	A	Division 1	1–1
1934	Wolverhampton Wanderers	H	Division 1	7–0
1945	Portsmouth	A	Football League – South	1–1
1951	Stoke City	A	Division 1	1–2
1956	Sunderland	H	Division 1	1–1
1962	Manchester City	A	Division 1	4–2
1973	Coventry City	H	Division 1	2–2
1976	Queen's Park Rangers	A	League Cup 5th round	1–2
1979	Nottingham Forest	A	Division 1	1–1
1981	Liverpool	H	League Cup 4th round	0–0
1984	Luton Town	H	Division 1	3–1

1985 Paul Merson signed his first professional contract.

1991	Tottenham Hotspur	H	Division 1	2–0
1992	Derby County	H	Coca-Cola Cup 3rd round replay	2–1

DECEMBER 2ND

1893	West Bromwich Albion	H	Friendly	5–0
1899	New Brighton Tower	A	Division 2	2–0
1905	Manchester City	H	Division 1	2–0
1911	Sheffield Wednesday	H	Division 1	0–2
1916	Tottenham Hotspur	A	London Combination	1–4
1922	Birmingham	A	Division 1	2–3

Frank Bradshaw's final senior match, he had played 132 (14 goals) League and 10 FA Cup games for the reds.
League debut for Andrew Kennedy.

1933	Liverpool	H	Division 1	2–1

1936 Ted Drake scored a hat-trick for England in the famous 6–2 victory over Hungary at Highbury. Ed Bowden won his 6th and last cap for England in the same game.

1939	West Ham United	H	League South 'A' Division	3–0
1944	Luton Town	H	Football League – South	9–3
1950	Bolton Wanderers	A	Division 1	0–3
1961	West Ham United	H	Division 1	2–2
1964	Exeter City	A	Friendly (Floodlight Opening)	4–1
1967	Burnley	A	Division 1	0–1
1970	Beveren–Waas	H	European Fairs Cup 3rd round 1st leg	4–0

Arsenal were drawn against Belgium side SK Beveren-Waas in the 3rd round of the Fairs Cup and the first leg was staged at Highbury. The Beveren players were given the incentive of £250 per man if they were to win but this became irrelevant as the Gunners won 4–0. George Graham started the match in place of Eddie Kelly and opened the scoring in the 11th when he stooped to head home a corner by George Armstrong. A minute earlier Peter Storey missed a penalty having his shot saved after Jon Sammels had been brought down. In the 30th minute Ray Kennedy increased the lead by heading in a Bob McNab cross. Jon Sammels scored Arsenal's third with a left-foot drive in the 55th minute and Kennedy scored his second with a lob 20 minutes from time to complete the victory.

1972	Leeds United	H	Division 1	2–1

1975	Liverpool	A	Division 1	2–2
1978	Liverpool	H	Division 1	1–0
1990	Liverpool	H	Division 1	3–0
1995	Aston Villa	A	Premier League	1–1

DECEMBER 3RD

1887	Grange Park	H	Friendly	
1891	Canadians	H	Friendly	4–0
1892	West Bromwich Albion	H	Friendly	2–4
1894	St Bernard's	H	Friendly	1–2
1898	Newton Heath	H	Division 2	5–1
1904	Small Heath	A	Division 1	1–2
1906	Cambridge University	A	Friendly	3–1
1910	Tottenham Hotspur	A	Division 1	1–3
1921	Blackburn Rovers	A	Division 1	1–0
1927	Huddersfield Town	A	Division 1	1–2
1932	Portsmouth	A	Division 1	3–1
1938	Birmingham	H	Division 1	3–1
1949	Wolverhampton Wanderers	H	Division 1	1–1
1955	Birmingham City	A	Division 1	0–4
1960	Wolverhampton Wanderers	A	Division 1	3–5
1966	Burnley	H	Division 1	0–0
1977	Middlesbrough	A	Division 1	1–0
1983	West Bromwich Albion	H	Division 1	0–1

Tommy Caton's first game for the club.

| 1989 | Manchester United | H | Division 1 | 1–0 |
| 1994 | Nottingham Forest | A | Premier League | 2–2 |

DECEMBER 4TH

1897	Leicester Fosse	A	Division 2	1–2
1909	Tottenham Hotspur	H	Division 1	1–0
1914	George Swindin was born in Campsall, Yorkshire.			
1915	Fulham	H	London Combination	2–1
1920	Chelsea	A	Division 1	2–1
1924	Alexander Graham sold to Brentford for £450.			
1926	Bury	H	Division 1	1–0
1933	Vienna XI	H	Friendly	4–2
1937	Birmingham	A	Division 1	2–1
1943	Southampton	A	Football League – South	2–1
1948	Manchester City	H	Division 1	1–1
1952	Bill Dodgin joined from Fulham for £4,000 (plus junior player).			
1954	Blackpool	A	Division 1	2–2
1956	West Ham United	H	Southern Floodlight Challenge Cup	3–2

John Barnwell played his first senior game.

1959	Terry Neill was signed from Bangor City for £2,500.			
1962	Kevin Richardson was born in Newcastle, Durham.			
1965	Aston Villa	H	Division 1	3–3

1968	Tottenham Hotspur	A	League Cup semi-final 2nd leg	1–1

The Gunners won 2–1 on aggregate.

1971	West Ham United	A	Division 1	0–0
1973	Wolverhampton Wanderers	H	Division 1	2–2
1976	Newcastle United	H	Division 1	5–3

Alan Ball made his final senior appearance for Arsenal.

1979	Swindon Town	H	League Cup 5th round	1–1
1982	Manchester City	A	Division 1	1–2
1985	Trinidad & Tobago	A	Jaliter Trophy	3–0
1988	Liverpool	H	Division 1	1–1
1991	Cliff Bastin died in Exeter.			
1993	Coventry City	A	Premier League	0–1
1996	Southampton	H	Premier League	3–1

DECEMBER 5TH

1891	Lincoln City	H	Friendly	3–1
1896	Lincoln City	A	Division 2	3–2
1903	Burnley	H	Division 2	1–0
1904	Parisian XI	H	Friendly	26–1
1908	Blackburn Rovers	H	Division 1	0–1
1914	Bury	A	Division 2	1–3
1925	Huddersfield Town	A	Division 1	2–2
1931	Sheffield Wednesday	A	Division 1	3–1
1936	Manchester City	H	Division 1	1–3
1942	Southampton	A	Football League – South	3–1
1953	Middlesbrough	A	Division 1	4–3
1959	Newcastle United	A	Division 1	1–4
1964	Fulham	A	Division 1	4–3
1967	Burnley	H	League Cup 5th round replay	2–1
1970	Manchester City	A	Division 1	2–0

For the first 75 minutes at Maine Road Manchester City had pinned Arsenal back but an error by City keeper Corrigan allowed George Armstrong to lob the ball into the goal to give the Gunners an undeserved lead. The game ended with John Radford scoring in injury time to ensure a 2–0 victory.

1981	West Ham United	A	Division 1	2–1

Debut for the 17-year-old Stewart Robson.

1987	Sheffield Wednesday	H	Division 1	3–1
1992	Southampton	A	Premier League	0–2

DECEMBER 6TH

1890	Casuals	H	Friendly	0–0
1902	Small Heath	A	Division 2	0–2
1913	Leeds City	H	Division 2	1–0

Herbert Chapman's first managerial game at Highbury, albeit in charge of the opposition!

1919	Chelsea	H	Division 1	1–1
1924	Preston North End	H	Division 1	4–0
1930	Grimsby Town	H	Division 1	1–0

1941	Brighton & Hove Albion	A	London League	3–2
1947	Manchester City	H	Division 1	1–1
1955	Tony Woodcock was born in Nottingham.			
1958	Portsmouth	A	Division 1	1–0
1969	Southampton	H	Division 1	2–2
1975	Leeds United	H	Division 1	1–2
1978	Red Star Belgrade	H	UEFA Cup 3rd round 2nd leg	1–1
1980	Wolverhampton Wanderers	H	Division 1	1–1
1986	Queen's Park Rangers	H	Division 1	3–1
1993	Tottenham Hotspur	H	Premier League	1–1
1997	Newcastle United	A	Premier League	1–0

Arsenal travelled to Newcastle with pressure mounting and questions being asked about Ian Wright who had struggled to find his goalscoring touch. Being at their most dangerous with their backs to the wall the Gunners produced a magnificent display, and it was no surprise when Ian Wright broke the deadlock after 35 minutes after some fine work from the two Dutchmen set him up. Despite a lot of possession in the second half Newcastle fail to break the defence with Keown and Adams outstanding, though all 11 must take credit. It was amazingly the first game of the season in which there had been no substitutes for the Gunners. They had now played 17 games and moved back up to 4th position in the Premiership.

DECEMBER 7TH

1889	Swifts	H	FA Cup qualifying round 4	1–5
1895	Leicester Fosse	H	Division 2	1–1
1896	Aston Villa	H	Friendly	1–3
1901	Lincoln City	A	Division 2	0–0
1903	Millwall Athletic	H	London League Premier Division	1–3
1907	Bolton Wanderers	A	Division 1	1–3
1908	Chelsea	A	London Professional Footballers Assoc Charity Fund	1–0
1911	Ronnie Rooke was born in Guildford, Surrey.			
1912	Derby County	A	Division 1	1–4
	League debut for Frederick Groves.			
1918	Tottenham Hotspur	A	London Combination	0–1
1932	David Jack won his 9th and last cap for England in the 4–3 victory over Austria at Stamford Bridge. He scored 3 goals in his international career.			
1939	Ian Ure was born in Ayr, Scotland.			
1940	Charlton Athletic	A	South Regional League	0–5
1946	Middlesbrough	A	Division 1	0–2
1957	Burnley	A	Division 1	1–2
1963	Liverpool	H	Division 1	1–1
1968	Everton	H	Division 1	3–1
1974	Carlisle United	A	Division 1	1–2
1982	Aston Villa	H	Division 1	2–1
1985	Southampton	A	Division 1	0–3
1996	Derby County	H	Premier League	2–2

DECEMBER 8TH

1886	Angus McKinnon was born in Paisley, Scotland.			
1888	Old St Paul's	H	London Senior Cup	3–1
1894	Darwen	H	Division 2	4–0
1898	Thames Ironworks	A	Friendly	2–1
1900	Burslem Port Vale	H	Division 2	3–0
1906	Birmingham	A	Division 1	1–5
1917	Crystal Palace	H	London Combination	0–2
1923	Blackburn Rovers	A	Division 1	0–2

1925 John Butler made his only international appearance for England in the 4–0 win over Belgium at The Hawthorns.

1926 Herbert Roberts joined from Oswestry Town for £200.

1928	Manchester United	H	Division 1	3–1
1934	Huddersfield Town	A	Division 1	1–1
1945	Portsmouth	H	Football League – South	4–3
1949	AIK Stockholm	H	Friendly	8–0
1951	Manchester United	H	Division 1	1–3
1953	Glasgow Rangers	A	Friendly	2–1
1956	Luton Town	A	Division 1	2–1
1958	Brentford	A	Southern Floodlight Challenge Cup	2–1
1962	Blackpool	H	Division 1	2–0
1973	Derby County	A	Division 1	1–1
1979	Coventry City	H	Division 1	3–1
1981	Liverpool	A	League Cup 4th round replay	0–3
1984	Southampton	A	Division 1	0–1
1990	Luton Town	A	Division 1	1–1
1991	Nottingham Forest	A	Division 1	2–3

Jimmy Carter made his senior debut coming on as substitute.

DECEMBER 9TH

1893	Northwich Victoria	A	Division 2	2–2

First League game for James Boyle.

1895	Sunderland	H	Friendly	1–2
1899	Southampton	H	Friendly	1–1
1905	Bury	A	Division 1	0–2
1911	Bury	A	Division 1	1–3
1916	Crystal Palace	H	London Combination	1–2
1922	Birmingham	H	Division 1	1–0

John Mackie made his League debut.

1933	Sunderland	A	Division 1	0–3
1935	Middlesbrough	H	Division 1	2–0
1939	Watford	A	League South 'A' Division	3–1
1944	Tottenham Hotspur	H	Football League – South	2–3
1950	Blackpool	H	Division 1	4–4
1961	Sheffield United	A	Division 1	1–2
1961	Paul Davis was born in Dulwich, London.			
1967	Sheffield Wednesday	H	Division 1	1–0

1971 Arsenal were due to play Burnley at Highbury in a League match that was postponed.

1972	Tottenham Hotspur	A	Division 1	2–1

1975	Feyenoord	H	Peter Storey's Testimonial	2–1
1978	Norwich City	A	Division 1	0–0
1981	Willie Young was sold to Nottingham Forest for £175,000.			
1985	Colchester United	A	Mike Walker Testimonial	2–1
	First senior outings given to Niall Quinn and Michael Thomas.			
1989	Coventry City	A	Division 1	1–0
1995	Southampton	A	Premier League	0–0

DECEMBER 10TH

1887	Brixton Rangers	H	Friendly	1–2
1891	2nd Royal West Kent Regiment	H	Friendly	1–2
1892	Clapton	H	FA Cup qualifying round 4	3–0
1898	New Brighton Tower	A	Division 2	1–3
1904	Manchester City	H	Division 1	1–0
1906	Millwall Athletic	H	Southern Professional Charity Cup	1–2
1910	Middlesbrough	H	Division 1	0–2
1921	Blackburn Rovers	H	Division 1	1–1
1926	Horace Cope bought for £3,125 from Notts County.			
1927	Newcastle United	H	Division 1	4–1
1932	Chelsea	H	Division 1	4–1
	The West Stand was officially opened by HRH the Prince of Wales. It cost £45,000 to build.			
1938	Manchester United	A	Division 1	0–1
1949	Portsmouth	A	Division 1	1–2
1955	West Bromwich Albion	H	Division 1	2–0
1960	Bolton Wanderers	H	Division 1	5–1
	George Eastham made his first-team debut.			
1963	Everton	H	Division 1	6–0
1966	Sheffield United	A	Division 1	1–1
1977	Leeds United	H	Division 1	1–1
1983	West Ham United	A	Division 1	1–3
1988	Norwich City	A	Division 1	0–0

DECEMBER 11TH

1886	Eastern Wanderers	A	Friendly	6–0
	Played on the Isle of Dogs, this was the first game played (as Dial Square), the team containing founding member Fred Beardsley.			
1893	Preston North End	H	Friendly	1–1
1897	New Brompton	H	FA Cup qualifying round 5	4–2
1902	Dan Lewis was born in Mardy, South Wales			
1909	Preston North End	A	Division 1	4–3
1915	Clapton Orient	A	London Combination	2–0
1920	Chelsea	H	Division 1	1–1
1926	Birmingham	A	Division 1	0–0
1937	Preston North End	H	Division 1	2–0
	Last game John Milne. He achieved 49 (19 goals) League and 3 FA Cup appearances.			
1943	West Ham United	H	Football League – South	1–1
	Jack Crayston's final game. Record: 168 (16 goals) League and 16 (1 goal) FA Cup. At			

the end of the war Crayston returned to Arsenal to work on the coaching staff and became assistant manager in 1947. He was appointed manager in November 1956 on the death of Tom Whittaker.

1948	Charlton Athletic	A	Division 1	3–4
1954	Charlton Athletic	H	Division 1	3–1
1960	John Lukic was born in Chesterfield, Derbyshire.			
1963	Nigel Winterburn was born in Nuneaton, Warwickshire.			
1965	Liverpool	A	Division 1	2–4
1971	Coventry City	H	Division 1	2–0
1979	Swindon Town	A	League Cup 5th round replay	3–4

DECEMBER 12TH

1891	Chiswick Park	H	Friendly	5–1
1892	FG Armitage's XI	H	Friendly	3–1
1896	Leyton	H	FA Cup qualifying round 4	5–0
1896	Loughborough Town	A	Division 2	0–8

Arsenal's record defeat in senior competitions.

1898	Bristol City	H	United League	1–3
1899	Charlie Jones was born in Troedyrhiw, South Wales.			
1903	Bristol Rovers	A	FA Cup Sup	1–1
1908	Bradford City	A	Division 1	1–4
1914	Preston North End	H	Division 2	1–2
1921	Bolton Wanderers	H	Division 1	1–1

Reg Boreham's first senior game.

1925	West Bromwich Albion	H	Division 1	1–0
1931	Huddersfield Town	H	Division 1	1–1
1936	Portsmouth	A	Division 1	5–1
1942	Millwall	H	Football League – South	6–0
1946	Ronnie Rooke at the age of 35 was signed from Fulham in a £1,000 deal with David Nelson and Cyril Grant going to Fulham as part of the exchange.			
1953	West Bromwich Albion	H	Division 1	2–1
1959	Burnley	H	Division 1	2–4
1964	Liverpool	H	Division 1	0–0
1970	Wolverhampton Wanderers	H	Division 1	2–1

Playing at home to Wolverhampton Wanderers, Arsenal dominated the match and ran out 2–1 winners but the game was never as close as the scoreline suggests. In 22nd minute George Graham scored from a Peter Storey through ball and John Radford increased the lead a minute after the break when he converted a George Armstrong corner. Against the run of play Dougan pulled a goal back for Wolves.

1977	Qadsia	A	Friendly	1–1
1991	Mickey Thomas was sold to Liverpool for £1,500,000.			
1992	Tottenham Hotspur	A	Premier League	0–1
1993	Sheffield Wednesday	H	Premier League	1–0
1994	Manchester City	A	Premier League	2–1

DECEMBER 13TH

| 1890 | Old Westminsters | A | London Senior Cup | 4–1 |
| 1897 | Rushden | H | United League | 3–1 |

1902	Brentford	A	FA Cup Sup	1–1
1913	Clapton Orient	A	Division 2	0–1
1919	Chelsea	A	Division 1	1–3
1924	Burnley	A	Division 1	0–1
1930	Liverpool	A	Division 1	1–1
1939	Army XI	A	Friendly	1–0
1941	Brentford	H	London League	1–3
1947	Grimsby Town	A	Division 1	4–0
1952	Burnley	A	Division 1	1–1
1958	Aston Villa	H	Division 1	1–2
1960	Glasgow Rangers	A	Friendly	2–4
1969	Burnley	H	Division 1	3–2
1975	Stoke City	A	Division 1	1–2

Final game for Geoff Barnett who had his contract cancelled by mutual consent (Feb 1976) and eventually went to play for Minnesota Kicks in the USA.

1976 Alan Hudson signed from Stoke City for £200,000 whilst John Radford left the club to join West Ham United in a deal worth £80,000.

1980	Sunderland	A	Division 1	0–2
1986	Norwich City	A	Division 1	1–1
1987	Coventry City	A	Division 1	0–0
1988	Shrewsbury Town	A	Bernard McNally Testimonial	2–1

Select XI

David Hillier's first appearance in the first-team.

1997	Blackburn Rovers	H	Premier League	1–3

Possibly one of the worst performances of the season as the League title seemed to be a forlorn hope. Overmars, running on to a through ball from Petit, lobbed Tim Flowers from 25 yards out to put the Reds ahead. Nigel Winterburn almost added to his Chelsea spectacular earlier in the season, but the ball floated just by the upright. The second half was a different story. As the game got more physical it was the visitors who took control and 3 goals in the last half an hour saw Blackburn take the points. Ian Wright was booked for a late challenge and was fortunate not to be red-carded as his frustration boiled over. After the game Wright was warned by the police about his abusive behaviour towards a group of Arsenal fans who had congregated below the players changing-room window in the East Stand.

DECEMBER 14TH

1889	Gravesend	A	Kent Senior Cup	7–2
1889	St Martins Athletic	H	London Senior Cup	6–0
1895	Burton Wanderers	A	Division 2	1–4
1901	Luton Town	H	FA Cup Sup	1–1
1907	Birmingham	H	Division 1	1–1
1912	Tottenham Hotspur	H	Division 1	0–3
1918	Chelsea	H	London Combination	3–0
1922	Don Roper was born in Botley, Hampshire.			
1929	Huddersfield Town	H	Division 1	2–0
1935	Aston Villa	A	Division 1	7–1

All seven of the Gunners goals were scored by centre-forward Ted Drake, a Division One record.

1937 John Vance Milne sold to Middlesbrough for £4,000.

| 1940 | Queen's Park Rangers | H | South Regional League | 3–2 |
| 1946 | Charlton Athletic | H | Division 1 | 1–0 |

Gunners debut for Ronnie Rooke.

1957	Preston North End	H	Division 1	4–2
1963	Wolverhampton Wanderers	A	Division 1	2–2
1968	Coventry City	A	Division 1	1–0
1974	Leicester City	H	Division 1	0–0
1985	Liverpool	H	Division 1	2–0

DECEMBER 15TH

1894	Manchester City	A	Division 2	1–4
1900	Leicester Fosse	A	Division 2	0–1
1903	Bristol Rovers	H	FA Cup Sup replay	1–1
1906	Everton	H	Division 1	3–1
1917	West Ham United	A	London Combination	2–3
1923	Huddersfield Town	H	Division 1	1–3

1926 Harold Peel signed from Bradford for £1,750.

1928	Leeds United	A	Division 1	1–1
1934	Leicester City	H	Division 1	8–0
1945	Nottingham Forest	H	Football League – South	2–2
1951	Huddersfield Town	A	Division 1	3–2
1956	Cardiff City	A	Division 1	3–2
1962	Leyton Orient	H	Division 1	2–0
1973	Burnley	A	Division 1	1–2
1976	Derby County	A	Division 1	0–0
1979	West Bromwich Albion	A	Division 1	2–2
1984	West Bromwich Albion	H	Division 1	4–0
1990	Wimbledon	H	Division 1	2–2

DECEMBER 16TH

1893	2nd Scots Guards	A	FA Cup qualifying round 4	2–1
1899	Burton Swifts	H	Division 2	1–1
1905	Middlesbrough	H	Division 1	2–2

1905 William Garbutt joined from Reading.

1911	Middlesbrough	H	Division 1	3–1
1922	Huddersfield Town	H	Division 1	1–1
1929	Sheffield United	A	Division 1	1–4
1933	Chelsea	H	Division 1	2–1
1939	Southend United	H	League South 'A' Division	5–1
1944	Aldershot	A	Football League – South	3–2
1950	Burnley	H	Division 1	0–1
1961	Burnley	A	Division 1	2–0
1964	Bath City	A	Friendly (Floodlight Opening)	4–2
1967	Stoke City	A	Division 1	1–0
1970	Beveren-Waas	A	European Fairs Cup 3rd round 2nd leg	0–0

Arsenal travelled to Antwerp in Belgium for the 2nd leg of their 3rd round Fairs Cup match against SK Beveren-Waas with a 4–0 lead from the first leg. The Arsenal fans were given the opportunity of a 1-day jet trip for £12 or 2 days for £17, however the match ticket was extra. The Gunners gave a very lacklustre performance but managed to gain a 0–0 draw and go through on aggregate. At half-time manager Bertie Mee withdrew John Radford and replaced him with Charlie George who made his first appearance since his injury on the opening day of the season at Goodison Park against Everton.

1972	West Bromwich Albion	H	Division 1	2–1
1978	Derby County	H	Division 1	2–0
1989	Luton Town	H	Division 1	3–2

1991 Michael Thomas, scorer at Anfield of the 1989 Championship-winning goal, was sold to Liverpool for £1,500,000.

1995	Chelsea	H	Premier League	1–1

DECEMBER 17TH

1887	Shrewsbury Park	A	Friendly	4–0
1892	Nottingham Forest	H	Friendly	2–3
1898	Lincoln City	H	Division 2	4–2
1902	Brentford	H	FA Cup Sup replay	5–0
1904	Notts County	A	Division 1	5–1
1910	Preston North End	A	Division 1	1–4
1921	Oldham Athletic	A	Division 1	1–2
1927	Manchester United	A	Division 1	1–4
1932	Huddersfield Town	A	Division 1	1–0
1938	Stoke City	H	Division 1	4–1

1944 Jimmy Robertson was born in Glasgow.

1949	Burnley	A	Division 1	0–0
1955	Blackpool	H	Division 1	4–1
1960	Burnley	H	Division 1	2–5
1966	Sunderland	H	Division 1	2–0
1969	Rouen	A	European Fairs Cup 3rd round 1st leg	0–0
1977	Coventry City	A	Division 1	2–1
1983	Watford	H	Division 1	3–1
1988	Manchester United	H	Division 1	2–1
1994	Leeds United	H	Premier League	1–3

DECEMBER 18TH

1897	Loughborough Town	A	Division 2	3–1
1901	Luton Town	A	FA Cup Sup replay	2–0
1909	Notts County	H	Division 1	1–2
1915	Watford	H	London Combination	3–1
1920	Bradford City	A	Division 1	1–3
1926	Tottenham Hotspur	H	Division 1	2–4

1931 William Harper was transferred to Plymouth Argyle.

1937	Liverpool	A	Division 1	0–2

Final appearance of Joe Hulme. His record: 333 (107 goals) League and 39 (17 goals) FA Cup. Another of the Gunners greats, he won 3 League Championship and 2 FA Cup winners medals as well as 9 full England caps.

1943	Tottenham Hotspur	A	Football League – South	1–2
1948	Huddersfield Town	H	Division 1	3–0
1954	Newcastle United	A	Division 1	1–5

1963	Standard Liege	A	Inter-Cities Fairs Cup 2nd round 2nd leg	1–3
1969	David Hillier was born in Blackheath, Greater London.			
1971	West Bromwich Albion	H	Division 1	2–0
1976	Manchester United	H	Division 1	3–1
1982	Sunderland	A	Division 1	0–3
1993	Leeds United	A	Premier League	1–2

DECEMBER 19TH

1891	Preston North End	H	Friendly	0–3
1896	Blackpool	H	Division 2	4–2
1903	Grimsby Town	H	Division 2	5–1
1908	Manchester United	H	Division 1	0–1
1912	Alf Common sold to Preston North End for £250.			
1914	Swindon Town	H	Friendly	1–2
1925	Birmingham	A	Division 1	0–1
1931	Middlesbrough	A	Division 1	5–2
1933	Jim Fotheringham was born in Hamilton, Scotland.			
1936	Chelsea	H	Division 1	4–1
1942	Luton Town	A	Football League – South	4–0
1953	Huddersfield Town	A	Division 1	2–1
1959	Sheffield Wednesday	A	Division 1	1–5
	League debut for Jimmy Magill.			
1964	Aston Villa	A	Division 1	1–3
1970	Manchester United	A	Division 1	3–1

Arsenal went into their match against Manchester United at Old Trafford 2 points behind Leeds United with a game in hand. The match was settled within 22 first-half minutes when the Gunners scored 3 goals. The United collapse started in the 14th minute when a George Armstrong corner was headed by Ray Kennedy to John Radford who in turn headed to Frank McLintock to hook the ball into the net from close range. Another Armstrong corner 7 minutes later was headed in by George Graham and shortly afterwards Kennedy headed home a Pat Rice cross. United managed to pull a goal back just before half-time through Sartori and Arsenal coasted to a 3–1 victory.

1987	Everton	H	Division 1	1–1
1989	Glasgow Rangers	A	Zenith Data British Challenge	2–1
1992	Middlesbrough	H	Premier League	1–1

DECEMBER 20TH

1897	Southampton	H	United League	1–1
1902	Manchester City	A	Division 2	1–4
1902	William Linward joined from West Ham United.			
1913	Glossop North End	H	Division 2	2–0
1919	Sheffield Wednesday	H	Division 1	3–1
1924	Leeds United	H	Division 1	6–1
1930	Newcastle United	H	Division 1	1–2
1947	Sunderland	A	Division 1	1–1
1952	Aston Villa	H	Division 1	3–1
1958	Preston North End	H	Division 1	1–2
1969	Sheffield Wednesday	A	Division 1	1–1
1975	Burnley	H	Division 1	1–0

| 1980 | Manchester United | H | Division 1 | 2–1 |
| 1986 | Luton Town | H | Division 1 | 3–0 |

DECEMBER 21ST

1889	Ilford	A	Friendly	2–0
1895	Burton Swifts	A	Division 2	2–3
1901	Burton United	H	Division 2	0–1
1903	Bristol Rovers	Tottenham		
			FA Cup Sup 2nd replay	1–0
1907	Everton	A	Division 1	1–1
1912	Middlesbrough	A	Division 1	0–2
1918	Crystal Palace	H	London Combination	3–3
1929	Liverpool	A	Division 1	0–1
1940	Crystal Palace	A	South Regional League	3–3
1946	Grimsby Town	A	Division 1	0–0
1957	Sunderland	H	Division 1	3–0
1963	Leicester City	H	Division 1	0–1
1963	Death of Andrew Lynd Kennedy.			
1968	West Bromwich Albion	H	Division 1	2–0
1974	Stoke City	A	Division 1	2–0
1979	Norwich City	H	Division 1	1–1
1985	Manchester United	A	Division 1	1–0

Gus Caesar made his League debut.

| 1991 | Everton | H | Division 1 | 4–2 |
| 1996 | Nottingham Forest | A | Premier League | 1–2 |

Andy Linighan's final appearance. His record: 118 League, 14 FA Cup, 14 FL Cup and 9 European games in which he scored a total of 8 goals. He took a long time to settle into a role at the club and was initially regarded as a flop who could not command a first-team place and was regularly prone to error. However, despite his obvious lack of pace, Linighan did win over his critics and became a dependable deputy for Adams and Bould.

Scoring the 1993 Cup final Winner did his reputation no harm either!

DECEMBER 22ND

1900	New Brighton Tower	H	Division 2	2–1
1906	Derby County	A	Division 1	0–0
1917	Queen's Park Rangers	H	London Combination	3–0
1923	Huddersfield Town	A	Division 1	1–6
1928	Burnley	H	Division 1	3–1
1934	Derby County	A	Division 1	1–3
1945	Nottingham Forest	A	Football League – South	2–3
1951	Wolverhampton Wanderers	H	Division 1	2–2
1956	Birmingham City	H	Division 1	4–0
1962	Manchester United	A	Division 1	1–0
1971	Alan Ball joined Arsenal from Everton for £220,000.			
1973	Everton	H	Division 1	1–0
1984	Watford	H	Division 1	1–1

Last League game for Colin Hill who played 46 (1 goal) League, 1 FA Cup and 4 FL

Cup matches. He was released on a free transfer at the end of 1985–86 and joined CS Maritimo in the Portuguese League.

DECEMBER 23RD

1893	Crusaders	H	Friendly	7–0
1895	Crewe Alexandra	A	Division 2	1–0
1899	Swindon Town	H	Friendly	2–1
1905	Preston North End	A	Division 1	2–2

Debut for William Garbutt.

1911	Notts County	A	Division 1	1–3

Final senior appearance for 'Baldie' Gray who finished with 184 League games.
Also last game for David Neave who made 154 (30 goals) League and 14 (2 goals) FA Cup appearances.

1916	Chelsea	H	London Combination	2–1
1922	Huddersfield Town	A	Division 1	0–4
1933	Sheffield United	A	Division 1	3–1
1939	Charlton Athletic	A	League South 'A' Division	0–0
1944	Brentford	H	Football League – South	5–2
1950	Tottenham Hotspur	A	Division 1	0–1
1960	Sheffield Wednesday	A	Division 1	1–1
1961	Tottenham Hotspur	H	Division 1	2–1
1967	Nottingham Forest	H	Division 1	3–0
1972	Birmingham City	A	Division 1	1–1

1976 Alan Ball transferred to Southampton for £60,000. Ball's record at Highbury stood at: League 177 (45 goals), FA Cup 28 (7 goals), FL Cup 12 appearances.

1978	Tottenham Hotspur	A	Division 1	5–0

Arsenal gave their fans an early Christmas present in a game at White Hart Lane in which they trounced Spurs and Liam Brady scored one of the best goals ever!

1988 Kenny Sansom was transferred to Newcastle United for a fee of £300,000.

1990	Aston Villa	A	Division 1	0–0
1995	Liverpool	A	Premier League	1–3

DECEMBER 24TH

1892	Burslem Port Vale	H	Friendly	1–3
1894	New Brompton	A	Friendly	0–5
1898	Barnsley	A	Division 2	1–2
1900	Walsall	A	Division 2	0–1
1904	Sheffield United	H	Division 1	1–0
1910	Notts County	H	Division 1	2–1
1921	Oldham Athletic	H	Division 1	0–1
1927	Everton	H	Division 1	3–2
1932	Sheffield United	H	Division 1	9–2

Jack Lambert scored 5 goals.

1938	Portsmouth	A	Division 1	0–0

1938 John Barnwell was born in Newcastle.

1949	Sunderland	H	Division 1	5–0
1955	Chelsea	A	Division 1	0–2

1958 Stan Charlton transferred to Leyton Orient.

DECEMBER 25TH

1886   At a meeting at the Royal Oak Public House in Woolwich, it was resolved that Dial Square FC change its name forthwith to Royal Arsenal FC, thus beginning the history of the club known today simply as Arsenal.

1889	Preston Hornets	H	Friendly	5–0
1891	Sheffield United	A	Friendly	3–3
1893	Burslem Port Vale	H	Division 2	4–1
1894	Burslem Port Vale	H	Division 2	7–0
1895	Burslem Port Vale	H	Division 2	2–1
1896	Lincoln City	H	Division 2	6–2
1897	Tottenham Hotspur	H	United League	2–3
1899	Lincoln City	A	Division 2	0–5
1900	West Ham United	H	Friendly	1–0
1901	Blackpool	H	Division 2	0–0
1902	Burton United	A	Division 2	1–2
1903	Bradford City	H	Division 2	4–1
1905	Newcastle United	H	Division 1	4–3
1906	Glasgow Celtic	H	Friendly	0–2
1907	Newcastle United	H	Division 1	2–2
1908	Leicester Fosse	A	Division 1	1–1
1909	Newcastle United	H	Division 1	0–3
1911	Tottenham Hotspur	A	Division 1	0–5
1912	Notts County	H	Division 1	0–0
1913	Bradford Park Avenue	A	Division 2	3–2
1914	Leicester Fosse	A	Division 2	4–1
1915	West Ham United	A	London Combination	2–8
1916	Queen's Park Rangers	A	London Combination	3–2
1917	Fulham	A	London Combination	1–1
1918	Clapton Orient	A	London Combination	2–3
1919	Derby County	A	Division 1	1–2
1920	Everton	A	Division 1	4–2
1922	Bolton Wanderers	A	Division 1	1–4
1924	Birmingham	A	Division 1	1–2
1925	Notts County	H	Division 1	3–0
1928	Blackburn Rovers	A	Division 1	2–5
1929	Portsmouth	A	Division 1	1–0
1930	Manchester City	A	Division 1	4–1
1931	Sheffield United	A	Division 1	1–4
1933	Leeds United	A	Division 1	1–0
1934	Preston North End	H	Division 1	5–3
1935	Liverpool	A	Division 1	1–0
1936	Preston North End	H	Division 1	4–1
1937	Blackpool	A	Division 1	1–2
1939	Clapton Orient	H	League South 'A' Division	3–0
1940	West Ham United	A	South Regional League	2–4
1941	Fulham	H	London League	2–0
1942	Chelsea	A	Football League – South	2–5
1943	Millwall	A	Football League – South	5–1
1944	Brentford	A	Football League – South	1–1

1945	Newport County	A	Football League – South	2–1
1946	Portsmouth	H	Division 1	2–1
1947	Liverpool	A	Division 1	3–1
1948	Derby County	H	Division 1	3–3
1950	Stoke City	H	Division 1	0–3
1951	Portsmouth	H	Division 1	4–1
1952	Bolton Wanderers	A	Division 1	6–4
1954	Chelsea	H	Division 1	1–0
1956	Chelsea	A	Division 1	1–1

DECEMBER 26TH

1889	Chatham	A	Friendly	2–2
1891	1st Lincolnshire Regiment	H	Friendly	6–0
1892	Stockton	H	Friendly	4–3

First game for Joseph Powell.

1893	Grimsby Town	A	Division 2	1–3
1894	Grimsby Town	A	Division 2	2–4
1895	Cliftonville Athletic	H	Friendly	10–1
1896	Gainsborough Town	A	Division 2	1–4
1898	Millwall Athletic	H	United League	0–1
1899	Loughborough Town	H	Division 2	4–0
1900	Newcastle United	H	Friendly	1–1
1901	Burslem Port Vale	H	Division 2	3–1
1902	Millwall Athletic	A	London League Premier Division	0–3

Debut of William Linward.

1903	Leicester Fosse	A	Division 2	0–0
1904	Aston Villa	A	Division 1	1–3
1905	Corinthians	H	Friendly	1–1
1906	Bury	H	Division 1	3–1
1907	Liverpool	H	Friendly	2–2
1908	Leicester Fosse	H	Division 1	2–1

1909 Charles Buchan signed as an amateur.

1910	Manchester United	A	Division 1	0–5

Debut of Thomas Winship.

1911	Tottenham Hotspur	H	Division 1	3–1
1912	Notts County	A	Division 1	1–2
1913	Bradford Park Avenue	H	Division 2	2–0
1914	Leicester Fosse	H	Division 2	6–0
1916	Queen's Park Rangers	H	London Combination	0–0
1917	Fulham	H	London Combination	1–1
1918	Clapton Orient	H	London Combination	9–2
1919	Derby County	H	Division 1	1–0
1921	Cardiff City	H	Division 1	0–0
1922	Bolton Wanderers	H	Division 1	5–0

First appearance of John Robson.

1923	Notts County	A	Division 1	2–1
1924	Birmingham	H	Division 1	0–1
1925	Notts County	A	Division 1	1–4

1928	Sunderland	H	Division 1	1–1
1929	Portsmouth	H	Division 1	1–2

Final senior appearance John Butler, played 267 (7 goals) League and 29 (1 goal) FA Cup games.

1930	Manchester City	H	Division 1	3–1
1931	Sheffield United	H	Division 1	0–2

Final senior game for Bill Seddon who finished with 69 League and 6 FA Cup appearances.

1932	Leeds United	H	Division 1	1–2
1933	Leeds United	H	Division 1	2–0
1934	Preston North End	A	Division 1	1–2
1935	Liverpool	H	Division 1	1–2
1936	Everton	A	Division 1	1–1
1939	Crystal Palace	A	League South 'A' Division	3–0
1942	Chelsea	H	Football League – South	1–5
1945	Newport County	H	Football League – South	7–0
1946	Portsmouth	A	Division 1	2–0
1949	Manchester United	A	Division 1	0–2
1950	Stoke City	A	Division 1	0–1

First senior match for Cliff Holton.

1951	Portsmouth	A	Division 1	1–1
1953	Blackpool	A	Division 1	0–2
1955	Wolverhampton Wanderers	A	Division 1	3–3
1956	Chelsea	H	Division 1	2–0
1957	Aston Villa	A	Division 1	0–3
1958	Luton Town	A	Division 1	3–6

Last League game for Jim Fotheringham. His record: 72 League and 4 FA Cup matches.

1959	Luton Town	H	Division 1	0–3
1960	Sheffield Wednesday	H	Division 1	1–1
1961	Fulham	H	Division 1	1–0
1964	Stoke City	H	Division 1	3–2
1966	Southampton	H	Division 1	4–1
1967	Chelsea	A	Division 1	1–2
1968	Manchester United	H	Division 1	3–0
1969	Nottingham Forest	A	Division 1	1–1
1970	Southampton	H	Division 1	0–0

Arsenal dropped their last point of the season at Highbury on a snow-covered pitch against Southampton. The ground staff had worked extremely hard to get the match played in order to avoid a fixture pile-up but the Gunners could not break down a resolute Southampton defence. The Arsenal team wore red shorts in place of their usual white and attacked throughout only to be thwarted by Martin in the visitors' goal. Bob McNab had his ankle put in plaster after the match as a precaution for an injury sustained late in the match.

1972	Norwich City	H	Division 1	2–0
1973	Southampton	A	Division 1	1–1
1974	Chelsea	H	Division 1	1–2
1975	Ipswich Town	A	Division 1	0–2

Final senior appearance of Eddie Kelly. He played 175 (13 goals) League, 17 (4 goals) FA Cup, 15 FL Cup and 15 (2 goals) European games.

1977	Chelsea	H	Division 1	3–0
1978	West Bromwich Albion	H	Division 1	1–2
1979	Tottenham Hotspur	H	Division 1	1–0
1980	Crystal Palace	A	Division 1	2–2
1983	Tottenham Hotspur	A	Division 1	4–2
1984	Norwich City	A	Division 1	0–1
1986	Leicester City	A	Division 1	1–1
1987	Nottingham Forest	H	Division 1	0–2
1988	Charlton Athletic	A	Division 1	3–2
1989	Southampton	A	Division 1	0–1
1990	Derby County	H	Division 1	3–0
1991	Luton Town	A	Division 1	0–1
1992	Ipswich Town	H	Premier League	0–0

1992 Jack Crayston died in Streetly.

| 1994 | Aston Villa | H | Premier League | 0–0 |

Stephen Hughes made his League debut.

1995	Queen's Park Rangers	H	Premier League	3–0
1996	Sheffield Wednesday	A	Premier League	0–0
1997	Leicester City	H	Premier League	2–1

After a run of bad results lady luck was due to fall on the Gunners and did in the game against Leicester. Arsenal attacked from the kick-off and Overmars went desperately close after a great run by Vieira down the left side of midfield. Heskey hit the bar for the visitors when it was easier to score a minute later. Ian Wright looked a lot sharper and in the 20th minute nearly broke the deadlock with a fine 20 yarder that had Keller scrambling to make a save. David Platt rose majestically to glance home a Bergkamp free kick in the 36th minute, but continued pressure before half-time failed to produce another goal. However, the game turned in the 56th minute in bizarre fashion when Steve Walsh under pressure from Ian Wright some 30 yards out from his own goal tried to clear the ball but only succeeded in skying the ball straight over Keller to give the Gunners a 2–0 lead. Like the game at Filbert Street earlier in the season Arsenal contrived to make hard work of their opponents and after a poor clearance by Seaman who tried to dribble his way out of trouble Neil Lennon tapped into an empty net. Exactly halfway through he campaign Arsenal were in 6th position their lowest of the season with 33 points.

DECEMBER 27TH

1889	Reading Town	H	Friendly	5–1
1892	Blackpool	H	Friendly	1–1
1897	Lincoln City	A	Division 2	3–2
1898	Luton Town	A	United League	1–1
1902	Burnley	H	Division 2	5–1
1904	Nottingham Forest	A	Division 1	3–0
1905	Aston Villa	A	Division 1	1–2
1909	Liverpool	H	Division 1	1–1
1913	Leicester Fosse	A	Division 2	2–1
1915	West Ham United	H	London Combination	3–2
1919	Sheffield Wednesday	A	Division 1	2–1
1920	Everton	H	Division 1	1–1
1921	Cardiff City	A	Division 1	3–4

Debut for Billy Milne and Robert Turnbull.

1923	Notts County	H	Division 1	0–0
1924	Nottingham Forest	H	Division 1	2–1
1926	Cardiff City	A	Division 1	0–2

League debut for Horace Cope and Harold Peel.

Final match for James Ramsay who had played 69 (11 goals) League and 6 FA Cup games.

1927	Liverpool	A	Division 1	2–0
1930	Blackpool	H	Division 1	7–1

George Male's first senior appearance.

1932	Leeds United	A	Division 1	0–0
1937	Blackpool	H	Division 1	2–1
1938	Charlton Athletic	A	Division 1	0–1
1941	Tottenham Hotspur	A	London League	2–1
1943	Millwall	H	Football League – South	1–1
1947	Liverpool	H	Division 1	1–2
1948	Derby County	A	Division 1	1–2
1949	Manchester United	H	Division 1	0–0
1954	Chelsea	A	Division 1	1–1
1955	Wolverhampton Wanderers	H	Division 1	2–2
1958	Luton Town	H	Division 1	1–0
1965	Sheffield Wednesday	A	Division 1	0–4
1966	Southampton	A	Division 1	1–2
1969	Newcastle United	H	Division 1	0–0
1971	Nottingham Forest	A	Division 1	1–1

Alan Ball's debut for Arsenal.

1972	George Graham was transferred to Manchester United for £120,000.			
1975	Queen's Park Rangers	H	Division 1	2–0
1976	Tottenham Hotspur	A	Division 1	2–2
1977	West Bromwich Albion	A	Division 1	3–1
1980	Ipswich Town	H	Division 1	1–1
1982	Tottenham Hotspur	H	Division 1	2–0
1983	Birmingham City	H	Division 1	1–1
1984	Death of Leslie Compton.			
1986	Southampton	H	Division 1	1–0
1993	Swindon Town	A	Premier League	4–0

DECEMBER 28TH

1895	Darlington	H	Friendly	6–2
1901	Barnsley	A	Division 2	0–2
1904	Sheffield United	A	Division 1	0–4
1907	Sunderland	H	Division 1	4–0
1908	Sheffield Wednesday	A	Division 1	2–6
1912	Liverpool	H	Division 1	1–1
1918	Queen's Park Rangers	A	London Combination	2–0
1926	Manchester United	H	Division 1	1–0
1929	Leeds United	A	Division 1	0–2
1935	Sunderland	A	Division 1	4–5
1936	Preston North End	A	Division 1	3–1

1939	Frank McLintock was born in Glasgow, Scotland.			
1940	Luton Town	H	South Regional League	8–1
1946	Wolverhampton Wanderers	H	Division 1	1–1
1953	Blackpool	H	Division 1	2–2
1957	Luton Town	A	Division 1	0–4
1959	Luton Town	A	Division 1	1–0
1963	Birmingham City	A	Division 1	4–1

Laurie Brown's last senior game. He had completed 101 (2 goals) League, 5 FA Cup and 3 European outings.

1964	Stoke City	A	Division 1	1–4
1965	Sheffield Wednesday	H	Division 1	5–2
1974	Sheffield United	A	Division 1	1–1
1982	Southampton	A	Division 1	2–2
1985	Queen's Park Rangers	H	Division 1	3–1
1987	Wimbledon	A	Division 1	1–3
1990	Paul Dickov was upgraded from trainee to professional.			
1991	Manchester City	A	Division 1	0–1
1992	Aston Villa	A	Premier League	0–1
1994	Ipswich Town	A	Premier League	2–0
1996	Aston Villa	H	Premier League	2–2
1997	Tottenham Hotspur	A	Premier League	1–1

Arsenal visited White Hart Lane where Spurs were boosted by the return of Jurgen Klinsmann in an attempt to revive their beleaguered team languishing at the foot of the table. The first half was mostly one-way traffic in favour of Spurs and inspired by Ginola they took the lead when Neilsen drove home a low cross from Fox after Winterburn slipped. A few minutes later Arsenal almost levelled after Anelka latching on to a Petit through ball beat Walker only to see the ball hit the post. The second half was more positive for the Gunners and they slowly took control and equalised through Man of the Match Ray Parlour driving home from the edge of the box to the delight of the few hundred Arsenal fans who managed to get a ticket. Arsenal continued to pile on the pressure but failed to get the winner.

DECEMBER 29TH

1888	Iona	A	Kent Senior Cup	5–1
1894	Dresden United	H	Friendly	1–0
1900	Gainsborough Trinity	A	Division 2	0–1
1906	Manchester City	H	Division 1	4–1
1917	Clapton Orient	A	London Combination	2–1
1923	Chelsea	H	Division 1	1–0
1928	Sheffield Wednesday	H	Division 1	2–2
1934	Portsmouth	H	Division 1	1–1
1945	Wolverhampton Wanderers	H	Football League – South	3–2
1951	Sunderland	A	Division 1	1–4
1956	West Bromwich Albion	A	Division 1	2–0
1973	Leicester City	A	Division 1	0–2
1979	Manchester United	A	Division 1	0–3
1981	Glentoran	A	Friendly	2–0
1982	Vladimir Petrovic signed from Red Star, Belgrade for £45,000. He had attempted to join			

the club prior to the start of the season but had been prevented by work permit problems.

| 1984 | Newcastle United | A | Division 1 | 3–1 |
| 1990 | Sheffield United | H | Division 1 | 4–1 |

Andy Cole's only League appearance (as substitute) for Arsenal.

| 1993 | Sheffield United | H | Premier League | 3–0 |

DECEMBER 30TH

1893	Ardwick	A	Division 2	1–0
1899	Leicester Fosse	A	Division 2	0–0
1905	Liverpool	A	Division 1	0–3
1911	Liverpool	A	Division 1	1–4
1916	Southampton	A	London Combination	1–0
1922	Stoke City	H	Division 1	3–0
1933	Birmingham	A	Division 1	0–0
1939	Norwich City	H	League South 'A' Division	2–2
1944	Southampton	H	Football League – South	2–4
1950	Sheffield Wednesday	A	Division 1	2–0
1961	Charlie Nicholas was born in Glasgow, Scotland.			
1967	Chelsea	H	Division 1	1–1
1972	Stoke City	A	Division 1	0–0
1978	Birmingham City	H	Division 1	3–1
1989	Aston Villa	A	Division 1	1–2
1995	Wimbledon	H	Premier League	1–3

DECEMBER 31ST

1887	Forest Gate Alliance	A	Friendly	1–2
1892	Leith Athletic	H	Friendly	1–1
1898	Luton Town	H	Division 2	6–2
1904	Newcastle United	H	Division 1	0–2
1907	Sheffield Wednesday	A	Division 1	0–6
1910	Bury	H	Division 1	3–2
1921	Chelsea	A	Division 1	2–0
1927	Bury	H	Division 1	3–1
1932	Birmingham	H	Division 1	3–0
1938	Huddersfield Town	H	Division 1	1–0
1949	Liverpool	A	Division 1	0–2
1955	Bolton Wanderers	H	Division 1	3–1
1960	Nottingham Forest	A	Division 1	5–3
1966	Aston Villa	A	Division 1	1–0
1977	Everton	A	Division 1	0–2
1983	Southampton	H	Division 1	2–2

1984 David Rocastle and Michael Thomas signed as professionals whilst former home-grown prodigy Brian McDermott was sold to Oxford United for £40,000.

On the same day Arsenal completed the signing of Steve Williams from Southampton for £550,000.

| 1988 | Aston Villa | A | Division 1 | 3–0 |
| 1994 | Queen's Park Rangers | H | Premier League | 1–3 |

Despite the miserable performance there was some joy as John Jensen finally scored after about 3,000 attempts in his previous 100 or so matches.